# The Political Economy of Monetary Circuits

*Also by Sergio Rossi*

LA MONETA EUROPEA: UTOPIA O REALTÀ?: L'emissione dell'ecu nel rispetto delle sovranità nazionali

MACROÉCONOMIE MONÉTAIRE: Théories et politiques

MODALITÉS D'INSTITUTION ET DE FONCTIONNEMENT D'UNE BANQUE CENTRALE SUPRANATIONALE: Le cas de la Banque Centrale Européenne

MONEY AND INFLATION: a New Macroeconomic Analysis

MONEY AND PAYMENTS IN THEORY AND PRACTICE

MACRO E MICROECONOMIA: Teoria e applicazioni (*with Mauro Baranzini and Giandemetrio Marangoni*)

MODERN THEORIES OF MONEY: the Nature and Role of Money in Capitalist Economies (*co-editor with Louis-Philippe Rochon*)

MONETARY AND EXCHANGE RATE SYSTEMS: a Global View of Financial Crises (*co-editor with Louis-Philippe Rochon*)

# The Political Economy of Monetary Circuits

## Tradition and Change in Post-Keynesian Economics

Edited by

Jean-François Ponsot

and

Sergio Rossi

palgrave
macmillan

First published 2009 by
PALGRAVE MACMILLAN

Palgrave Macmillan in the UK is an imprint of Macmillan Publishers Limited, registered in England, company number 785998, of Houndmills, Basingstoke, Hampshire RG21 6XS.

Palgrave Macmillan in the US is a division of St Martin's Press LLC, 175 Fifth Avenue, New York, NY 10010.

Palgrave Macmillan is the global academic imprint of the above companies and has companies and representatives throughout the world.

Palgrave® and Macmillan® are registered trademarks in the United States, the United Kingdom, Europe and other countries.

ISBN 978–0–230–20337–2 hardback

This book is printed on paper suitable for recycling and made from fully managed and sustained forest sources. Logging, pulping and manufacturing processes are expected to conform to the environmental regulations of the country of origin.

A catalogue record for this book is available from the British Library.

A catalog record for this book is available from the Library of Congress.

10 9 8 7 6 5 4 3 2 1
18 17 16 15 14 13 12 11 10 09

Printed and bound in Great Britain by
CPI Antony Rowe, Chippenham and Eastbourne

# Contents

# List of Tables

# List of Figures

# Foreword

*Faruk Ülgen*

## Introduction

To date, the dominant conceptions of money and monetary phenomena remain fundamentally related to classical and neoclassical views of the market economy. As a matter of fact, the abundant research work carried out in this field over the second half of the twentieth century following alternative theoretical approaches, such as the post-Keynesian view and the monetary circuit school, do not seem to be explicitly accepted and integrated in the current principles on which macroeconomists usually agree. The divide between what the mainstream considers as the principles of economic theory and what these alternative views suggest persists. At the same time, the monetary problems of our economies are yet to be solved, and haunt both economists and governments.

A good summary of the current state of economic theory is provided by a paper entitled 'The principles of macroeconomics at the millennium', written by Parkin (2000) and published in the *American Economic Review*. Surveying the main current advanced macroeconomics textbooks,[1] Parkin (2000) puts to the fore four propositions on which macroeconomists would agree:

1. Macroeconomic phenomena may be considered as the equilibrium results or consequences of choices made by rational economic agents in a stochastic world. This proposition is the outcome of the 'great synthesis' regarding macroeconomics on the ground of some microeconomic foundations given by neoclassical rational individual choice theory.
2. The classical dichotomy is a powerful and empirically relevant approach to explain economic phenomena. This second proposition means that the quantity theory of money is the relevant economic model that allows us to analyse, on the one hand, economic equilibrium in real terms (based on rational individual behaviour) and, on the other, money as an exogenous variable without any effect on long-run real equilibrium.

3. Although the previous proposition holds in general, correlations among monetary variables and real variables reveal that monetary policy interventions have short-run effects on real magnitudes. Indeed, different economic theories seek to explain these correlations in order to guide economic policy decisions, but none of the suggestions stemming from these theories is universally accepted. Consequently, no agreement has yet been reached on the efficiency properties and on the expected effects of these alternative views. This means that, in the short run, there can be some monetary disruption (owing mainly to wrong economic policies or, in the new-Keynesian perspective, to information asymmetries), which could be corrected or adjusted over the long run when interferences are neutralized by market-friendly 'good' policies or 'good' institutions.
4. Following the first proposition and notwithstanding the third, economic policy could be defined as a process, not as a given objective event. To make this last point clearer, one could state that economic policy should mainly have a role as a market-accompanying device against shocks, and should not provoke unexpected disequilibria in the economic system.

These propositions raise two major questions:

- Do fluctuations in economic activity result from efficient intertemporal individual choices (as is the case in real-business-cycle models) or are they due to coordination failure problems in the whole economy (as in new-Keynesian and post-Keynesian models)?
- Can we use the correlations between real variables and monetary variables as a tool for choosing 'good' economic policies? Usually, the admitted answer is positive for the short run and negative for the long run, except for rational-expectations models.

In order to deal with these issues, the main current advanced macroeconomics textbooks provide common definitions and a way of measuring economic aggregates via a circular-flow model. They quote Keynes very often as the reference for a short-run conception of the economy, while they refer to Friedman when adopting a long-term fundamental focus. Prominent macroeconomists see Keynes's influence as almost entirely political, whereas they consider Smith, Arrow, Friedman, and Samuelson as the fathers of modern macroeconomics.

This orientation leads to a specific analytical choice, which consists in considering the market economy as fundamentally non-monetary and self-equilibrating, except for short-run disequilibrium interferences coming essentially from 'bad' economic policies. As a result, the well-known models of the neoclassical synthesis assign to governments a conservative role in their monetary and fiscal policies. Therefore, '[w]hen students enter a post-Keynesian class in monetary economics, their minds have been so much distorted by the neoclassical fallacy of an exogenous supplied stock of money that they find difficult to understand even the simplest story about demand-led endogenous money' (Lavoie, 2003, p. 506). In fact, there is a prolific post-Keynesian research work, which provides relevant alternative results.[2] Thus, the aim of the first international workshop on monetary circuit theory and on post-Keynesian approaches to monetary economics, held at the Pierre-Mendès-France University in Grenoble, France, on 24 April 2007, was to search for common elements of these two approaches, in order to provide a general outline for a unitary theory of money in a capitalist market economy. In this vein, several papers presented at this workshop reiterated the principles of monetary economics of the Keynesian heterodoxy, and showed that the theoretical agenda in this regard was far from being fulfilled.

Let us first recall the main features of the alternative monetary theories presented in this volume, and then state the core of the conceptual questions related to a monetary theory of the market economy.

## The theory of the monetary circuit, the monetary theory of production, and the (post-) Keynesian monetary approach

The theory of the monetary circuit is grounded in the process of money emission and constitutes a monetary macroeconomics paradigm. Its analytical aim is analogous to the post-Keynesian approach, that is, to provide a relevant explanation for the working of a monetary economy of production. Analysing the process of capital accumulation, such a monetary theory of production apprehends a number of macroeconomic problems in our capitalist economies, like inflation and unemployment, referring to some pathologies of the structural characteristics of our monetary systems.

Such a vision constitutes an alternative to neoclassical economics, considering that the market economy is not a real-exchange equilibrium economy but indeed a monetary economy of production, where expenditure decisions result from the choices and expectations of various and distinct economic agents. More precisely, as Claude Gnos explains in Chapter 1, the theory of the monetary circuit underpins Keynes's principle of effective demand and emphasizes that in an entrepreneur or money-wage economy entrepreneurs play the crucial role.

In this regard, we can notice some Kaleckian principles ('workers spend what they earn, while entrepreneurs earn what they spend') explaining the overwhelming position of entrepreneurs in any economic system. This position is the result of specific monetary relations between banks and entrepreneurs. Indeed, money is considered an endogenous item such that its creation comes from the bank-financing/firm-borrowing operations, which make entrepreneurs independent of the balances accumulated by saving agents. Therefore, money comes into the picture not thanks to a Machiavellian willingness of a *deus ex machina* but through the willpower of banks and entrepreneurs. Both monetary circuit theorists and post-Keynesian economists adopt the endogenous-money stance, and reject the classical view of commodity money involved in real-exchange models. The methodology adopted in the theory of the monetary circuit consists in showing that any monetary transactions occurring in the economy should be thought of as part of either the flux or the reflux of money wages constituting the circuit, money emission occurring through mere bookkeeping entries, that is, debits and credits that banks record in their books as argued by Schmitt (1975). The origins of this view are to be found in Keynes's writings on the finance motive, pointing out the very role of money and banks in a market economy. In Keynesian words, bank advances (that is to say, commitments to finance) are necessary in order for entrepreneurs to embark on investment projects without absorbing any pre-existent resources. In this perspective, Gnos shows that the production process generates a financial relationship tying up firms and their workers through banks. All complex economic transactions are grounded in the process of formation and spending of incomes. Consequently, the level of employment is not determined by the interplay of labour supply and labour demand but mainly by entrepreneurs, who take production decisions in light of the demand they expect for their own output. Voluntary unemployment, the sole kind of unemployment that can be envisaged in neoclassical real-equilibrium models, has no analytical relevance in this alternative approach.

Further, using Schmitt's empty-wages schema and the circular process that Keynes (1930) called 'widow's cruse', Gnos emphasizes the ability of circuit theory to take up the challenge of explaining economic disequilibria. When firms accumulate profits in a process that allows the production of goods that they are bound to accumulate in the form of capital goods (or in the form of inventories of unsaleable consumption goods), overaccumulation enters the picture. The mismatches in the monetary and financial operations occurring in the process of firms' capital accumulation can explain, at least to a great extent, the 2008 economic and financial crisis originating in the United States.

In Chapter 2, after recalling the historical perspective of the opposition between the 'monetary view' and the 'real view' of money, Jesper Jespersen points out that Keynes's foundations of monetary circuit theory and the post-Keynesian monetary view share three main characteristics, which distinguish them from mainstream economics methodologically:

1. A macroeconomic approach that, following the evolutionist, institutionalist, and regulationist approaches, may be summarized by the objective, which consists in establishing and analysing the historical/institutional settings of the economy as a whole. This amounts to searching for the macroeconomic foundations of different forms of microeconomic behaviour of the various components of a market economy in which individual decisions take place in a pre-ordered context and evolve through interdependencies between collective/state-guided rules and private/decentralized economic calculus;
2. An approach that assigns a decisive role to monetary decisions of economic agents and relations among them as permissive conditions of the desired economic activity level;
3. A dynamic approach that considers the economy as an evolutionary process whose final result, at any given point of time, is an *ex post* observation about the global compatibility (or incompatibility) of private and separated monetary decisions of agents. The more fundamental decisions are those of banks and entrepreneurs.

Through the major characteristics of monetary circuit theory and post-Keynesian theory, Jespersen shows that these two monetary theories of production complement each other in order to develop a relevant macroeconomic analysis focusing on the economy as a whole in an uncertain and open entrepreneurial framework. Hence, modern monetary macroeconomics is based on four building blocks, namely:

- liquidity-preference theory, where uncertainty plays a crucial role;
- money-in-advance (circuit) theory, explaining the creation, circulation, and destruction of money within the economic system;

- endogenous money-supply process, through the role of the banking sector (banks' response to entrepreneurs' need for financing their production/investment plans affecting the path of economic evolution);
- rate of interest theory, combining central bank policy, liquidity preference, and uncertainty, in opposition to the loanable-funds approach of the investment-financing process and the determination of interest rates through supply and demand of savings.

The theoretical starting point for this analytical synthesis is the bookkeeping description of the money-emission process, considering that the credit lines that banks decide to grant to entrepreneurs lead to the formation of bank deposits in the whole economy. In Chapter 3, Sergio Rossi shows that such a framework reveals the logical need to move from a sequential to a simultaneous approach to monetary circuits, as banks create the macroeconomic flow (that is, money) while the object of the circulation is related to production in Keynes's entrepreneur economy. Rossi's analysis reveals that banks issue money but that money's purchasing power is the result of an integration of banking and production systems, which concur together to the creation of value. However, for the sake of rigorous statement, Rossi points out that one should distinguish between bank money (a flow) and bank deposits (stocks); banks issue money as the purely numerical means of payment whereas deposits are the result of the monetization by banks of the production costs that firms may incur in the current or future period. Following Schmitt on this point, and in order to establish the very characteristics of the workings of our capitalist economies, Rossi emphasizes that bank loans create deposits with no need of any pre-existent savings. The object of these bank deposits is not money as such but indeed produced output. Hence, the purchasing power of money results from production, and not from the banks' magic of 'credit creation'.

In Chapter 4, Louis-Philippe Rochon addresses an important issue in the monetary circuit approach, to wit, the existence of profits within the monetary circuit. Rochon comments on some recent solutions and suggests his own answer to this issue, which is to allow investment to be financed by bank credit and reimbursed over several periods, thereby allowing for the formation of monetary profits.

In a monetary economy, as Rochon recalls, money supply is credit-driven and demand-determined. Production is, above all, a process of debt creation, while economic events unfold in a sequence over historical time, where the past cannot be changed and the future is the other name for uncertainty. Both firms and banks bet on the future ability of financed firms' plans to raise revenue and to extinguish their debt. In an endogenous-money model, the logical problem that arises at the macroeconomic level is that when production is financed by the emission of credit money by banks, the amount of money that firms may recover by selling products would at the most be equal to the amount by which they have been financed by banks. As a result, the reflux problem is a key issue of the monetary circuit. The market must generate sufficient income, and firms must be able to capture this income in order for them to reimburse their debt and earn a profit. Recalling various solutions proposed from different perspectives in numerous post-Keynesian and monetary circuit approaches, Rochon underlines several problems arising from these solutions, that is to say, they all rely on some asymmetrical or external assumptions. By including investment finance in the monetary circuit approach, Rochon shows that there is sufficient money to account for the realization of profits. He assumes that investment is partly financed by bank credit, but reimbursed over several periods. Indeed, this is the Kaleckian principle that Rochon's model includes.

Within the monetary conception of the entrepreneurial economy, the nagging problem of the equality between investment and saving is thought out in a radically different way with respect to loanable-funds theory. The limits to economic growth do not depend on savings but on monetary and financial systems (bank credit, effective demand, monetary and fiscal policies, level of development of financial markets, return rate of the production and financial system), which affect investment expectations and their realization over time. As Jean-Luc Bailly explains in Chapter 5, the causality between investment and saving is not unidirectional. Through their expectations (the principle of effective demand) financed by bank credit, entrepreneurs create new sources of spending without waiting for output sale and the use of savings for funding their expenditures. As Keynes puts it, saving is not the source of investment, as the former is a result of the latter when entrepreneurs can embark on new productions or investment. If entrepreneurs waited for the spending of households and for their subsequent savings, there would indeed be no income creation in the whole economy, and the level of economic activity would stagnate, as Schumpeter underlined in his theory of economic development. The crucial role of entrepreneurs in a market economy, through the money emission process carried out by banks, is thus explained in a general macroeconomic setting. Bailly argues that the formation of fixed capital in a monetary production economy follows a process that leads firms to capture a fraction of current output. This is why firms are wholly independent economic agents and may have contradictory interests regarding those of households.

In Chapter 6, Riccardo Bellofiore and Marco Passarella argue that, in the setting of a monetary economy of production, one can better appraise the issues raised in Rosa Luxemburg's theory of the capitalist economy. Even if the analytical schema developed by Luxemburg in order to show how money enters the system and where extra money realizing surplus value comes from is defective, her works contain a clear model of the monetary circuit where the notion of finance is a basic feature of the analysis. Bellofiore and Passarella show that Michal Kalecki's and Joan Robinson's readings of Rosa Luxemburg's works can provide an interpretation that links Luxemburg's problem with Keynes's principle of effective demand. Kalecki indeed emphasizes that independently of the critiques that can be directed at her theory, Luxemburg succeeds in outlining the necessity of covering the savings gap by home investment or exports, and this before Keynes's *General Theory*. Parallel to this, the rereading of Luxemburg's work by Robinson allows us to state that if the propensity to save by the capitalist class exceeds the accumulation rate dictated by technical progress, crisis can be averted only if there is an outlet for investment outside the capitalist system. When income distribution and the propensity to save of capitalists generate savings in excess of new investment, there is a chronic excess of the potential supply of real capital over its demand. The system has therefore to fall into a chronic depression.

However, Bellofiore and Passarella emphasize that Kalecki and Robinson, as Luxemburg's socialist critics, did not confront the fact that in Luxemburg's reasoning it is the capitalist class itself that sets off the capitalist process as a monetary circuit through injections of purchasing power. While her model is a simple circuit model, there are two differences with respect to modern circuit theory: Luxemburg assumes gold producers rather than banks as monetary capitalists as well as the existence of a historically determined real wage, while circuit authors assume that the real wage is set by capitalists' autonomous decisions about the structure of output. Nevertheless, Bellofiore and Passarella maintain that the *Anti-Critique* of Luxemburg can be considered as one of the forerunners of monetary circuit theory. Indeed, it explains the capitalist process as a monetary circuit. In this view, capital accumulation does not mean producing an increasing number of commodities, but converting more and more commodities into money capital.

Therefore, Bellofiore and Passarella point out that the capitalist class (identified with the firm sector) is the only point of origin for money, and show that the Luxemburg problem may be restated in a different setting, the conceptual framework privileged by old (Schumpeter and Keynes, for instance) and new (Schmitt and Graziani, among others) theories of the monetary circuit, as they all reject the view of money as a commodity, and separate firms, banks, and wage earners as constitutive groups of our capitalist systems. The myth of the representative agent aiming to maximize his utility (or profit) under given techniques and preferences in a real-exchange market having self-equilibrating mechanisms is therefore rejected for a heterogeneous society in which the place of each category of economic agents is determined through their access to money. Schumpeter also argued that agents can accede to the social stock of goods and services only by means of money. More explicitly, one cannot become an entrepreneur without obtaining money as the means of financing one's production activities, and one cannot buy consumption goods without obtaining money wages. There is no exchange without production, there is no production without credit, and there is no accumulation without money. The capitalist economy is fundamentally a monetary economy of production.

Several extensions of this alternative approach to the workings of our economic systems can be proposed by considering the analysis worked out by some institutional economists. Guglielmo Forges Davanzati and Riccardo Realfonzo show in Chapter 7 that the monetary theory of production can also be considered in Veblenian terms. Following Parker Foster and Ranson (1987), Forges Davanzati and Realfonzo argue that production is governed not by real exchanges but by the institution of money, and that it is carried out only as long as banks grant credit to firms in order to finance investment. Forges Davanzati and Realfonzo argue that Veblen's view of the dynamics of institutional change can be considered as driven by social conflict, generated by a significant and long-term increase in the ratio between financial rents and real wages. This conflict occurs between the rent-keeping leisure class and the productive system (notably, the employees). One can find this reasoning in Smithin (2003), who studies the dynamics of interest rates and financial markets as a transformation of market economies in pure financial-rent economies aiming to make different market niches profitable usually through public debt with high risk premium. This dynamics creates a social conflict when workers perceive income distribution as being unfair, notably when rents and profits are no longer legitimate on moral grounds.

Now, new concepts and theories imply new conceptions of institutions, which could nevertheless be found in the writings of past prominent economists such as Wicksell. Therefore, Stefano Figuera analyses in Chapter 8 the renewal of interest in Wicksell's writings regarding the monetary authorities' interventions on different markets. Some mainstream economists, in the New-Consensus view, maintain that the monetary policy instrument of central banks is a short-run nominal rate of interest, and assume that the endogeneity of money supply is of particular importance (see, for instance, Woodford, 2003). However, this stems from the assumption that money supply aims to satisfy the demand for liquid balances by economic agents and not to finance production activities. Reconsidering Wicksell's analysis of a pure credit economy from the perspective of the monetary theory of production, Figuera calls for a reform of central banks' policies in a more preventive perspective, aiming to reduce the instability of modern economies. This issue has become urgent at the time of writing.

Adopting an analogous view of the monetary circuit, Steve Keen puts to the fore in Chapter 9, through a continuous-time formulation, a dynamic model related to Graziani (1989). Keen's analysis provides two main results: positive profits are compatible with the monetary circuit in a Wicksellian pure credit economy, and the endogenous creation of money is not incompatible with the phenomenon of borrowing purely for the sake of speculation, as occurs in modern times. Therefore, the Ponzi-financing activities pointed out by Minsky's financial-instability hypothesis may be considered as the driving force underlying the unprecedented accumulation of debt that characterizes contemporary economies.

Keen notes that from the point of view of explaining the modern phenomenon of the recent speculative bubble period, borrowing purely for the sake of speculation has to be added to the production-oriented borrowing that is the focus of monetary circuit theory. This speculative borrowing is driven by expectations of asset price appreciation and the bubble itself drives that price appreciation. Keen states, therefore, that in stark contrast to Greenspan's assertion that an asset bubble cannot be identified until after it has burst (which is true by definition in a real-equilibrium framework), the bubbles in both the share and housing markets were obvious, from a Minskian standpoint, by mid-1994 and 1996 respectively.

The evolution of monetary economies and financial instability constitute, at the time of writing, a central issue for economists and economic institutions such as central banks and the International Monetary Fund.

In this perspective, questioning the current liberal economic transformations, in Chapter 10 Marc Pilkington develops the theory of money emissions and argues that Polanyi's concept of *haute finance* allows us to apprehend a new institutional sector that can be integrated into the Lavoie and Godley stock–flow model, in order to single out the far-reaching macroeconomic consequences of the financialization of our economies.

It thereby becomes evident that this framework does not concern only the purely theoretical issue of the very nature of a capitalist market economy; a number of issues also arise regarding monetary policies. Admittedly, mainstream models nowadays consider monetary authorities' interventions on the markets in terms of variations in the central bank's interest rates and no longer with respect to an exogenous money supply scheme (as was the case for monetarists in the 1970s and 1980s). Their conception of the economy, however, is still related to real-equilibrium hypotheses, while they determine the efficiency of monetary policies on the ground of some 'technical' norms such as central bank independence, price stability (arguing that inflation is mainly a 'bad' monetary-policy phenomenon), inflation-targeting policies, and so on, conveying the neutral-money view[3] and leaving the monetary and financial instability issue behind (or considering it as an exogenous accident). This is why it is necessary to renew the debate on economic policies following the results of monetary circuit and post-Keynesian studies, which can provide different policy prescriptions from the usual economic policy agenda resulting from conventional economic analyses.

On the whole, the contributions to this volume show that there are numerous raw and finished materials for elaborating a relevant theory of a monetary capitalist/market economy that could have a great impact on our understanding of modern societies. One of the central objectives of these alternative approaches is the development of a unitary theory of a capitalist/market economy as a monetary economy. Such a target, however, should also provide a convincing alternative framework to the dominant approach. The next section presents very briefly some major elements of an integrated conception of the (monetary) market economy, which could unify different heterodox views on the subject matter.

## Unifying heterodoxies for 'a' theory of a monetary economy

First of all, at the methodological level, one has to conceive of a monetary economy not in terms of issues like inflation and the conduct of monetary policies, but in terms of concepts, such as money and equilibrium, in order to reveal the source of the theoretical controversy. The conception of money has been dealt with in various ways in economic theory. The well-known equilibrium theories (neo-Walrasian, monetarist, business cycles/rational expectations, real business cycle models) consider an exchange economy in real terms and try to integrate money into the real equilibrium after the latter is reached. In such a framework, money is irrelevant and is considered in general as an exogenous magnitude given by government or the central bank. In contrast, monetary circuit and post-Keynesian models,[4] in the tradition of the papers that Keynes published between 1937 and 1939, and some non-equilibrium monetary approaches,[5] although heterogeneous, analyse the capitalist market economy on the basis of money and monetary relations and not from a given real-equilibrium situation. In these models, which we may range in the category of 'monetary approaches', money is a non-neutral endogenous magnitude, a primary concept of a market economy. In contrast to the real-equilibrium beliefs and following the Keynesian tradition, these monetary approaches have the potential to represent an alternative paradigm, arguing that, in any economic system, money plays a part of its own, and determines and affects the economic agents' motives and decisions.

To recapitulate the fundamental features of the (post-) Keynesian monetary approach, and to present a general theoretical alternative formulation with respect to mainstream models, we postulate that the market economy, as a decentralized economy composed of private and independent agents, should be conceived of through money, so that exchange relations between economic units presuppose the existence of some monetary relations between them. These relations are grounded in a set of monetary rules. To be sure, money is neither a physical good to satisfy the wants of customers nor a service supplied by entrepreneurs in order to facilitate people's lives. It is a generic noun of a set of rules that allow agents to make their own economic decisions and to put them into practice. One of the essential aspects of the Keynesian revolution in economic theory is indeed 'the integration of money and finance in determining economic variables (doing without the postulate of the reals and therefore of the neutrality of money)' (Minsky, 1996, p. 71).

In this monetary approach, the decision power in economic activity is assigned to entrepreneurs. Consequently, if an entrepreneur decides to spend more (either for increasing his stock of raw materials or for paying higher wages, for instance) and if he obtains the funds he asks for, his higher expenditure will be reflected automatically in an increase in the deposits of those agents that are thus paid. As far as this expenditure is financed through a new loan arrangement (by banks), there will be an increase in money supply. Keynes (1936) argued that granting bank credit to entrepreneurs allows them to increase current investment (hence economic activity), which would not have otherwise occurred. Most important, Schumpeter (1961) pointed out that economic development is not a stationary-state phenomenon with saving flows that would permit the financing of investment. Therefore, the fundamental economic relations are tied up between banks and entrepreneurs, and not between undifferentiated representative agents as in the mainstream approach to macroeconomics. The supply of money is determined by the need of firms for loans to expand their operations and by the need of banks to earn profits from making loans. So, in such a credit-money economy, changes in the money supply are endogenous, because they are determined by fluctuations in the demand for money and not by deliberately induced variations of the central bank's open-market operations.

A monetary economy is an economy of contracts that are used to organize production and exchange relations. Money indeed comes into the picture via private debt contracts. Davidson (1994, p. 104) notes that there are three necessary conditions in order for a private debt to operate as a medium of contractual settlement: (1) private debts must be denominated in terms of the money unit; (2) a settlement institution for these private debts must exist; (3) a belief that unsettled debts are convertible at a known parity into the legally enforceable medium of contractual settlement should hold.

The first condition is the establishment of an accounting unit. Indeed, a unit of account allows economic relations to be measured in economic terms. As Keynes stated in his *Treatise on Money* (1930), the primary concept of a monetary economy is money as a unit of account that allows people to be defined socially as economic units. Individuals need money in order for them to enter the economic scene.

The second and the third conditions must hold when economic relations are not founded on an a priori market-clearing schema. The private and uncertain nature of economic relations calls for a socially generally accepted means of payment. Individuals need a common medium denominated in terms of their unit of account. This characteristic of money as a fully discharging medium comes from the decentralized nature of private relations based on the creation of debts at any point of time in economic life. In this respect, a monetary economy can be represented through two main constraints: the financing constraint and the repayment constraint. The financing constraint means that all economic decisions need to be funded by money in order to become effective. The repayment constraint is the obligation to return the amount borrowed when the debt is due. These constraints reflect the working of a monetary economy. In such an economy, the payments system, that is to say, the monetary circulation process, consists of a money-creation process (the emission of general means of payment), the modalities of the use of monetary signs, and a rule of settlement (repayment of debts and destruction of credit-money granted) (see Ülgen, 1995).

More precisely, when an agent wants to produce a real good or service in an economic system, that agent has to finance this decision, because the equipment, raw materials, wages, and so on must be paid before the product can be sold on the market. These decisions are founded on subjective individual expectations on the future state of markets. There is no centralized planning process that establishes a priori a set of interdependent equilibrated supplies and demands. Logically, when agents elaborate specific projects, they have to borrow funds from banks. Banks are the unique agents that can finance economic activities without having accumulated saving funds: they can create credit money in order to finance entrepreneurs' activities. Banks do not need to have accumulated savings in order to grant credit to businesses. They will create credit money (hence bank deposits) only if they consider that the entrepreneurs' projects are profitable. The credibility of the projects, the debt burden, the expected development of markets, and interest rates are some of the constraints that may keep banks from funding future production activities. This view conforms to the classical definition of a market economy, in which private economic decisions are free from collective planning, because they depend only on agents' expectations and on the access to money created by banks to fund them. In this view, the new-Keynesian argument of asymmetric information problems of a market economy (see Jaffee and Stiglitz, 1990) may hold, because banks are not forced to satisfy the financing needs of individuals. Banks grant loans only when they expect a sufficient return on them. If there is asymmetric information about some agents' capacities or intentions to perform under contract, which is the general case in a decentralized market economy where the information set is incomplete and differentiated, banks cannot rely only on the interest-rate vector to distinguish deficit units according to quality. Therefore, banks may ration credit (that is, they may not be willing to satisfy all demand for credit) in order to limit the amount of cheating by borrowers. This shows the active role of banks, and constitutes a decisive monetary limit to economic development.

Entrepreneurs undertake activities according to the level of aggregate demand they expect on product markets. They are only constrained by the needs of disposing of money. This is the free market economy and not a well-established coordination economy. This private credit money circulates in the whole economy as a general means of payment, that is, as money, because it is used to pay for wages and other necessary expenditures in the production process. Hence, macroeconomic magnitudes depend on the willingness of entrepreneurs and banks to undertake and to finance the relevant production projects respectively. Following the principle put forward by Kalecki (1971), aggregate profits or, in more general terms, economic development are determined by the spending decisions of the capitalist class. This class of entrepreneurs is motivated by what Keynes (1936) called 'animal spirits'. If their profit expectations increase, entrepreneurs will be more inclined to enter into additional forward contracts. Their demand for credit money (Keynes's finance motive) will increase even before any additional employment and income are generated (see Keynes, 1937).

Entrepreneurs receive as profit what they spend, and the total wage bill is determined by effective demand. There is no reason, however, why individual decisions should allow the economic system to be in general equilibrium. Changes in the level of credit demand are linked to entrepreneurs' and banks' expectations on future sales figures, and not to portfolios' adjustments of saving holders. Economic magnitudes are the result of debt contracts stemming from the credit-money creation process. Banks temporarily remove the budget constraint of entrepreneurs. Actually, the means of payment, denominated in the unit of account, is lent to entrepreneurs for the period indicated in a contract. Budget constraints are indeed not removed indefinitely.

Credit money is based on private contracts and does not have a social attribute: a set of social rules is thus required in order to give private banks' monies a generally accepted validity within the whole economy. Private commitments to pay circulating in the whole economy have to be established on explicit conditions of repayment. The repayment constraint expresses the impossibility for borrowers to fund their own activities via their own debts. This is a problem of convertibility between individual debts. Any agent has to accept the independent and subjective decisions (hence the debts) of other agents as general means of payment. In the same manner, the clearing of banks' accounts – which are the consolidated accounts of all economic relations – requires the introduction of a third party that must be independent of private agents. This third party, not implied in any contracts, is given in a monetary economy by the central bank and its 'money base'. The 'high-powered' money base gives monetized private-debt contracts a social attribute and allows banks' balances to be finally settled on the interbank market.

Entrepreneurs can repay their loans if they realized their plans as expected (thereby their debt is extinguished and credit money is destroyed). When entrepreneurs cannot repay their debts, an imbalance occurs. In this respect, three cases can be considered. In the first case, when entrepreneurs cannot repay their debts, they file for bankruptcy. Banks get all what they can from failed agents. The second case is the rescheduling of the debt maturity by banks with a higher interest charge in general. The third case occurs when entrepreneurs try to obtain savings from households. In this case, the short-term bank debts of entrepreneurs are transformed into long-term debts on financial markets. At this stage, banks engage in liability management, as they must first grant loans, and later on search for funds to replace those deposits that are leaking out of their balance sheets. When banks increase their loan portfolio, they try to find means to face deposit withdrawals for settlement needs.

Compulsory reserve requirements on bank deposits imposed by monetary authorities belong to the possible rules aiming to increase the safeness of the payment system. At the time of writing, most economic systems are imperfect overdraft regimes. Financial markets are developed and central banks intervene through open-market operations, while banks still borrow partly from the central bank and finance a relatively important part of economic activity. Therefore, central banks may apply frown costs (that is, raise the discount-window borrowing charges) when they consider that banks' loans become too expansive. As the central bank is the lender of last resort, its frown costs can affect interest rates on the interbank market. As Goodhart (1989) noted, however, restrictive monetary policies through so-called quantitative restraints on high-powered money led to a farcical situation, as the central bank is always obliged to provide the required monetary base according to the level of bank loans. This is true in an overdraft economy as well as in an open one: independently of the existing financial institutions, the logical monetary requirement of a capitalist market economy is based on the same relations. The central bank does not supply exogenous money; it only validates and controls, for the sake of the whole economic system, private financing relations, which imply the circulation of debts as money.

## Conclusion

In light of the alternative views presented in this book, it would seem wise to note that the analytical grounds provided by the theories of a monetary economy of production, through their logical framework as a relevant way of considering a market economy, seem to be able to sharpen economists' wits. This is even more so as, at the time of writing, the global economic system is experiencing a global recession, owing to the financial crisis that originated in the United States in the second half of 2007.

Indeed, money and monetary rules characterize a market economy and allow private agents to undertake separate free economic actions. If so, then two main conclusions have to be emphasized. First, as Hahn (1965) pointed out, the possibility of bankruptcy is a real possibility of discontinuity in the economic system. In an economic system where contracts are made in monetary terms and where the recontracting is neither obvious nor automatic, an equilibrium solution may not exist. Secondly, in this monetary setting, financial markets and savings (the Wicksellian loanable funds) do not enter into the picture at the beginning of the economic process but at the repayment point. Further, the interest rate appears to be determined previously, namely, through the credit-money creation process between banks and entrepreneurs. The financial markets' or the loanable funds markets' interest rate is therefore an *ex post* variable. Yet, it can be considered by individuals as one of the informational vectors when they make their borrowing decisions.

Studying the economy as a circuit of complex interactions among heterogeneous macro-groups in which the result of economic relations is an *ex post* observation depending on the compatibility (or not) of these decentralized decisions, one can argue that these interactions inevitably lead to conflict within the sphere of production. Hence, the role of economic policies should also be to stabilize the economic system according to specific distributional objectives. If so, then the rate of interest is an exogenous variable in the hands of the central bank, while money supply is endogenous, determined in the loans market as firms obtain credit from banks to finance production. However, the relation between interest rates and inflation is rather complex, and monetary policy is not the only tool to curb inflation in an economic system, contrary to what mainstream models do by relying exclusively on monetary policy.

Economic policies (mainly monetary policy interventions of central banks on markets through interest-rate announcements) supply private agents with common information in a decentralized context. Monetary policy does not aim to set an exogenous quantity of money. This logic leads us to conceive of some fundamental causal relationships in an opposed direction with respect to the money-neutrality view (Lavoie, 2004): interest rates become an exogenous variable determined by the central bank, because they are the prime or reference cost of borrowing; price levels and production levels determine the money stock (to wit, the total amount of bank deposits); financial conditions and debt burdens allow (or not) economic activity to develop. Therefore, a central bank's interventions should not be viewed as exogenous quantity-setting operations, but as monetary policies in order (or with the hope) to affect markets according to general economic policies. Of course, central banks intervene in markets and can affect, under certain circumstances, the evolution of monetary aggregates. But this does not mean that money becomes exogenous, although the central bank and its interest rate are both exogenous elements with respect to private markets, by definition.

From these general principles one easily concludes that in order to avoid the confusion between the effects of a central bank's open-market operations and the banking system's role in the economy, the first analytical step is to understand the very nature of money in a market economy. Further, the age-long debate on the real versus the monetary conception of a capitalist economy must give up the scene to the study of relevant conditions in which we can expect the economic system to behave more efficiently in respect of the development problems of our societies, otherwise monetary and financial crises will continue to exist without any coherent exit solution.

It turns out that the monetary circuit and post-Keynesian schemes can provide more relevant policy prescriptions than the usual economic policy agenda founded on the conventional economic analysis that considers crises as hitches in a (non-monetary) market-equilibrium economy. The monetary research agenda is neither simple nor obvious when confronted with several centuries of rigorous development in real-equilibrium economic theory, but as this volume testifies work is in progress and has the potential to become the new paradigm in modern macroeconomics.

## Acknowledgements

The author would like to thank Billur Altin and Sergio Rossi for their helpful comments on and meticulous reading of a previous draft of this foreword.

## Notes

1. Here we voluntarily exclude alternative textbooks such as Taylor (2004).
2. For recent references, among others, see Deleplace and Nell (1996), Holt and Pressman (2001), Rochon and Rossi (2003), Smithin (2003), Arestis et al. (2005), Fontana and Realfonzo (2005), Arestis and Sawyer (2006), Gnos and Rochon (2006), and Setterfield (2006).
3. Setterfield (2005, p. 32) points out that those new-Keynesian models that adopt an interest-rate-oriented policy to describe the conduct of monetary policy (instead of the manipulation of money supply) reach a new consensus on the same mainstream macroeconomics principles: the long-run neutrality of money and the automatic reversion of the real economy towards a unique supply-determined equilibrium. Yet, this is 'not the result of any new body of monetary theory. Rather, its source is pragmatism' (Setterfield, 2005, p. 32).
4. See Davidson (1978), Kaldor (1982), Moore (1988), Arestis (1992), Lavoie (1992), and Graziani (2003), among others.
5. See, for instance, Minsky (1986), Dymski and Pollin (1994), and Cartelier (1996, 2008).

## References

Arestis, P. (1992), *The Post-Keynesian Approach to Economics: an Alternative Analysis of Economic Theory and Policy* (Aldershot: Edward Elgar).

Arestis, P., Baddeley, M. and McCombie, J. (eds) (2005), *The New Monetary Policy: Implications and Relevance* (Cheltenham: Edward Elgar).

Arestis, P. and Sawyer, M. (eds) (2006), *A Handbook of Alternative Monetary Economics* (Cheltenham: Edward Elgar).

Cartelier, J. (1996), 'Payment systems and dynamics in a monetary economy', in G. Deleplace and E.J. Nell (eds), *Money in Motion: the Post-Keynesian and Circulation Approaches* (London: Macmillan).

Cartelier, J. (2008), 'Money: the case for an alternative economic theory and beyond', Working Paper, University of Paris X-Nanterre.

Davidson, P. (1978), *Money and the Real World*, 2nd edn (London: Macmillan).

Davidson, P. (1994), *Post Keynesian Macroeconomic Theory: a Foundation for Successful Economic Policies for the Twenty-First Century* (Aldershot: Edward Elgar).

Deleplace, G. and Nell, E.J. (eds) (1996), *Money in Motion: the Post-Keynesian and Circulation Approaches* (London: Macmillan).

Dymski, G. and Pollin, R. (eds) (1994), *New Perspectives in Monetary Macroeconomics: Explorations in the Tradition of Hyman P. Minsky* (Ann Arbor: University of Michigan Press).

Fontana, G. and Realfonzo, R. (eds) (2005), *The Monetary Theory of Production: Tradition and Perspectives* (Basingstoke: Palgrave Macmillan).

Gnos, C. and Rochon, L.-P. (eds) (2006), *Post-Keynesian Principles of Economic Policy*, vol. 2 (Cheltenham: Edward Elgar).

Goodhart, C.A.E. (1989), 'The conduct of monetary policy', *Economic Journal*, 99 (396), 293–346.

Graziani, A. (1989), 'The theory of the monetary circuit', *Thames Papers in Political Economy*, Spring.

Graziani, A. (2003), *The Monetary Theory of Production* (Cambridge: Cambridge University Press).

Hahn, F.H. (1965), 'On some problems of proving the existence of an equilibrium in a monetary economy', in F.H. Hahn and F.P.R. Brechling (eds), *The Theory of Interest Rates* (London: Macmillan).

Holt, R.P.F. and Pressman, S. (eds) (2001), *A New Guide to Post Keynesian Economics* (London: Routledge).

Jaffee, D.J. and Stiglitz, J. (1990), 'Credit rationing', in B.M. Friedman and F.H. Hahn (eds), *Handbook of Monetary Economics*, vol. II (Amsterdam: Elsevier Science).

Kaldor, N. (1982), *The Scourge of Monetarism* (Cardiff: University College Cardiff Press).

Kalecki, M. (1971), *Selected Essays in the Dynamics of the Capitalist Economy* (Cambridge: Cambridge University Press).

Keynes, J.M. (1930), *A Treatise on Money* (London: Macmillan).

Keynes, J.M. (1936), *The General Theory of Employment, Interest and Money* (London: Macmillan).

Keynes, J.M. (1937), 'The "ex-ante" theory of the rate of interest', *Economic Journal*, 47 (188), 663–9.

Lavoie, M. (1992), *Foundations of Post-Keynesian Economic Analysis* (Aldershot: Edward Elgar).

Lavoie, M. (2003), 'A primer on endogenous credit-money', in L.-P. Rochon and S. Rossi (eds), *Modern Theories of Money: the Nature and Role of Money in Capitalist Economies* (Cheltenham: Edward Elgar).

Lavoie, M. (2004), *L'économie postkeynésienne* (Paris: La Découverte).

Minsky, H.P. (1986), *Stabilizing an Unstable Economy* (New Haven: Yale University Press).

Minsky, H.P. (1996), 'The essential characteristics of Post Keynesian economics', in G. Deleplace and E.J. Nell (eds), *Money in Motion: the Post-Keynesian and Circulation Approaches* (London: Macmillan).

Moore, B.J. (1988), *Horizontalists and Verticalists: the Macroeconomics of Credit Money* (Cambridge: Cambridge University Press).

Parker Foster, G. and Ranson, B. (1987), 'Thorstein Veblen on money and production', *Economics and Societies*, 67 (9), 221–8.

Parkin, M. (2000), 'The principles of macroeconomics at the millennium', *American Economic Review*, 90 (2), 85–9.

Rochon, L.-P. and Rossi, S. (eds) (2003), *Modern Theories of Money: the Nature and Role of Money in Capitalist Economies* (Cheltenham: Edward Elgar).

Schmitt, B. (1975), *Théorie unitaire de la monnaie, nationale et internationale* (Albeuve: Castella).

Schumpeter, J.A. (1961), *The Theory of Economic Development* (Cambridge: Harvard University Press).

Setterfield, M. (2005), 'Central bank behaviour and the stability of macroeconomic equilibrium: a critical examination of the "New Consensus"', in P. Arestis, M. Baddeley and J. McCombie (eds), *The New Monetary Policy: Implications and Relevance* (Cheltenham: Edward Elgar).

Setterfield, M. (ed.) (2006), *Complexity, Endogenous Money and Macroeconomic Theory: Essays in Honour of Basil J. Moore* (Cheltenham: Edward Elgar).

Smithin, J. (2003), *Controversies in Monetary Economics*, rev. edn (Cheltenham: Edward Elgar).
Taylor, L. (2004), *Reconstructing Macroeconomics: Structuralist Proposals and Critiques of the Mainstream* (Cambridge: Harvard University Press).
Ülgen, F. (1995), 'Endogénéités de la monnaie. Fondements et définitions d'un concept: un bilan critique', *Economie Appliquée*, 48 (4), 29–59.
Woodford, M. (2003), *Interest and Prices: Foundations of a Theory of Monetary Policy* (Princeton: Princeton University Press).

# Preface

This volume offers a modern approach to monetary macroeconomics that is deeply rooted in the post-Keynesian tradition outside mainstream economics. It presents an original and controversial argument, which ought to stimulate debate on the topic within the economics profession.

Keynes is generally considered as the father of modern macroeconomics. The great step forward made by Keynes consisted in the choice of money as the numerical standard of value. His innovation was that of working out a *monetary theory of production*, and in this respect Keynes's work really stands at the origin of modern macroeconomics. As a number of contributions gathered in this book show, Keynes's message can be reinterpreted in light of the modern theory of the monetary circuit. In particular, it can be shown that macroeconomics is logically independent of microeconomics, and that it is macroeconomics that forms the hard core of any economic analysis, which is both real and monetary all at once.

The aim of this book is to provide further analytical evidence to support the real as well as monetary analysis provided by the modern theory of the monetary circuit. Together with the work of other authors taking part in this research programme (Graziani, Lavoie, Moore, and Schmitt, among others), this volume is a contribution to a new approach to economics, which will provide an original insight into the complex field of monetary macroeconomics.

Early drafts of the chapters gathered in this volume were first presented at an international conference held at the University Pierre-Mendès-France in Grenoble on 24 April 2007. On that occasion, participants engaged in open and lively discussions that helped shape the contributions collected in this book. The editors are particularly grateful to all the scholars who participated in the conference, as well as the local organizing committee for having provided an ideal framework within which scientific debate was possible in an open and pleasant environment. They also wish to express their gratitude to Palgrave Macmillan and notably to Taiba Batool and Gemma Papageorgiou for their enthusiastic and professional support during the development of the book. Finally, they also are grateful to Denise Converso-Grangier for her tireless efforts in preparing the ultimate version of the whole typescript.

JEAN-FRANÇOIS PONSOT
SERGIO ROSSI

# Notes on the Contributors

**Jean-Luc Bailly** is Associate Professor of Economics at the University of Burgundy in Dijon, France. He is a member of the Centre for Monetary and Financial Studies in Dijon. His research interests are in the area of monetary macroeconomics and history of economic thought. He has contributed several chapters to books and has published in academic journals.

**Riccardo Bellofiore** is Professor of Political Economy at the University of Bergamo, Italy, and Research Associate in the History and Methodology of the Economics Group at the Faculty of Economics and Econometrics, University of Amsterdam, the Netherlands. His current research interests include the economics of globalization, the development and crisis of contemporary capitalism, theories of endogenous money, Marxian value and crisis theory, and economic philosophy.

**Stefano Figuera** is Associate Professor of Economics at the University of Catania, Italy. He has a DPhil degree from the University of Burgundy, Dijon, France. His research interests are in the area of monetary macroeconomics and history of economic thought. He is the author of several books and has published in academic journals.

**Guglielmo Forges Davanzati** is Associate Professor of Economics at the University of Salento, Italy. His current research interests concern the post-Keynesian theory of money and the labour market. He has recently published *Ethical Codes and Income Distribution: a Study of John Bates Clark and Thorstein Veblen* (2006).

**Claude Gnos** is Associate Professor of Economics at the University of Burgundy, and Director of the Centre for Monetary and Financial Studies in Dijon, France. He has authored a number of articles on monetary macroeconomics, circuit theory, and the history of economic thought in books and academic journals.

**Jesper Jespersen** is Professor of Economics at Roskilde University, Denmark. He received his PhD from the European University in Florence, Italy, and was Jean Monnet research fellow at the European University

Institute in 1984–85. In 2001–2 and 2004–5 he was awarded the Carlsberg Overseas Fellowship at Churchill College, Cambridge, UK. His main interests of research are post-Keynesian macroeconomic theory, policy, and methodology.

**Steve Keen** is Associate Professor of Economics and Finance at the University of Western Sydney, Australia. His research speciality is developing complex-systems models, and in particular models of Minsky's financial-instability hypothesis. He has written *Debunking Economics* and is co-editor of *Commerce, Complexity and Evolution*. His next book will be entitled *Finance and Economic Breakdown*.

**Marco Passarella** is a post-doctoral researcher at the University of Bergamo, Italy. He has a PhD degree from the University of Florence, Italy. His research interests are in the area of monetary macroeconomics and the theory of value. He has already contributed some forthcoming chapters to international books and has published in academic journals.

**Marc Pilkington** is a Lecturer at Nice-Sophia-Antipolis University, France, where he holds the position of *Professeur Agrégé*. He has a PhD degree from the University of Burgundy in Dijon, France. His interests are currently in monetary macroeconomics and the economics of international business. He has published in international journals such as *Global Business & Economics Anthology* and *International Review of Business Research Papers*.

**Jean-François Ponsot** is Associate Professor of Economics at the University Pierre-Mendès-France, Grenoble, France. He was a Post-Doctoral Researcher at the Central Bank of Ecuador, and an Assistant Professor at Laurentian University, Canada. He has published in international journals and scientific books, on dollarization, currency boards, international monetary integration, and Keynes's economics.

**Riccardo Realfonzo** is Professor of Economics at the University of Sannio, Benevento, Italy. His research interests concern monetary circuit theory, the theory of income distribution, Marxian economics, and the history of economic analysis. He has published many books and papers in international journals such as *Économie Appliquée, History of Economic Ideas, History of Economics Review, International Journal of Political Economy*, and *Review of Political Economy*.

**Louis-Philippe Rochon** is Associate Professor of Economics at Laurentian University, Canada. He holds a PhD from the New School for Social Research. His research interests are in monetary theory and policy, macroeconomics, and development. He has published numerous books and articles on post-Keynesian economics.

**Sergio Rossi** is Professor of Economics at the University of Fribourg, Switzerland. He has a DPhil degree from the University of Fribourg and a PhD degree from University College London. His research interests are in the area of monetary macroeconomics, where he has authored and edited a number of books, contributed several chapters to books, and widely published in academic journals.

**Faruk Ülgen** is Assistant Professor of Economics at the University Pierre-Mendès-France in Grenoble, France. He has a PhD degree from the University Paris X-Nanterre. He specializes in monetary theory, macroeconomics, monetary policy, and in industrial and organizational economics. He has authored two books on market theories and on the coordination problems in market economies, contributed several chapters to books, and published in academic journals.

# 1

# Circuit Theory Supplementing Keynes's Genuine Analysis of the Monetary Economy of Production

*Claude Gnos*

## Introduction

When elaborating the *General Theory*, particularly in his 1933 writings, Keynes (1933/1979) showed his intention of working out a 'theory of the monetary economy of production' that would sharply depart from the neoclassical (or 'classical' in his words) theory of a 'real exchange economy'. He then essentially laid focus on the role of the entrepreneur and the functions of money in the actual economy, which is, he argued, an 'entrepreneur' or 'wage-economy'. On the neoclassical view, as is well known, the entrepreneur is a mere intermediary between the market for productive services and the market for manufactured goods, and money is a neutral medium of exchange, so much so that, in a state of equilibrium, the entrepreneur and money may be disregarded.[1] The volume of output and its distribution are determined by the interplay of supply and demand in markets, in a way that, under free competition, allegedly achieves an optimal allocation of resources. This is not so on Keynes's view:

> [a]n entrepreneur is interested, not in the amount of product, but in the amount of money which will fall to his share. He will increase his output if by doing so he expects to increase his money profit, even though this profit represents a smaller quantity of product than before. (Keynes, 1933/1979, p. 82)

> [t]he firm is dealing throughout in terms of sums of money. It has no object in the world except to end up with more money than it started with. That is the essential characteristic of an entrepreneur economy. (Keynes, 1933/1979, p. 89)

However, this feature of Keynes's economics has not been taken seriously into consideration. According to the conventional view, 'the hallmark of Keynesian economics is the absence of continuous market clearing' (Snowdon and Vane, 2005, p. 361). Unemployment would be caused by price and wage rigidities that prevent markets from clearing when there is a fall in nominal demand (for a critical review, see Rotheim, 1998, and Gnos, 2003b).

In his biography of Keynes, Moggridge accounts for Keynes's developments on a theory of the monetary economy of production in a way that is fairly typical of the way Keynesian economists, whether 'Old' or 'New', may think of the Keynesian revolution. According to him, Keynes's 'attempt to make his break with traditional theory more explicit through a "monetary theory of production" was to become more elaborate in his 1933 lectures until he dropped the whole notion as unable to do the job he wanted it to – to isolate the distinguishing characteristics of what he called classical economics' (Moggridge, 1992, p. 561). Then, Keynes would have turned to the development of his key notions of liquidity preference, effective demand and the equilibrating role of fluctuations in output. In the final analysis, these latter key concepts developed in the *General Theory* would be alien to Keynes's attempt to work out a theory of the monetary economy of production.

This is not the way proponents of circuit theory see the Keynesian revolution. On the contrary, they point out that the principle of effective demand, which is in Keynes's words 'the essence of the General Theory of Employment' (Keynes, 1936/1973, pp. 24–5), is precisely based on the successive spending and proceeds of sales entrepreneurs are to incur for a given volume of employment (see Gnos, 2006). Actually, they aim at showing that together with insights on money that Keynes developed during a time period extending from his 1930 *Treatise on Money* (Keynes, 1930/1971) to his 1941–43 'Proposals for an International Clearing Union' (Keynes, 1942/1980), the principle of effective demand allows them to work out a theory of the monetary circuit that supplements Keynes's genuine views on the monetary economy of production.

The aim of this chapter is to introduce circuit theory in making reference to Keynes's analysis of the monetary economy of production, its actual source of inspiration. With reference to the principle of effective demand, the next section will show that Keynes's ambition to break with the neoclassical approach to economics paved the way for elaborating on the concept of the circuit. The third section will hammer the point home with reference to Keynes's genuine insights on money. The fourth section will expand on a crucial feature of circuit theory, to wit, the distribution theory it entails. The fifth section will show the relevance of circuit theory with regard to the analysis of unemployment that Keynes grounded in demand deficiency. It will also examine the way circuit theory may implement the latter analysis. The last section will conclude.

## Keynes's ambition to break with the neoclassical approach to economics

Let us consider the principle of effective demand that Keynes introduced in this way:

> in a given situation of technique, resources and factor cost per unit of employment, the amount of employment, both in each individual firm and industry and in the aggregate, depends on the amount of proceeds which the entrepreneurs expect to receive from the corresponding output. For entrepreneurs will endeavour to fix the amount of employment at the level which they expect to maximise the excess of the proceeds over the factor cost. (Keynes, 1936/1973, pp. 24–5)

This quotation is no doubt in keeping with Keynes's 1933 conception of the monetary economy of production: it is the entrepreneur who decides on the volume of employment, and he does so considering the money he will gain in excess of its factor cost. However, to ascertain that the principle of effective demand is at odds with the neoclassical view, we have to examine Keynes's theory of employment in further detail.

Keynes goes on with the presentation of his theory in defining two functions. On the one hand, he defines the aggregate supply function, $Z = \o(N)$, where $Z$ stands for the aggregate supply price of the output of a given employment ($N$), that is, 'the expectation of proceeds which will just make it worth the while of the entrepreneurs to give that employment' (Keynes, 1936/1973, p. 24). On the other hand, he defines the aggregate demand function, $D = f(N)$, where $D$ stands for the proceeds which entrepreneurs are expecting to receive when selling the output of a given employment ($N$). He finally defines the effective demand that determines employment, as '[t]he value of $D$ at the point of the aggregate demand function, where it is intersected by the aggregate supply function' (p. 25).

According to the mainstream or 'orthodox' interpretation of Keynes's principle of effective demand, all this amounts to putting emphasis onto quantity rather than price adjustment (see Snowdon and Vane, 2005, p. 58). The difference between the neoclassical and the Keynesian analysis would be one of focus. To show the irrelevance of this interpretation, we can put forward two main arguments.

First, Keynes's aggregate demand and supply functions are in no way similar to the demand and supply functions defined within the neoclassical model. This is a point that Keynes emphasized in his 1937 lectures when rejecting the adjustment process between investment and saving depicted by his opponents. He namely argued that: '[e]x ante decisions in their influence on effective demand relate solely to *entrepreneurs'* decisions. Ex ante saving a very dubious concept – the decisions don't have to be made' (Keynes, 1937a/1973, pp. 182–3). On Keynes's view, the entrepreneur has to make a decision with respect to production at a time when incomes are not yet available – 'income, investment and saving [...] are *ex post* concepts' (p. 183). Factors are hired when production is launched; they are paid afterwards, when the production process is under way. The profit of the entrepreneur is formed when the goods produced are sold in the market. Accordingly, individuals do not make *ex ante* decisions with regard to the spending of incomes. As Keynes puts it, '[t]o begin with, they do not know what their incomes are going to be, especially if they arise out of profit' (Keynes, 1937b/1973, p. 216). Thus, there are no distinct supply and demand forces, which would be based on the behaviour of two different categories of agents, entrepreneurs and individuals, and which would adjust to each other and determine employment (see Gnos, 2004b). *Ex ante* is solely the domain of entrepreneurs' decisions, with the latter having to foresee what the demand will be.

In support of our argument we may observe that Walras, in order to conceive of the adjustment process of supply and demand, which is centre stage in the general equilibrium model, had to go as far as ignoring the time dimension of production: '[p]roduction, however, requires a certain lapse of time. We shall resolve the [. . .] difficulty purely and simply by ignoring the time element at this point' (Walras, 1874/1954, p. 242). This solution was coherent with his general equilibrium approach, by which production amounts to an exchange of productive services for goods. Contrariwise, Keynes takes time into consideration. He actually brings forth a sequential analysis, which is in no way a matter for Walras's simultaneous equations. It is true that supply and demand play their role in markets for goods, but it is not at the time when entrepreneurs have to make their decisions with regard to production:

> Time usually elapses, however – and sometimes much time – between the incurring of cost by the producer (with the consumer in view)

> and the purchase of the output by the ultimate consumer. Meanwhile the entrepreneur (including both the producer and the investor in this description) has to form the best expectations he can as to what the consumers will be prepared to pay when he is ready to supply them (directly or indirectly) after the elapse of what may be a lengthy period; and he has no choice but to be guided by these expectations, if he is to produce at all by processes which occupy time. (Keynes, 1936/1973, p. 46)

Secondly, Keynes denies the supposedly positive effect of changes of wages on employment praised by neoclassical theory:

> The argument simply is that a reduction in money-wages will *cet. par.* stimulate demand by diminishing the price of the finished product, and will therefore increase output and employment [. . .]. In its crudest form, this is tantamount to assuming that the reduction in money-wages will leave demand unaffected. [. . .] It is from this type of analysis that I fundamentally differ. (Keynes, 1936/1973, pp. 257–8)

As Keynes (1936/1973, p. 23) emphasizes, '[t]he factor cost is, of course, the same thing, looked at from the point of view of the entrepreneur, as what the factors of production regard as their income'. This means that wages fuel demand. To cut them is to diminish demand accordingly: the neoclassical assumption by which demand is left unaffected should be dismissed. Keynes is quite clear on this: 'if the wage-unit changes, the expenditure on consumption corresponding to a given level of employment will, like prices, change in the same proportion' (p. 92). We thus observe that in Keynes's theory, wages are in no way conceived of as an adjustment variable that would ill-advisedly be kept fixed (see Gnos, 2004a, 2005). As Keynes (1936/1973, p. 27) puts it, '[t]he essential character of the argument [Keynes refers here to his theory of employment] is precisely the same whether or not money-wages, etc., are liable to change'.

The arguments we have just examined in order to show how Keynes's theory breaks with the neoclassical analysis no doubt confirm the relevance of the circuitist approach to economics. Just as the principle of effective demand, circuit theory is namely built up with reference to firms' successive outlays and receipts and the resulting formation and spending of money income. In this way, circuit theory shares Keynes's sequential analysis, which starts with entrepreneurs' expectations with regard to factor costs and proceeds of sales in markets, and the correlated dismissal of Walras's real-exchange economy. Let us now turn to Keynes's insights on money that also laid the foundations of circuit theory.

## Circuit theory and Keynes's insights on money

First and foremost, circuitists refer to the 'finance motive' that Keynes defined in his 1937 articles on interest rate theory (Keynes, 1937b/1973, 1937c/1973). Keynes namely explained that entrepreneurs considering investing in a new production have to secure a 'financial provision', which they will use to meet their spending on production costs. He emphasized that banks and the new issue market alike can provide this financial provision that is designed to bridge the gap 'between the time when the *decision* to invest is taken and the time when the correlative investment and saving actually occur' (Keynes, 1937b/1973, p. 208). To grasp what is at stake, let us consider the sequence depicted in the previous section of this chapter.

As a first step, the entrepreneur has to make a decision with regard to the level of production and hence of employment he is going to implement. What Keynes's finance motive emphasizes is the fact that the entrepreneur has simultaneously to secure finance in order to pay for the factor cost he will meet when actually launching production. To that end, if we abstract from the deposits that the firm may hold with its bank (we shall reconsider this assumption below), the entrepreneur will borrow money from banks or the general public in the financial market. But, contrary to all appearances, the entrepreneur does not, in this way, borrow savings from the banks or the general public. As Keynes (1937b/1973, p. 209) puts it:

> 'finance' has nothing to do with saving. [...] 'Finance' and 'commitments to finance' are mere credit and debit book entries, which allow entrepreneurs to go ahead with assurance. [...] Credit, in the sense of 'finance', looks after a flow of investment. It is a revolving fund which can be used over and over again. It does not absorb or exhaust any resources [...]. Each new net investment has new net saving attached to it. The saving can be used once only. It relates to the net addition to the stock of actual assets.

To make sense of this argument, let us first consider overdraft facilities that banks commonly provide to firms. The very notion of overdraft facility is explicit enough: it is a commitment by banks to pay for the expenses incurred by their customers. Entrepreneurs are thus allowed

*Table 1.1* Entries resulting from the payment of wages from bank loans

| Bank | | | |
|---|---|---|---|
| *Assets* | | *Liabilities* | |
| Loans to firms | £*w* | Deposits of workers | £*w* |

to go ahead. When they actually pay for the wage bill of their workers, firms become indebted to banks while workers are credited with deposits in the banks' books. Just as Schmitt (1984) within circuit theory and Moore (1988) on the post-Keynesian side argue, banks' deposits are savings. Double-entry bookkeeping that denotes the equality of sources and applications of funds is namely deciding: banks cannot grant credit to borrowers without simultaneously securing credit from depositors. Keynes himself emphasized this feature of banks' operations in the *General Theory*.[2] Thus, when paid, firms' workers earn wages that they save until they spend them on the goods market. Keynes's analysis of the finance motive is clearly confirmed. Banks provide firms with finance in the form of drawing rights in order to allow them to launch a production and pay for their factor cost. The subsequent payment of the wage bill results in the formation of savings corresponding to the investment of money performed by firms. Then, firms become indebted to banks up to the sums of money paid to their workers. The production process thus generates a financial relationship tying up firms and their workers through banks, which is easy to understand (Table 1.1).

Workers, who will *in fine* be paid in goods (whatever the actual part of the output they will finally obtain), grant credit to firms until the goods being produced can be brought to and sold in the market. Just as the principle of effective demand claims, firms commit themselves in the operation with a view to sell the goods at a profit, that is, to appropriate a share of output. The financial relationship under examination is cancelled when workers spend their deposits on goods. Workers part with the deposits they spend while firms, which got indebted to banks when they had to pay for their workers' wage bill, become creditors of the banks (Table 1.2). Then, they can repay the loans granted by banks, or keep the deposits that result in drawing rights, in order to finance a new production.

It should be noted that, in actual economies with numerous banks, the homogeneity and convertibility of bank monies allow the development of a complex network of transactions allowing every worker and his

*Table 1.2* Entries resulting from the spending of wages on goods

| **Bank** | | | |
|---|---|---|---|
| *Assets* | | *Liabilities* | |
| Loans to firms | £*w* | Deposits of firms | £*w* |

*Table 1.3* Entries resulting from firm F2 paying wages from deposits borrowed in financial markets

| **Bank** | | | |
|---|---|---|---|
| *Assets* | | *Liabilities* | |
| Loan to firm F1 | £*x* | Deposits of F2's workers | £*x* |

dependants to buy whichever goods best meet their needs, regardless of the particular goods he actually produced. Further, the overlapping of production processes in the economy allows workers to spend wages regardless of the time it takes to produce and commercialize the particular good they produced.

Let us now consider the payment of wages from the general public's loans. We may suppose that firm F2 borrows deposits amounting to £*x* that were generated by a first firm, F1, when the latter paid for its workers' wage bill, and that are still unspent. To pay F2's wage bill, the bank debits F2's account and credit its workers' accounts. The resulting entries in the bank's books are shown in Table 1.3.

The bank's role ends there, but what actually occurs is a twofold financial operation. Income holders lend deposits to F2 in the financial markets, which simply means that they convert their savings from bank deposits into F2's liabilities. Their savings actually remain unspent: F1 has not sold the goods it produced and is still indebted to its workers through the bank. On their part, F2's workers are credited with deposits to which there corresponds a new output. We then understand that although the money is provided by income holders, firm F2 obtains a mere drawing right on banks, the use of which results in the formation of new savings. Of course, as mentioned earlier, firms may hold deposits with banks that they spend on wages. This does not mean that firms spend savings on wages. They simply give up the opportunity of spending their savings on goods.

From the two cases just examined, interesting conclusions may be drawn. First, the usual view is denied, by which bank deposits are one and the same thing holding concurrently the functions of means of payment and store of value. On the one hand, we observe that bank deposits, just as overdraft facilities, constitute drawing rights on banks by which depositors may ask banks to perform payments on their behalf, which banks will achieve in debiting and crediting accounts in the unit of account (for a detailed analysis of bank payments, see Rossi, 2006, 2007). On the other hand, bank deposits are savings by which depositors grant credit to borrowers through the intermediation of banks. Actually, the role of banks is twofold: they are both monetary and financial intermediaries. As monetary intermediaries they perform what Keynes in his 'Proposals for an International Clearing Union' termed 'the essential principle of banking' (Keynes, 1942/1980, p. 171), to wit, they simply debit and credit accounts with equal amounts of the unit of account.

Secondly, we observe that one and the same operation, namely the lending of deposits, may have differentiated meanings. If the deposits are spent on wages, it turns out that the borrower obtained a mere drawing right on banks: no pre-existent resources have been exhausted. On the contrary, new savings are formed. It is only when deposits are spent on goods that pre-existent savings are spent. In that case, the borrower spends the lender's saved income, and will pay off his debt later on out of his own future income.

These are findings that circuit theory has got hold of; it namely insists on the distinction between money and savings, and promotes a methodology inspired from Keynes's *Treatise on Money* (1930/1971, see in particular pp. 120–1), by which complex economic transactions derive significance from a restricted number of operations, to wit, the formation and the spending of incomes (see Gnos, 2003a). This is precisely the point illustrated at this juncture.

## Distribution according to circuit theory

Distribution is another main issue raised by Keynes's analysis of the entrepreneur economy. Keynes observes that in a 'real-wage' or 'co-operative economy', 'the factors of production are rewarded by dividing up in agreed proportions the actual output of their co-operative efforts' (Keynes, 1933/1979, p. 77). It is, he emphasizes, the case presupposed by the (neo)classical economists according to whom the determination of employment is linked to the interplay of supply and demand in the labour market, with supply and demand 'depending upon the expected amount of their reward in terms of output in general' (p. 76). In this case, there is no difference whether or not the services of the factors of production are paid in kind or in money. This is actually a conclusion drawn by Walras within the general equilibrium model (Walras, 1874/1954), according to whom labour, capital goods, and land are three factors the productive services of which are commonly exchanged for goods produced in accordance with the contribution of these services to production.

Keynes's view is quite different. Keynes discards the neoclassical tripartite definition of factors, and proposes to 'regard labour, including, of course, the personal services of the entrepreneur and his assistants, as the sole factor of production, operating in a given environment of technique, natural resources, capital equipment and effective demand' (1936/1973, pp. 213–14). He then consistently chooses the wage-unit as an appropriate yardstick for measuring the output of the economy as a whole. How are we to make sense of this proposal?

First, with reference to the analysis developed in the previous section, we may notice that spending money on capital goods is not equivalent to spending money on wages. When a firm pays for the wage bill of its workers, it forms new incomes. Contrariwise, when spending money on capital goods (including natural resources that are somehow produced by the firms which bring them to market) it spends incomes. It is worth noting that in order to apply the distinction he made between the factors and their services to capital, Walras had to assume that capitalists own capital goods the productive services of which they exchange for goods produced. There is no doubt that it is a quite artificial assumption that Walras himself had to discard when depicting reality further on in his book:

> [c]apital goods, proper, [. . .] are hired out not in kind, but in money. The capitalist accumulates his capital by successive savings and lends money to the entrepreneur for a given period; the entrepreneur converts his money into capital proper and at the expiration of the contract he returns the money to the capitalist. This operation constitutes credit. (Walras, 1874/1954, p. 228)

According to this quotation, Walras actually acknowledges that contrary to what he argued when building up the general equilibrium model, firms in reality do not buy productive services of capital goods owned by capitalists, but buy capital goods for money they borrow from capitalists. This does not amount to denying the role capital goods play in production; it means that money and credit shape the economy in a way that is accounted for in Keynes's theory and not in Walras's general equilibrium model. The physical features of production are namely second in comparison with the monetary and financial conditions of production. As for land, it too is not to be distinguished from its physical productive services; whatever its physical contribution to production, in a monetary economy of production, it is a real asset that entrepreneurs buy or rent (for a more detailed analysis of this issue, see Gnos, 2006).

Secondly, we may recall that according to Keynes the objective of the entrepreneur is to make a profit, that is, to receive proceeds in markets in excess of the reimbursement of the factor cost of the goods produced. Factor cost being equal to the wage bill, profit is necessarily the source of interest and rent. This is a point that Keynes explicitly considers although he does not expand much on it, when referring to 'that part of his profit which the entrepreneur has to hand on to the rentier' (Keynes, 1936/1973, p. 290). The issue, then, is to explain the formation of profits, which can be done as follows.

Since profits arise from sales, we may argue that they are a redistributed part of wages, transferred from workers to firms when sale proceeds exceed factor costs. To that extent firms and their backers are substituted for workers and will spend wages in their place: profits are included in the circuit of wages. Keynes outlined this conception in his *Treatise on Money*, when explaining that a fall in the selling price of goods below their factor cost would mean a loss for entrepreneurs, causing 'a transfer of wealth from the pockets of the entrepreneurs into the pockets of the general public' (Keynes, 1930/1971, p. 159). The same reasoning may be applied to profits that are symmetrical to losses, formed when prices in the market exceed factor costs (see Gnos, 1998).

In recent literature, some writers have wondered how wages formed in the economy and amounting to, say, £$x$ can pay for goods sold for £$x+y$ (for comments see notably Renaud, 2000, and Rochon, 2005). To address the issue, let us first insist on the fact that the homogeneity and convertibility of bank monies allow workers and their dependants to buy whichever goods best meet their needs. With respect to profit formation, this means that firm F will have no difficulty in selling a batch of goods G at a price of £1250, in the production of which it spent £1000 on wages, provided wage earners and their dependants are prepared to buy these goods for this sum of money. The extra £250 are made up of wages that are reckoned as F's profit in its books and were paid in the production of other goods in another firm. They cannot be spent finally but on these latter goods. This means that F's backers, to whom F will distribute its monetary profit, will buy these goods. It should be observed that part of the wages paid by F on the production of the G goods, may be spent on another batch of goods produced by another firm, form the profits of the latter firm, and be eventually spent on the G goods. The difficulty under examination actually arises from a methodological error (see Gnos, 2003a). Sale proceeds in excess of factor cost do not result, as commentators seem to assume, from a single transaction, to wit, the once and for all spending of £*x* on the produced goods, but from a series of transactions over time with individual production processes overlapping each other, some of them starting when others are ending. Circuit theory is not questioned by the diversity of the economic transactions taking place in the real world; it is on the contrary confirmed as a representation of the deep structure underlying observable transactions. In the final analysis, there is no question that wages are formed and spent in the production of goods and their subsequent sale in markets. The distribution of output as a whole takes place in circuits defined on each firm.

## A renewed analysis of demand deficiency

The circuit of wages that underpins Keynes's theory when the latter is focusing on entrepreneurs successively paying out factor cost and then recouping that cost from proceeds, entails that production generates wages, as well as incomes derived from wages, that are sufficient to pay for the whole output. In the example above, whether firm F sells the goods produced at a price higher or lower than their labour cost amounting to £1000, it incurs a profit or a loss that comes down to a transfer of income from the pockets of wage earners into its pockets, or vice versa. This means that whatever their price in markets these goods have a macroeconomic price of £1000 necessarily. This is why Keynes could address the mainstream argument by which a reduction in money-wages would boost sales by cutting production costs and hence the price of output (see above). The attempt by Keynesians, whether 'Old' or 'New', to reduce Keynes's originality to price and wage rigidity is all the more surprising. It may perhaps be explained by the fact that when comparing the expected costs and receipts connected to any quantity of employment, entrepreneurs take into account the current wages they are likely to pay out. Just as Keynes (1936/1973, p. 24) puts it, the factor cost per unit of employment is then to be considered as given, together with the situation of technique and resources. Now, with reference to the general equilibrium model, to consider wages as given amounts to assuming that markets are impeded to adjust in an optimal way. That is precisely the way standard Keynesians put it. Yet, in Keynes's genuine theory, employment is not determined as part of a system of simultaneous equations depicting the behaviour of economic agents; it is determined by entrepreneurs, who compare the expected costs and receipts they are going to meet when hiring workers. This makes all the difference.

How are we to explain unemployment? Keynes acknowledges that on his view unemployment cannot result from a lack of income: production generates the income that is necessary and sufficient to pay for the goods produced. This is why Keynes (1936/1973) pointed at a possible demand deficiency resulting from a deficiency of spending both on consumption and investment goods relative to current income, which he linked to consumers' propensity to consume and entrepreneurs' inducement to invest. In Keynes's (1936/1973, p. 27) own words:

> [t]he outline of our theory can be expressed as follows. When employment increases, aggregate real income is increased. The psychology of the community is such that when aggregate real income is increased aggregate consumption is increased, but not by as much as income. Hence employers would make a loss if the whole of the increased employment were to be devoted to satisfying the increased demand for immediate consumption. Thus, to justify any given amount of employment there must be an amount of current investment sufficient to absorb the excess of total output over what the community chooses to consume when employment is at the given level. For unless there is this amount of investment, the receipts of the entrepreneurs will be less than is required to induce them to offer the given amount of employment.

One of the prominent proponents of circuit theory, Schmitt (1984), has undertaken to show that circuit theory allows a revamping of Keynes's approach to unemployment, in exhibiting a fundamental source of demand deficiency that is not grounded in consumers' and entrepreneurs' forms of behaviour but in the way banks carry out monetary and financial operations involved in the process of firms' accumulation of capital.

To introduce the argument, it may be helpful to consider the way economists usually conceive of the formation and amortization of firms' capital. Particularly in the Austrian tradition (see Snowdon and Vane, 2005, pp. 474–9), capital goods are allegedly intermediate goods produced by firms and used in the process of production. They are gradually amortized, which means that from one period of time to another, firms sell produced goods the price of which includes the amortization of the cost of capital goods. In this way income holders buy used capital goods as component parts of the newly produced goods. Eventually, firms spend the sums of money obtained from amortization on new capital goods that will replace the used goods.

However, this account of the process of capital formation and amortization is only a rough account of the actual process. Let us namely consider the financing of production. We have noticed that when paying for wages, firms get indebted to workers through banks. This clearly applies to the production of consumption goods that workers will appropriate when spending wages (see above). It also applies to the production of goods that will be appropriated by firms' backers out of redistributed profits, because the latter are just substituted for workers, profits being a redistributed part of wages. But the case of capital goods is substantially different. To appropriate and accumulate these goods, that is, to get them free of debt, firms cannot but pay for the wages of the workers employed in the production of these goods out of their retained profits. It is true that, in practice, the purchase of capital goods amounts to inter-firm transactions. However, it is only the surface of things. Fundamentally, firms as a whole cannot be both buyers and sellers of the same goods. Then, if they are to appropriate capital goods, what actually happens is that they cannot but buy these goods when paying for workers' wages out of their own incomes, to wit, profits. Another way to make the point is to acknowledge that when spending profits on goods, firms retroactively fund the wage bills of the workers who produced these goods out of their profits. As an illustration, let us assume that firm F earns profits up to £500 that it spends on capital goods. This means that this firm appropriates goods and that, simultaneously, the debt of the firm that produced these goods, which had been generated in the payment of the wage bill of its workers, is cancelled accordingly. Of course, firms can either spend profits they earned beforehand or sums of money they borrow and will pay back in the future out of their profits. Anyway, a crucial consequence results from the appropriation of capital goods by firms.

Firms namely accumulate capital goods that are, so to say, outside the purchasing power of wages. In Schmitt's (1996, p. 102) words, the wages paid in the production of such goods are 'empty': 'from the moment they are handed out by firms, [they] are completely empty of all purchasing power, that is, devoid of any output'. Capital goods are literally fixed in firms' assets. This is due to the retroactive effect we have just mentioned. In our example, workers producing capital goods earn £500 wages the spending of which will not allow them, their dependants, or any other income holders, to appropriate the corresponding goods. The debt of the firm that employs them has notably been cancelled when firm F spent profits on the goods. The formation of 'empty' wages thus defines an inflationary gap (see Rossi, 2001), which will be repeated from one period to another through the amortization process. In our example, the wage bill in the current period amounts to £2000, while profits spent on wages amount to £500. Then, workers earn £2000 as wages that will allow them (or income holders in general) to buy goods worth £1500 only. Demand is in excess of supply. It is true, however, that when spending profits on the payment of the wages of the workers producing capital goods, firms do not buy those goods that correspond to their profits and therefore leave them available. The formation of excessive demand is thus offset by the latter goods. But that works once and once only, that is, when profits are spent on the payment of wages. As soon as capital goods are being amortized, the excess demand is confirmed.

To make the latter point, let us start with considering the amortization process of capital goods. Firms add the cost of the used capital goods, due to wear and obsolescence, that Keynes (1936/1973, pp. 66–73) labelled 'user cost', in the price of the goods they sell in markets. In this way, on the conventional view, income holders buy used capital goods as component parts of the produced goods. Eventually, firms spend the sums of money obtained from amortization on new capital goods that will replace the used goods. However, as already emphasized, firms cannot appropriate goods except in spending profits on the wages of the workers producing them. When paying for the user cost of consumption goods, income earners form (gross) profits to the benefit of firms that will be (retroactively) spent on the wage bill of the workers employed in the production of replacement goods. This implies that 'empty' wages are generated when firms buy replacement goods. Demand is then in excess of supply, and results in increased prices in markets and in the related formation of additional (net) profits to the benefit of firms. As Schmitt argues (1984, p. 222, our translation), '[t]he conclusion to be drawn from this, is that the amortization of fixed capital does not amount to simply reproducing capital goods [. . .] but that it generates a surplus equivalent to the depreciation taken into account'. Instead of a strict compensation of the loss of value in firms' fixed capital due to wear and obsolescence, the amortization process thus systematically induces additional profits for firms.

What is at stake, then, is what firms do with these additional profits. Several alternatives may be considered. First, firms can invest them in a new production, particularly in the production of additional capital goods. So far so good, but we may surmise that this alternative may prove unsustainable. Notably, the part of the output falling to firms cannot expand indefinitely, so much so that up to a certain point firms cannot but give up accumulating capital goods due to a decreasing rate of return on capital. If so, they may of course decide to invest their profits in the production of consumption goods. But, as shown above, it turns out that when funding the production of goods out of their profits, firms give rise to empty wages. This means that they would produce consumption goods that they would be unable to sell (these goods would namely be out of the purchasing power of wages). Firms would then be bound to accumulate inventories. This is not, of course, an appropriate alternative.

Secondly, and this sounds a plausible alternative when further investment in production is worthless, firms can redistribute profits to shareholders or lend them in financial markets. The problem, then, is that the spending of profits formed in the amortization process on consumption goods would generate equivalent profits to the benefit of the firms that sell these goods. As explained above, there is namely no debt in firms' liabilities that would be counterpart to empty wages. Therefore, when receiving the money firms become net creditors to banks. From a macroeconomic viewpoint, profits formed in this way cannot be definitively spent. A circular process is induced, which Keynes in his *Treatise on Money* labelled a 'widow's cruse' (Keynes, 1930/1971): the spending of such profits generates profits over and over again. In fact, just as Keynes then argued, although he was not considering the amortization process of capital goods, profits formed in this process 'must be regarded, not as part of the earnings of the community [...] but as increasing [...] the value of the accumulated wealth of the entrepreneurs' (p. 112). The process of capital accumulation is enhanced and, as a collateral damage, generates inflation in the economy.

All in all, the analysis of the formation and amortization of firms' fixed capital, as developed by Schmitt within circuit theory, proves quite informative. As we know, Keynes's analysis of demand deficiency has been blamed for being unable to account for stagflation, that is, the concomitance of deflation and inflation that was prevailing in the 1970s. Circuit theory no doubt takes up the challenge. The formation of empty wages, which defines an inflationary gap, simultaneously results in deflation. It is so because firms accumulate profits in a process that allows the production of goods that they are bound to accumulate in the form of capital goods or inventories of unsaleable consumption goods. A production process gets started whose aim is not consumption, as we would be expecting, but its own enlargement. Sooner or later this is bound to result in overaccumulation, and induces firms to cut employment. However, one may object that inflation has currently been eradicated in developed countries. Is the analysis stated here still relevant? There is no doubt that it is. Notably, inflation is not simply to be assessed with reference to increases in prices of goods. We have explained that firms accumulate profits they are induced to lend in financial markets. Then, inflation is also to be assessed with reference to developments in prices and amounts in financial markets. In that light, circuit theory no doubt appears quite relevant for explaining the 2008 financial and economic crisis experienced all over the world.

How is this issue to be addressed? We have no space left here to deal with this subject matter thoroughly. Let us simply mention that Schmitt (1984) has in this way worked out an approach to inflation and deflation that incriminates the way banks, as they presently stand, manage money and credit flows and stocks. It is an approach that had been initiated by Ricardo (1824/1951), and that inspired the Bank Act passed in the United Kingdom in 1844 (see Bradley, 2001). The cure, here, consists in changing the way entries are recorded in banks' books, in order to make monetary and financial stocks and flows consistent with the analytical distinction between money, credit, and capital. This would result in the implementation of three departments in banks: a first one devoted to money creation, a second one dealing with the management of savings, and a third department dedicated to the recording and management of firms' profits. In Schmitt's words, this third department would 'manage all income–expenditure flows relating to profits, in such a way that, henceforth, all remunerations handed out by enterprises to the factors of production will be real incomes' (Schmitt, 1996, p. 105). The challenge is namely to avoid the formation of empty wages when firms purchase capital goods.

## Conclusion

In this chapter we have introduced circuit theory with reference to Keynes's representation of a monetary economy of production. We have shown that Keynes's ambition to break with the neoclassical approach to economics and his insights on money undoubtedly paved the way for theorizing about the circuit of the wages that entrepreneurs pay out in the production process and recoup in sales. However, circuit theory is not simply a duplicate of Keynes's theory. It actually supplements Keynes's genuine views, especially with respect to his theory of unemployment. Circuit theory, at least in the version of it developed by Schmitt, notably provides a sound revamping of the analysis of demand deficiencies. It shows that unemployment is not simply a matter of economic behaviour, but primarily the result of mismatches in the monetary and financial operations occurring in the process of firms' capital accumulation. Then, the solution to unemployment lies in a structural change of the way banks carry out and record monetary and financial flows and stocks. The circuitist approach to deflation is all the more accurate in that it accounts for the circumstances that resulted in the 2008 worldwide financial and economic crisis. It namely accounts for the accumulation of liquidities and the related inflation in prices in financial markets as well as for persistent unemployment.

## Notes

1. '[W]ith exchange and production in a state of equilibrium we may abstract, if not from numéraire, at least from money, provided that the land-owners, labourers and capitalists receive from the entrepreneurs a certain quantity of products in the form of rent, wages and interest in exchange for a certain quantity of productive services in the form of land-services, labour and capital-services. Assuming equilibrium, we may even go so far as to abstract from entrepreneurs and simply consider the productive services as being, in a certain sense, exchanged for one another, instead of being exchanged first against products, and then again against productive services' (Walras, 1874/1954, p. 225).
2. 'The prevalence of the idea that saving and investment, taken in their straightforward sense, can differ from one another, is to be explained, I think, by an optical illusion due to regarding an individual depositor's relation to his bank as being a one-sided transaction, instead of seeing it as the two-sided transaction which it actually is. It is supposed that a depositor and his bank can somehow contrive between them to perform an operation by which savings can disappear into the banking system so that they are lost to investment, or, contrariwise, that the banking system can make it possible for investment to occur, to which no saving corresponds' (Keynes, 1936/1973, p. 81).

## References

Bradley, X. (2001), 'An experience in banking departmentalisation: the Bank Act of 1844', *Research Papers of the Research Laboratory of Monetary Economics at the Centre for Banking Studies*, no. 5, June.

Gnos, C. (1998), 'The Keynesian identity of income and output', in A. Jolink and P. Fontaine (eds), *Historical Perspectives on Macroeconomics: Sixty Years after the General Theory* (London: Routledge).

Gnos, C. (2003a), 'Circuit theory as an explanation of the complex real world', in L.-P. Rochon and S. Rossi (eds), *Modern Theories of Money: the Nature and Role of Money in Capitalist Economies* (Cheltenham: Edward Elgar).

Gnos, C. (2003b), 'The employment issue: Post Keynesian economics challenging New Keynesian economics', in E. Hein, A. Heise and A. Truger (eds), *Neu Keynesianismus: der neue wirtschaftspolitische Mainstream?* (Marburg: Metropolis).

Gnos, C. (2004a), 'Analysing and fighting recession with reference to Keynes', in L.R. Wray and M. Forstater (eds), *Contemporary Post Keynesian Analysis* (Cheltenham: Edward Elgar).

Gnos, C. (2004b), 'Is *ex-ante ex-post* analysis irrelevant to Keynes's theory of employment?', *Review of Political Economy*, 16 (3), 335–45.

Gnos, C. (2005), 'Circuit theory and the employment issue', in G. Fontana and R. Realfonzo (eds), *The Monetary Theory of Production: Tradition and Perspectives* (Basingstoke: Palgrave Macmillan).

Gnos, C. (2006), 'French circuit theory', in P. Arestis and M. Sawyer (eds), *A Handbook of Alternative Monetary Economics* (Cheltenham: Edward Elgar).

Keynes, J.M. (1930/1971), *A Treatise on Money* (vol. I *The Pure Theory of Money*) (London: Macmillan). Reprinted in *The Collected Writings of John Maynard Keynes* (vol. V *A Treatise on Money: the Pure Theory of Money*) (London: Macmillan).

Keynes, J.M. (1933/1979), 'The distinction between a co-operative economy and an entrepreneur economy', draft of *The General Theory*, Chapter 2, in *The Collected Writings of John Maynard Keynes* (Vol. XXIX *The General Theory and After: a Supplement*) (London: Macmillan).

Keynes, J.M. (1936/1973), *The General Theory of Employment, Interest and Money* (London: Macmillan). Reprinted in *The Collected Writings of John Maynard Keynes* (vol. VII *The General Theory of Employment, Interest and Money*) (London: Macmillan).

Keynes, J.M. (1937a/1973), 'Ex post and ex ante', 'Notes from Keynes' 1937 Lectures', in *The Collected Writings of John Maynard Keynes* (Vol. XIV *The General Theory and After: Part II, Defence and Development*) (London: Macmillan).

Keynes, J.M. (1937b/1973), 'Alternative theories of the rate of interest', *Economic Journal*, 47 (186), 241–52. Reprinted in *The Collected Writings of John Maynard Keynes* (Vol. XIV *The General Theory and After: Part II, Defence and Development*) (London: Macmillan).

Keynes, J.M. (1937c/1973), 'The "ex ante" theory of the rate of interest', *Economic Journal*, 47 (188), 663–9. Reprinted in *The Collected Writings of John Maynard Keynes* (Vol. XIV *The General Theory and After: Part II, Defence and Development*) (London: Macmillan).

Keynes, J.M. (1942/1980), 'Proposals for an International Clearing Union', in *The Collected Writings of John Maynard Keynes* (Vol. XXV *Activities 1940–1944. Shaping the Post-War World: the Clearing Union*) (London: Macmillan).

Moggridge, D.E. (1992), *Maynard Keynes: an Economist's Biography* (London: Routledge).

Moore, B.J. (1988), *Horizontalists and Verticalists: the Macroeconomics of Credit Money* (Cambridge: Cambridge University Press).

Renaud, J.-F. (2000), 'The problem of the monetary realization of profits in a Post Keynesian sequential financing model: two solutions of the Kaleckian option', *Review of Political Economy*, 12 (3), 285–303.

Ricardo, D. (1824), *Plan for the Establishment of a National Bank* (London: J. Murray). Reprinted in P. Sraffa and M. Dobb (eds) (1951), *The Works and Correspondence of David Ricardo* (Vol. IV *Pamphlets and Papers 1815–1823*) (Cambridge: Cambridge University Press).

Rochon, L.-P. (2005), 'The existence of monetary profits within the monetary circuit', in G. Fontana and R. Realfonzo (eds), *The Monetary Theory of Production: Tradition and Perspectives* (Basingstoke: Palgrave Macmillan).

Rossi, S. (2001), *Money and Inflation: a New Macroeconomic Analysis* (Cheltenham: Edward Elgar).

Rossi, S. (2006), 'The theory of money emissions', in P. Arestis and M. Sawyer (eds), *A Handbook of Alternative Monetary Economics* (Cheltenham: Edward Elgar).

Rossi, S. (2007), *Money and Payments in Theory and Practice* (London: Routledge).

Rotheim, R.J. (1998), 'New Keynesian macroeconomics and markets', in R.J. Rotheim (ed.), *New Keynesian Economics/Post Keynesian Alternatives* (London: Routledge).

Schmitt, B. (1984), *Inflation, chômage et malformations du capital: macroéconomie quantique* (Paris and Albeuve: Economica and Castella).

Schmitt, B. (1996), 'Unemployment: is there a principal cause?', in A. Cencini and M. Baranzini (eds), *Inflation and Unemployment: Contributions to a New Macroeconomic Approach* (London: Routledge).

Snowdon, B. and Vane, H.R. (2005), *Modern Macroeconomics: Its Origins, Development and Current State* (Cheltenham: Edward Elgar).

Walras, L. (1874/1954), *Elements of Pure Economics or the Theory of Social Wealth*, translated by W. Jaffé (London: George Allen & Unwin), first French edition 1874.

# 2

# Bridging the Gap between Monetary Circuit Theory and Post-Keynesian Monetary Theory

*Jesper Jespersen*

## Introduction

It is quite easy to make even rather straightforward issues complicated. By contrast, to make complex theoretical issues comprehensible is much less straightforward. Be that as it may, we will try to keep the discussion of how to bridge the gap between monetary circuit theory and the post-Keynesian monetary theory as simple as possible. For that purpose, the collection of papers edited by Rochon and Rossi (2003) is a very useful anthology.

Within monetary circuit theory the analysis of money and production occurs with regard to credit money. The focus of this theory is on how banks create money by extending borrowing facilities to firms and households. Banks have a unique institutional position especially with regard to business, because initial production costs can be covered by bank lending, which gives rise to bank deposits. It was really a major shift in financial institutional set-ups, when first commodity money (namely, gold) and later outside money (that is, central-banknotes) were substituted as means of payment in the business sector by bank credit. In that case, money – represented by bank credit – had become endogenously supplied by private banks and was only partly regulated by law and institutional requirements (see Graziani, 2003, and Realfonzo, 2003). By concentrating on bank credit, many circuit theorists only look at the specific property of 'money' as those financial instruments that have an immediately accepted purchasing power. By contrast, and generally speaking, post-Keynesian economists have a broader institutional and functional approach to money. They prefer to set off from the treatment of money by Keynes's two major contributions: *A Treatise on Money* (1930) and *The General Theory* (1936), where liquidity preference theory is presented as one of the distinct novelties wherein 'money' (bank deposits, overdraft facilities, and outside money) is an aggregate of financial instruments that can facilitate production and at the same time are considered as the liquid part of a financial portfolio.[1]

The monetary aspects of macroeconomic theory can be easily mixed up, if the macroeconomic intention of the analysis is not made clear. In traditional textbooks, money is said to have (at least) three different functions: it is a unit of account, a means a payment (immediate purchasing power), and a store of wealth. This might have been true in old-fashioned societies where gold (or corn) was the dominant and the only widely circulated monetary instrument. Today private banks have taken the major role of suppliers of means of payment – bank lending (and guarantee) represents a means of payment. Bank credit can be granted in different units of domestic or foreign currencies.

Within circuit theory the important aspect of money is whether or not bank credit can be used as final payment (unconditional purchasing power). Thus, in this chapter we shall concentrate on the second function of money, that is, as means of payment (representing unconditional purchasing power). This demarcation is a fair choice, because being a means of payment is today the most distinct property of money, as people have learned to calculate in real terms, and firms and households have also learned about portfolio selection theory – namely, that it is costly to keep wealth in the form of immediate purchasing power.

Having defined money as bank credit, we will concentrate on the demand for money and not go into any details behind bank lending. Very briefly, one could say that the supply of bank credit is determined by banks' portfolio selection, risk exposure, and the institutional working of the banking sector as a whole (see for instance Lavoie, 2003).

Monetary circuit theory concentrates on the monetary theory of production (Graziani, 2003), that is, on money as means of payment accepted by workers as final payment of wages. Production cannot be undertaken unless firms have access to means of payment, which are accepted by wage earners as immediate purchasing power. This is why money in monetary circuit literature is so closely related to production: without means of payment, no production can take place or be sold. Therefore, circuit theorists also make an effort to present a well-functioning banking sector (the financial technology) as a very important institutional condition for economic growth (Rossi, 2003). In a modern society, where specialization and labour sharing are pronounced, production cannot be undertaken unless means of payment are ready to be used for the wage bill. When wage earners have been paid, they are 'ready' to consume. Hence, when 'money' (as different from any other financial instrument) has been issued in the payment of wages, the transaction on the factor market is done. Wage earners know that the relevant means of payment can be used unconditionally later on, which, from a circuit point of view, is the important property of 'money'.

It is well known that Keynes (1930) was a breakaway from the orthodox theory of rate of interest by the introduction of his liquidity preference theory. This theory was further elaborated by Keynes (1936), when he emphasized the importance of money as a store of wealth. In this respect, Keynes was not very explicit on the institutional definition of money, but in a footnote he declared himself willing to accept short-term treasury bonds as being part of the money supply. Hence, the store-of-wealth perspective is overwhelming, which is very understandable: Keynes wanted to demonstrate as a theoretical novelty that the rate of interest is a financial phenomenon that cannot in any respect guarantee that investment and savings are equal at the level of full-employment output. The role of money that Keynes (1936) had in mind is the role fulfilled by a secure financial asset, which does not necessarily play the role of immediately available purchasing power. Within his new theory, Keynes did not concentrate on money as a means of payment, because that was the orthodox view. In *The General Theory* he disregarded the discussion of endogenous money supply by assuming the supply of money as given.

In this chapter we shall argue that, instead of contradicting each other, the theory of the monetary circuit and the post-Keynesian monetary approach complement each other. In our view, the theory of the monetary circuit should be considered as an important deepening of the understanding of the demand for, and supply of, money for the transaction motive within the broader framework of post-Keynesian liquidity preference theory, which emphasizes the store-of-wealth motive.

A unifying theme for both approaches to monetary macroeconomics is the theory of endogenous money supply and the role of banks within a monetary economy of production. This common analytical field was probably not understood until the breakaway from the old-fashioned assumption of an exogenously given money supply, which was a standard assumption within the neoclassical/Keynesian synthesis. The theory of endogenous money within post-Keynesian economics is most convincingly presented by Moore (1988). In his book, Moore (1988) proposes a theoretical model where the finance motive for demanding money is unfolded within a macroeconomic framework and integrated into a theory of the supply of private bank money. As Moore (1988) points out, any expansion of production at the macroeconomic level requires bank credit. Private banks play a pivotal role in providing loans, which give rise to bank deposits as soon as borrowers draw on the relevant credit lines.

Modern monetary macroeconomics consists therefore of four building blocks:

1. Liquidity preference theory inherited from Keynes (1936). This is a theory of a stock-and-flow demand for money where uncertainty plays an important role;
2. 'Money-in-advance' theory (circuit theory). This theory explains the creation, circulation, and destruction of money for transactions purposes;
3. Endogenous money supply (banking institutions and circuit theory);
4. Interest rate theory (combining central bank policy, liquidity preference, and uncertain expectations about future inflation).

This chapter is structured as follows. In the next section, we provide a brief historical perspective, showing that the divide between exogenous and endogenous money supply theory is 'old hat' and can be found in the debate between the Currency and the Banking schools of the nineteenth century. The third section is devoted to Keynes (1936) and the post-Keynesian monetary theory, with emphasis on uncertainty and the rate of interest as a financial phenomenon causing persistent unemployment. This view is contrasted with circuit theory (of production), which mainly focuses on money (considered as bank credit) as a necessary vehicle for undertaking production. In the last section we stress that circuit theory is a useful elaboration of the transaction (and finance) motive for demanding money, and an important expansion of the theory of (endogenous) money supply through bank credit.

## Monetary macroeconomics: a brief historical perspective

Money and monetary theory have been a central part of many heated debates through more than 200 years. One can detect a development within the history of monetary thought from Hume's specie-flow-prices theory to the fully fledged post-Keynesian monetary macroeconomics explaining money, production, prices, and rates of interest within one coherent theoretical framework (see Smithin, 2003).

Undoubtedly, Keynes (1923, 1930, 1936) provided important stepping stones for the theoretical development from the old-fashioned 'money as a veil' approach to the modern 'monetary (macroeconomic) theory of production'. But it was not until the endogenous money supply theory was developed that money, finance, and production were theoretically fully integrated into a coherent framework. Monetary circuit theory played an important role in order for this integration to occur (see for instance Graziani, 1990).

Looked upon in this perspective of theoretical development, one could claim that monetary theory is mainly mirroring changes in financial structures and technology. In the nineteenth century, the financial sector was much less sophisticated than at the time of writing. Money was either made out of valuable metal or paper notes based on a legal right of convertibility into silver (and later into gold), and issued in limited amount. Further, at that time there were hardly any trustworthy financial assets (except those with well-defined real collateral) for hoarding. In such a financially 'primitive' society, money represented purchasing power, and more money (or a higher velocity of money) meant increased purchasing power for goods (and services). Also, production was at that time restricted by supply-side considerations. Hence, it was a rather easy case to argue that money (especially monetary expansion) had no real, but only inflationary, consequences. In addition, organized lending and borrowing were rather rare at that time. Only people in acute need of purchasing power were forced to borrow and would in that case have little or no collateral, which explains why usury laws were relevant to prevent social misery and abuse. In any case, there were hardly any well-functioning financial markets (except for government bonds in a few countries), and the rate of interest was in most cases more influenced by flows rather than stock considerations. This explains why the flow-of-funds theory was thought relevant at that time.

The primitive financial sector and the dominant agricultural sector explain why the quantity theory of money and prices had some theoretical bearing in the past (see Blaug, 1995). Production was a real-sector phenomenon determined by supply-side conditions, namely, land, weather, and demography. Any excess of money would lead to inflation, independently of whether the cause was more gold or more paper money.

Historically, there is one major exception to this rather rigid monetarist way of thinking of money as a 'veil' and the only causality running from money to prices. This exception is the Banking School back in the early nineteenth century (see Hicks, 1967, and Smithin, 2003, pp. 87ff.), which claimed that the amount of bank money determined by business through discounted real bills could not be the cause of inflation.

Indeed, the partisans of the Banking School knew from daily practices in an emerging industrialized society that production was not an exogenously given volume of output. Production (and specialization) would in most cases grow and just keep the same rate of growth as the money supply, because credit money is needed in order to secure the financing of production. Banks could fulfil that role by granting loans without legal restriction, if they were allowed to do so.

In the Banking School we find the embryonic elements of the endogenous money supply theory to be developed later on in the history of monetary thinking. In many ways, the Banking School was a rather modern theory of endogenous money supply. Money was supplied only when it was needed, hence banks would always work in the right way. Only bank lending to dubious/uncertain activities might cause trouble. Yet, at that time (as today) banks had difficulty restraining their lending activities and not to grant credit beyond what was needed for the real-sector expansion. Therefore, followers of the Banking School acquired a bad reputation owing to the activity of too optimistic bank governors occasionally causing bank failures and financial misery.

By contrast, the Currency School, emphasizing the causality at the core of the quantity theory of money and prices developed by Ricardo (and Hume), appeared much more simple, understandable, and responsible – like currency boards today. This constrained rule for the money supply could limit the number of bank failures; therefore, the policy applying that rule was called 'sound money'. A restrictive bank policy, however, might have kept economic growth in a tighter straitjacket than what was needed. Be that as it may, the quantity theory of money became the undisputed theoretical foundation of monetary 'macroeconomics' until the early twenty-first century. (For instance, Alfred Marshall did not express any reservations with regard to this doctrine.) Keynes and the post-Keynesian School are the only challenge to the Currency School in modern times.

## Money, financial circulation, and macroeconomic reality in Keynes's view

Financial infrastructures and technologies were changing in the early twentieth century. In particular, the introduction of bank cheques together with overdraft facilities made money's velocity of circulation variable (Ingham, 2004). Further, it became increasingly indisputable that produced output was growing and followed an irregular path, which was not immediately explainable by the availability of supply factors

(Jespersen, 2002). On top of that, Keynes (1923) demonstrated empirically in his *Tract on Monetary Reform* that the velocity of money was unstable. As a result, there was no close relation between the development in the stock of high-powered money and the general price level.

These empirical findings were a theoretical puzzle as long as Keynes worked within the neoclassical framework of partial/general equilibrium models. In *A Treatise on Money*, Keynes (1930) tried to bridge the gaps within the quantity theory of money and prices between the real-sector development, prices, and the rate of interest by providing, on the one hand, the Fundamental Equation and, on the other hand, a more elaborate theory of money demand. According to the Fundamental Equation, in the short run price changes were generated by a mismatch of savings and real investments (real-sector phenomena). How could a mismatch between savings and investment be explained theoretically? For that purpose, Keynes (1930) introduced a distinction between industrial circulation and financial circulation of the money supply. Industrial circulation was intended to satisfy the flow-demand for money that was needed for undertaking and selling the production to consumers (and firms for real investment). By contrast, financial circulation concerns the stock of money that is demanded by those agents who make portfolio decisions.

The important theoretical innovation provided by Keynes in his *Treatise on Money* was the demonstration that the rate of interest in the short run was dominated by portfolio considerations, that is to say, expectations, which could make the financial rate of interest deviate from the natural rate of interest (Leijonhufvud, 1968). Keynes (1930) defined the (financial) rate of interest as the expected opportunity cost of holding money, which is the (relative) price between liquid and non-liquid financial assets. Accordingly, there will in practice be a full spectrum of rates of interest depending on the degree of liquidity and the expected rate of inflation.

> [In my *Treatise on Money*] I had, however, overlooked the fact that in any given society there is [...] a *different* natural rate of interest for each hypothetical level of employment. [...] I had not then understood that, in certain conditions, the system could be in equilibrium with less than full employment. (Keynes, 1936, pp. 242–3)

In *The General Theory*, Keynes at last realized that the macroeconomic development of output and prices could not be analysed within a general equilibrium, closed model – not even in the long run. The rate of interest was not solely determined by savings and real investment.

The financial focus was on the 'speculative demand for money', and speculative behaviour is generated as a consequence of different opinions caused by uncertainty with regard to the future. Uncertainty is an ever-present phenomenon with regard to economic decision making. Uncertainty, Keynes realized, will never go away. Therefore, a closed-system analysis, that is to say, general equilibrium analysis, cannot in most cases be relevant. Expectations are changing, because there is no long-run fixed point on which one can focus. As a matter of fact, the further away into the future one looks, the more uncertainty dominates. This is the methodological heritage from Keynes that post-Keynesian economists carry along.

## Major characteristics of post-Keynesian monetary economics

Contrary to mainstream economics, post-Keynesian macroeconomics focuses on the economy 'as a whole'. This means that macroeconomics cannot and should not rely only on aggregate microeconomic magnitudes. In fact, macroeconomic models can have different microeconomic underpinning, depending on the historical and institutional context, which is ever-changing. In correspondence with this methodological point of view, post-Keynesian economists emphasize the following key characteristics of macroeconomic analysis (see Jespersen, 2009):

1. Uncertainty is an unavoidable and ever-present ontological fact.
2. Macroeconomic models do evolve through real time and require an open-system analysis (for instance, a path-dependent analysis).
3. The post-Keynesian challenge is to develop an empirically relevant macroeconomic model.
4. According to King (2003, pp. 5–6), there are at least four distinct characteristics of post-Keynesian macroeconomic analyses, namely:
   - (i) Effective demand is the driving force of production and employment.
   - (ii) Real investment causally determines saving.
   - (iii) The rates of interest depend mainly on monetary and financial conditions.
   - (iv) There are no reasons to expect the macroeconomic system to be self-adjusting, and with regard to the long run 'we simply do not know'.

In some way all four points are interrelated. One cannot say that the last point is caused by the other three, because each of these points is influenced by the fact that the macroeconomic system is not self-adjusting, and with regard to the long run 'we simply do not know'.

In light of the above list, one cannot doubt that the analysis of the real economy and the financial sector is highly interrelated. Therefore, it would have been an improvement from the very beginning of the macroeconomic revolution after Keynes, if money and especially bank credit had been pinpointed as a precondition for making aggregate demand effective. Without bank credit, firms can only finance their demand for labour through accumulated profits. In early post-Keynesian theory there is an institutional missing link between money and production: one cannot really set up a 'monetary theory of production' without having the banking sector as a facilitating institution within that theory. The development of the institutional and legal framework concerning the banking system had an important impact on macroeconomic development, but this fact has not been systematically investigated from a post-Keynesian perspective (Chick (1986) and Chick and Dow (1997) are some of the rather few exceptions in this regard). Banks have the exclusive (internal) power of creating money (in the sense of generally accepted means of payment) by granting loans to creditworthy non-bank agents.

On the other hand, the store-of-wealth element of liquidity preference theory is one of the main features linking uncertain expectations about the future via the rate of interest to produced output. This is the novelty that still keeps post-Keynesian macroeconomic theory at a distinct footing from neoclassical theory. It is by adding the perspective of uncertainty to macroeconomic analysis that enables Keynes to explain why markets do not necessarily clear at the macroeconomic level even when prices (and wages) are fully flexible. A proper macroeconomic analysis with fundamental uncertainty integrated in a significant way requires an 'open system' approach (see for instance Jespersen, 2009). Such an open-system methodology makes it easier to understand that prices, the rate of interest, and the money wage rate might be 'wrong' from a neoclassical point of view. When uncertain expectations with regard to the future are taken into account, then it is not the lack of price flexibility that explains, for instance, persistent underutilization of available factors of production.

Uncertainty is, of course, an important element of the post-Keynesian monetary theory of production; but it is not the only relevant aspect. There is still the other element, consisting in the transaction demand for money. From that perspective, one may add that the better and with less friction the banking system is working, the less uncertainty can be attached to the fulfilment of the demand for money as means of payment.

## Specific features of monetary circuit theory

As mentioned above, in *The General Theory* Keynes left the theory of money supply rather underdeveloped, unfortunately. This was perhaps all right as long as the main purpose of his monetary theory was to argue that the rate of interest is mainly a financial phenomenon. According to Keynes, there is a different natural rate of interest for each hypothetical level of employment, which is determined by the level of investment and the propensity to save. One could wish that the theory of money supply had been more elaborate in *The General Theory*, because the financial arguments behind the principle of effective demand are left underdeveloped in that book.

This lack of elaboration was only to some extent rectified in Keynes's (1937) paper on the agents' finance motive for demanding money (and credit). In fact, it was not until the development of the post-Keynesian theory of endogenous money supply and circuit theory that the close connection between money and production was understood clearly.

Production cannot expand if the needed bank credit facilities are not made available at 'reasonable' conditions. Hereby, banks play a unique role with regard to the industrial circulation of liquidity. Their importance is better explained by circuit theorists than by post-Keynesian economists (see for instance Gnos, 2003, and Rossi, 2003). On the other hand, monetary circuit theory is rather lopsided by stating that 'bank deposits are the alter ego of physical output, and come to light as soon as the latter is monetised via the remuneration of wage-earners by firms' (Rossi, 2003, p. 344). A more general statement about banks' activities cannot exclude bank credit used for portfolio reshuffling. If the state of confidence is becoming more insecure, there will be a tendency within society as a whole to demand more short-term financial instruments. Banks could expand their balance sheets by acquiring bonds and shares at the expense of accepting more deposits. This banking behaviour would be statistically registered as an increased money supply, but will have no direct impact on the real economy.

Now let us have a closer look at monetary circuit theory, where banks play a pivotal role in providing working capital to businesses (that is, Keynes's industrial circulation) (see Realfonzo, 2003).

1. Monetary circuit analysis is (often) limited to one production period. Firms ask for and obtain loans from banks in order for

them to have the necessary working capital to pay for production costs (mainly the wage bill). If all goods are sold, these loans are repaid at the end of the period. This analysis gives a static impression compared with reality, because production is a continuously ongoing process. Wages are paid either weekly or monthly, and goods are sold continuously. As long as production is going on, the needed amount of bank loans during (say) one month is unchanged. Of course, during the month there might be waves on the overdraft account, but this has no real impact on the economic system.

2. When goods are unsold, firms are making losses and have to ask for more loans to continue their production. If unsold goods are piling up, there is an increased risk of bankruptcy. Banks will have to decide when to stop 'throwing good money after bad', and accept that some of the loans cannot be paid back to their full amount. This microeconomic risk related to any loan is at least partly compensated through the payment of interest on bank loans, which may be considered as a kind of risk premium.
3. Hence, the payment of interest (like any other insurance premium) is a cost that is added to wages and sales taxes, and has to be covered through a price mark-up. Higher rates of interest (in excess of productivity gains and expected inflation) have (like an increased sales tax) a contractive macroeconomic effect, unless the banks' profit (like sales tax) is 'reinjected' into the circuit.

Following this monetary circuit approach, we note that the post-Keynesian concept of effective demand cannot be made 'effective' unless working capital is made available. Firms may be ready to undertake production, because they think that sale proceeds will exceed costs – this is a necessary condition – but until finance is made available to them by banks, the sufficient condition for making production real is not present. As a matter of fact, to make production effective, not only will firms have to find this profitable, but also bankers have to be convinced of this profitability. If the bankers do not grant credit, aggregate demand cannot become effective.

Hence, in a monetary production economy banks have the last word when an expansion of production (and employment) is planned by firms. If banks decide not to grant credit for working capital, firms cannot expand production. Similarly, in case of (wage) cost inflation, firms have to cut back on production (or to accept a fall in the profit rate), if banks refuse to grant them new credit.

## The determination of the rate of interest

Keynes (1936) made us understand that the rate of interest is a macroeconomic variable determined in the economy 'as a whole' (see Jespersen, 2009). In practice, the rate of interest is the 'inverted' price of bonds. Now from microeconomics one knows that the price of an asset is determined by its demand and supply and by the prices of its closest substitutes – according to Keynes, other financial assets and especially money. These microeconomic considerations have to be put into a macroeconomic context, because the rate of interest is a macroeconomic variable. Therefore, the rate of interest is also influenced by the development of investment and saving. To make his case persuasive in *The General Theory*, Keynes (1936) assumed the money supply as given, and bonds and money to be close substitutes. In this very simplified framework, the rate of interest featured as a financial variable mainly determined as the cost of holding money.

When the assumption of a given supply of money is given up and substituted by the endogenous money supply hypothesis, the determination of the (long-run) rate of interest becomes much more complicated, as it is determined by the whole economic system. In this fundamentally changed framework, the short-run rate of interest fixed by the central bank becomes the 'financial anchor'. The interbank market rate of interest becomes the 'basic' price for banks when they decide which rate(s) of interest they will charge on loans and pay on deposits. As we know from liquidity preference theory, in the financial sector there is a spectrum of rates of interest. The shape of the money supply curve varies with a number of factors, the most important of them being the expected rate of inflation (and uncertainty related to this expectation).

Hence, if the endogenous element of money supply becomes dominant, which is the case in a well-functioning banking sector, then monetary theory comes close to the horizontalists' stance as cogently described by Smithin (2003, pp. 202–3):

> The 'supply of money' function therefore becomes a horizontal line at the administratively determined short-term nominal interest rate [. . .]. There may be limits to bank lending, reflected in higher interest charges or credit rationing, at the microeconomic level of the individual bank or individual client, but the same restrictions do not apply to the overall system expanding in concert.[2]

As a consequence, liquidity preference theory plays a significant but minor role with regard to the theory of interest. In fact, much less is said today about the long-run rate of interest than was the case in *The General Theory*. When the assumption of a given stock of money is given up, the long-run rate of interest is not only determined by the relative price of money and bonds within the private sector's portfolio: all relevant (financial) assets play a role in this respect, and their relative prices are mainly driven by the uncertain expectations of future inflation together with the short-run rate of interest. In the short-run perspective, nothing can prevent the short- and long-term rates of interest from departing from one another. The so-called 'perverse' yield curve has been observed more often than not. The main point to emphasize in this connection, however, is that even with endogenous money supply the long-run rate of interest is not determined by loanable funds alone, as portfolio (stock) considerations are still of great importance in this respect.

In this form, Keynes's liquidity preference theory of the rate of interest has survived to date. At the same time, one understands why the monetary policy tool of 'open market operations' has gone out of fashion: at the time of writing, the market for corporate and government bonds, together with markets for other close financial substitutes, is immense and driven by expectations to such an extent that no central bank governor would imagine going against the market through direct interventions. Hence, the only monetary policy instrument left is the short-run rate of interest, which has quite an impact on the cost of bank credit and, through this, on the cost of the 'monetary circuit'.

## Is there a gap to be bridged? Some concluding remarks

In our interpretation, monetary circuit theory is a useful and essential elaboration on, and expansion of, the monetary theory of production. Monetary circuit theorists focus mainly on the flow dimension of the money creation process related to production. They emphasize correctly that production costs usually have to be paid before goods (and services) can be sold to consumers. Hence, it is a money-in-advance theory, and in that respect the modern organization of the banking sector is instrumental. The banking system is able to create a nearly unlimited amount of credit, because any excess or deficit of deposits can be levelled out via the interbank market. In its crude, stylized form, the banking system cannot by itself become illiquid. Whenever a bank grants a loan, the borrower will draw on his credit line, and by that activity a bank deposit is created. This self-contained banking system was in practice as long as industrialized countries shielded themselves financially through international capital controls. In that period it was not easy to get foreign bank credit to pay for imports, which led to the establishment of the European Payments Union in the 1950s. Today, one might consider the entire cross-border banking system as an interrelated system, but with exchange-rate uncertainty attached to it.

Monetary circuit theorists were in some way the first group of post-Keynesian economists to emphasize the specific role of the banking system as provider of the needed money-in-advance to make Keynes's principle of effective demand 'effective'. This happened through the focus of monetary circuit theorists on the banking system (as a whole) as being indispensable to understanding how Keynes could speak so consequently of a 'monetary' theory of production.

On the other hand, it is true that monetary circuit theory did not concentrate on money as a store of value and on the rate of interest, which is left to post-Keynesian monetary theory to explain through its emphasis on uncertainty and expectations in relation to portfolio choices. This latter aspect, however, does not change the overall impression that monetary circuit theory has filled a gap, which has made post-Keynesian monetary theory more consistent and brought it closer to reality.

## Acknowledgements

This chapter was presented at the first international workshop on monetary circuit theory and post-Keynesian monetary economics, held at the Pierre-Mendès-France University in Grenoble, France, on 24 April 2007. The author has benefited from a number of relevant comments from workshop participants, who, of course, have no responsibility for his own interpretation of the issues discussed in this chapter.

## Notes

1. Keynes was so concerned with showing that the rate of interest was a financial (and not a real) phenomenon that he lumped the demand for means of payment together with the demand for a risk-free financial asset.
2. Hence, also in this case, the 'whole' is different from the sum of its constituent parts.

## References

Blaug, M. (ed.) (1995), *The Quantity Theory of Money: From Locke to Keynes and Friedman* (Cheltenham: Edward Elgar).

Chick, V. (1986), 'The evolution of the banking system and the theory of saving, investment and interest', *Économies et Sociétés* (Série Monnaie et Production, 3), 20 (8–9), 111–26.
Chick, V. and Dow, S.C. (1997), 'Competition and integration in European banking', in A. Cohen, H. Hagemann and J. Smithin (eds), *Money, Financial Institutions and Macroeconomics* (Boston: Kluwer).
Gnos, C. (2003), 'Circuit theory as an explanation of the complex real world', in L.-P. Rochon and S. Rossi (eds), *Modern Theories of Money: the Nature and Role of Money in Capitalist Economies* (Cheltenham: Edward Elgar).
Graziani, A. (1990), 'The theory of the monetary circuit', *Économies et Sociétés* (Série Monnaie et Production, 7), 24 (6), 7–36.
Graziani, A. (2003), *The Monetary Theory of Production* (Cambridge: Cambridge University Press).
Hicks, J. (1967), *Critical Essays in Monetary Theory* (Oxford: Clarendon Press).
Ingham, G. (2004), *The Nature of Money* (Cambridge: Polity Press).
Jespersen, J. (2002), 'Why do economists disagree on the EMU?', in P. Arestis, M. Desai and S. Dow (eds), *Money, Macroeconomics and Keynes: Essays in Honour of Victoria Chick*, vol. 1 (London: Routledge).
Jespersen, J. (2009), *Macroeconomic Methodology: a Post-Keynesian Perspective* (Cheltenham: Edward Elgar).
Keynes, J.M. (1923), *A Tract on Monetary Reform* (London: Macmillan).
Keynes, J.M. (1930), *A Treatise on Money* (London: Macmillan).
Keynes, J.M. (1936), *The General Theory of Employment, Interest and Money* (London: Macmillan).
Keynes, J.M. (1937), 'The general theory of employment', *Quarterly Journal of Economics*, 51 (2), 209–23.
King, J. (ed.) (2003), *The Elgar Companion to Post-Keynesian Economics* (Cheltenham: Edward Elgar).
Lavoie, M. (2003), 'A primer on endogenous credit-money', in L.-P. Rochon and S. Rossi (eds), *Modern Theories of Money: the Nature and Role of Money in Capitalist Economies* (Cheltenham: Edward Elgar).
Leijonhufvud, A. (1968), *Keynesian Economics and the Economics of Keynes* (New York: Oxford University Press).
Moore, B.J. (1988), *Horizontalists and Verticalists: the Macroeconomics of Credit Money* (Cambridge: Cambridge University Press).
Realfonzo, R. (2003), 'Circuit theory', in J. King (ed.), *The Elgar Companion to Post-Keynesian Economics* (Cheltenham: Edward Elgar).
Rochon, L.-P. and Rossi, S. (eds) (2003), *Modern Theories of Money: the Nature and Role of Money in Capitalist Economies* (Cheltenham: Edward Elgar).
Rossi, S. (2003), 'Money and banking in a monetary theory of production', in L.-P. Rochon and S. Rossi (eds), *Modern Theories of Money: the Nature and Role of Money in Capitalist Economies* (Cheltenham: Edward Elgar).
Smithin, J. (2003), *Controversies in Monetary Economics*, rev. edn (Cheltenham: Edward Elgar).

# 3

# Monetary Circuit Theory and Money Emissions

*Sergio Rossi*

## Introduction

This chapter focuses on the emission of money and its relation with the working of the banking system in a monetary economy of production and exchange. Referring to the main contributions in this field, this chapter shows that bank money is a macroeconomic flow, while income is a macroeconomic stock in the form of bank deposits. This chapter notably explains that banks can and do issue money but that money's purchasing power is the result of an integration of banking and production systems, both of which contribute to the creation of value. In particular, this chapter addresses the conceptual and factual distinction between money, credit, and income from a monetary macroeconomics point of view, going back to Keynes's insights in both *A Treatise on Money* and *The General Theory*, and referring to the work of post-Keynesian authors as well as monetary circuit theorists, considered in light of the theory of money emissions (see Rossi, 2006, for a survey of the latter theory).

The theory of money emissions is a paradigm of monetary macroeconomics that in the late 1950s emerged in France and Switzerland under the lead of Schmitt (1960), who gave rise to what he called 'quantum theory of production' (see Schmitt, 1982, 1984, 1988; Cencini, 1985a, b, 1988, 2001, 2005; Rossi, 1998, 2001, 2003, 2007). This school of thought inspired the French–Italian theory of the monetary circuit, led by Graziani (1985, 1987, 1994a, b, 2003) in Italy and by Parguez (1975, 1982, 1984, 1986, 1987) in France, which also enthused a group of scholars in Canada under the leadership of Lavoie (1984a, b, 1985a, 1987) (see Seccareccia, 1996; Rochon, 1999b, 2000; Parguez and Seccareccia, 2000). The founding fathers of the modern monetary circuit approach (see Parguez, 1975, and Graziani, 1990) recognized in their early writings on this subject matter that their own research work had been inspired by Schmitt's. Indeed, Graziani (1994b, p. 13, our translation) goes so far to acknowledge that Schmitt 'is the author who has developed most rigorously both the theoretical and the terminological principles of the circuit doctrine, and who has adhered to them with steadfast consistency'. He further observes that 'Schmitt is the author who has gone more deeply into the analysis of banking activity' (Graziani, 1990, p. 32, fn. 7). Also, Le Bourva (1962) – who is quite often considered as a forerunner of the post-Keynesian theory of endogenous money *à la* Kaldor–Moore (see Lavoie, 1992, p. 436) – refers to Schmitt (1960) when he adopts the terminology that has been introduced by the latter author to express the monetary circuit in a 'money-wage' or 'entrepreneur' economy in Keynes's (1933/1973, p. 89) sense (that is to say, a monetary economy of production; in this respect see Graziani, 2003).

This chapter starts off from the fact that, in a monetary economy, '[a]ny transaction involves three parties, namely a payer, a payee, and a banker', as pointed out by Hicks (1967, p. 11). It thereby introduces in the next section the analysis of money advocated by the proponents of the theory of money emissions, and investigates the workings of a monetary economy of production with this paradigm, confronting it with the French–Italian circuit school in an attempt at cross-fertilization. In doing so, it explains in the third section how '[m]oney is introduced into the economy through the productive activities of the firms, as these activities generate income' (Lavoie, 1984b, p. 774).

Grounded in Keynes's (1930, p. 134) view that 'human effort', that is, production, and 'human consumption are the ultimate matters from which alone economic transactions are capable of deriving any significance', the third section presents an investigation of the production–consumption process in which production is not a function of time, but an instantaneous event – in economic, though not in physical, terms – which 'quantizes' time. Indeed,

> in economics, production is an instantaneous event relating to a finite and indivisible period of time (a quantum of time) and its result, the product, is nothing other than this quantum. [...] In particular, the payment of wages is an instantaneous event which, defining a positive income formation, refers to a finite period of time [that is, the period over which wages accrue on a contractual basis]. (Cencini, 2001, pp. 116–17)

This amounts to saying that if the payment of wages occurs (say) once per calendar month, then each month is defined as a finite and indivisible period of time in economic analysis, and the corresponding income is formed as a net magnitude for the economy as a whole. Indeed, what workers earn is not lost by firms: even when firms use a pre-existent bank deposit to pay out wages, thus activating a wage fund (that is, circulating capital), the emission of money for the remuneration of wage earners occurs as if it started from a *tabula rasa*. As a matter of fact, distinguishing money (a purely numerical 'vehicle') from bank deposits (a liquid store of wealth) leads us to explain that any wage payments, even those carried out in practice with a circulating capital, need the emission of a purely numerical means of payment in order to be finalized.

As a matter of fact, when a final payment occurs, the banking system has to intervene in order for it to provide the contracting (non-bank) agents with the number of money units necessary to measure the very object of the transaction economically, and to settle debt between them. Without money, in reality, no numerical standard would be available to measure the value of those objects that agents exchange, and, more important for the contracting parties, in order to settle their debt obligations resulting from exchange. The point to be underlined in this perspective is that money is in reality the means, not the object, of payments. Banks themselves cannot provide the 'content' of payments: this is always and everywhere the result of production necessarily, that is to say, the efforts accomplished by workers whose outcome (that is, produced output) the banking system monetizes when a firm uses the credit line that a bank has granted to it for that purpose.

The conclusion that we reach in this chapter is that investigating money, credit, income as well as production within the so-called 'circuitist' framework shows the logical need to move from a sequential (that is to say, defined in time) to an instantaneous approach to a monetary circuit. The bottom line is notably that bank money is a macroeconomic flow whose instantaneous circuit has a stock of income as its object, and that banks create the flow but not its object, which is intimately related to production. Let us proceed step by step towards this conclusion, which will provide the *macroeconomic* foundations of macroeconomics, thus opening a whole new field of investigation for macroeconomic policy making, focusing on conceptual rather than mathematical reasoning in economics (see Schmitt, 1986). To be sure, real-world macroeconomic problems have a monetary–structural origin, and can only be appraised through a truly macroeconomic approach, to wit, one which avoids 'microfounding' it on the agents' forms of behaviour and thereby the 'fallacy of composition' that any economists ought to keep in the back of their minds when doing any macroeconomic analyses (see Rossi, 2008, for analytical elaboration in this regard).

## On money emissions and monetary circuits

Advocates of the monetary circuit approach put money at the centre of their analyses of the workings of our capitalist economies of production. They emphasize the sequential nature of monetary flows in the circular process of production–consumption involving the set of firms and the set of households with the intervention of the banking system considered as a whole (see Gnos, 2006, and Realfonzo, 2006, for recent surveys of this approach). To date, it is quite usual in the literature to assimilate the theory of money emissions to monetary circuit theory, considering the former as a different version of the same paradigm (see for instance Chick, 2000). In fact, these are two absolutely different paradigms within heterodox monetary economics. In particular, Graziani and Parguez's approach on one side and, on the other, Schmitt's conception of bank money and monetary macroeconomics strongly differ and are also in sharp contrast to one another. These differences are so deep that, as noted by Deleplace and Nell (1996, p. 38, fn. 8), Schmitt has come to refuse to define the paradigm he has been working on since 1956 as being a 'circuitist' approach. As Gnos and Rasera (1985) explain, the principal reason for this refusal resides in the fact that, for monetary circuit authors, the circuit of money takes time to be completed, whilst for Schmitt and his scholars money is defined as an instantaneous circular flow from and to its issuing bank. In other words, according to a monetary 'circuitist' money *flows* within the economic system – as in the famous Robertson (1937, p. 29) view that considers 'money on the wing' as opposed to 'money at rest' – whilst for a proponent of the Schmitt approach money *is* a flow essentially, to be distinguished from bank deposits, which are stocks (of purchasing power). As Lavoie (1987, pp. 71–2, our translation) notes in this regard, '[i]nitially, money appears in the form of a flow. It is only at the end of the circuit that money will become a stock.'

The distinction between bank money (a flow) and bank deposits (stocks) is not rhetorical, but factual as well as conceptual: in both theory and practice, banks (can) issue money as the purely numerical means of payment – deprived of any value as such – but cannot create bank deposits on their own, as these deposits are the *result* of the monetization by banks of those production costs that one or more firms may incur in the current or some future period. In fact, monetary circuit theorists and proponents of the theory of money emissions agree, although for different reasons, that 'there is a payment which banks can carry out without having at their disposal any previous deposit' (Cencini, 1997, p. 274): this payment is the remuneration of wage earners for the labour services the latter provide to firms during (say) a calendar month, which occurs according to the now so famous principle that 'loans create deposits'. Indeed, the logical analysis of money emission starting from a *tabula rasa* shows that bank loans create deposits with no need of any preexistent savings (see Schumpeter, 1954, pp. 1110–17). Yet, the object (or the 'content') of these bank deposits, on which wage earners possess a claim (or 'drawing right') is not money as such (which is a purely double-entry item, that is, an 'asset–liability' (Schmitt, 1975, p. 13)) but indeed produced output. Hence, the purchasing power of money (stored in a bank deposit) results from production, and not from the banks' 'abracadabra'.[1] The 'life cycle' of money is limited to an instant, to wit, the instant required to record a payment in the double-entry bookkeeping of the issuing bank, as a result of which a bank deposit is created for the economy as a whole when a business pays out the wage bill. 'Having played its role as a means of payment, money disappears leaving behind a book-keeping entry representing a positive amount of income deposited within the banking system' (Cencini, 1997, p. 274).

The bookkeeping nature of bank money is a fact to which monetary circuit theory and indeed any monetary theory of production have to conform, in order for them to provide a relevant (that is, a realistic) explanation of the workings of our capitalist economies. Circuit theorists are therefore on the right track when they argue that money is created when a payment has to be carried out – and not earlier than that. 'Money therefore *only comes into existence the moment a payment is made.* At that moment, in one and the same act, money is created, the borrower becomes a debtor to the bank and the agent receiving a payment becomes the creditor of the same bank' (Graziani, 1990, p. 11). Advocates of the French–Italian monetary circuit school, however, do not go far enough to consider that money is simultaneously created and destroyed in each payment, which lasts the space of an instant and so does money. 'Money and payments are one and the same thing' (Schmitt, 1996, p. 88), because money exists *within* payments whilst bank deposits exist *between* payments. This amounts to saying that bank money *carries out* payments – and it takes an instant, to wit, a zero duration in time, for a bank to enter a payment in its ledger – while bank deposits *finance* payments (see Rossi, 2007, Chs 1–2 for analytical elaboration on this point).

*Table 3.1* Loan and deposit resulting from a payment between two clients of the same bank

| **Bank** | | | |
|---|---|---|---|
| *Assets* | | *Liabilities* | |
| Loan to the payer | £*x* | Deposit of the payee | £*x* |

The origin of the lack of distinction between money and bank deposits in monetary circuit theory, which thereby impedes its scholars from seeing clearly the nature of money as instantaneous circular flow, is to be found in their assimilation of bank money and bank credit: '[m]oney is in the nature of credit money and in modern times is represented by bank credit' (Graziani, 2003, p. 25). In fact, money and credit ought to be distinguished in both theory and practice (see Rossi, 2007, Ch. 1) – even though the emission of bank money is tied to bank credit in the sense that 'loans create deposits'. As proponents of the theory of money emissions argue, 'money is a flow whose instantaneous circulation has a stock of income (or capital) as its object. Banks create the flow but not its object, which is closely related to production. This is to say that money and credit are not one and the same thing' (Cencini, 2001, p. 3). When a bank issues money, as a matter of fact, it owns a claim against the payer that is balanced by an equivalent claim that the payee owns against the bank – which is therefore a mere 'go-between' between any two non-bank agents: the position of the payer offsets the position of the payee in the bank's ledger. Now, the claim owned by the payee in the form of a bank deposit defines his/her credit against the issuing bank. This, nevertheless, does not mean that the bank *lends* the number of money units that it *issues* in a payment. In fact, the underlying loan concerns the two non-bank agents involved in the payment: the payee indeed grants a credit to the payer via the bank (or the banking system) acting as an intermediary, even though both non-bank agents might not be aware of this financial intermediation by the bank (Gnos, 1998). To be sure, the bank is neither a net creditor nor a net debtor of the economy as a whole when it issues money in any payments, as it is simultaneously debited as well as credited with the number of ($x$) money units (say, pounds) that it issues in the payment that one of its clients asks it to carry out within the relevant economic system (Table 3.1).

Being an instantaneous circular flow from and to its issuing bank, which issues it in the payment of an economic transaction between two non-bank agents – the payer and the payee, who, for expositional ease, we suppose here to be clients of the same bank (see Rossi, 2005, for an analysis of multi-bank systems and interbank payments) – money is clearly not to be mixed up with credit, which, of course, has a positive duration in time (over which interest accrues) and whose actual circuit may (or may not) be closed later on, depending on the borrower's ability to repay his/her debt. As a matter of fact, the closure of this circuit, that is, the repayment of debt, is a recurring issue in monetary circuit literature, whose proponents explain it by referring to agents' forms of behaviour, in particular, their liquidity preference (as pointed out by Keynes (1936) and adhered to by several monetary post-Keynesians (see, for instance, Dalziel, 2001, and Bibow, 2009)).[2] According, for example, to Rochon (1999a, p. 35), '[l]iquidity preference represents a problem for the closure of the system [that is to say, the monetary circuit]'. In reality, it is wrong to maintain that an increase in bank deposits 'poses a problem for the closure of the monetary circuit [and that] hoarded saving represents a leakage' (p. 35). In fact, owing to its bookkeeping nature, no bank deposit can leak out of the banking system where it is recorded, until it is spent on the market for produced goods and services and thus destroyed. What Rochon labels 'hoarded savings' are in reality immediately lent – by the bank where they are recorded on the liabilities side of its balance sheet – to those businesses that can recover their factor costs neither on the product market nor on the financial market (via a sale of securities). Rochon (1999a, p. 36) seems to notice this point when he argues that '[a]t the end of the monetary circuit, firms owe banks the exact amount that households have decided to entrust to banks as saving deposits. Banks will use these funds to refinance firms' debt under longer term conditions.' What he does not (at least explicitly) recognize is that this financial intermediation by banks has nothing to do with their forms of behaviour and is not 'an exception to the rule' (p. 37).

In fact, modern banking cannot but abide by the logical principle of money emission pointed out above: every payment is a monetary as well as a financial intermediation from the banks' point of view. The *monetary* intermediation concerns money as a flow, and is based on the principle that 'loans make deposits' (as explained above). *Financial* intermediation concerns money as a stock (to wit, bank deposits), and is based on the principle that 'deposits make loans': as soon as a bank deposit is formed in a bank's balance sheet, this bank cannot but provide a loan to some borrower, owing to the basic principle of *double-entry* bookkeeping. To be sure, banks are both money and credit purveyors (see Keynes, 1973, p. 91), which means that they are monetary as well as financial intermediaries. When banks provide money, loans create deposits; as credit providers, they act upon the reverse principle, that is, deposits make loans, although this does not require any pre-existent deposits (as in the 'loanable funds' theory) when the payment is carried out on the factor market as pointed out above. Indeed, as a result of the instantaneous circular flow defining the emission of money from and to a bank, the bank deposit resulting from this emission on the factor market – which actually defines a payment between a firm and its wage earner(s) – provides the *initial* finance that the former needs to pay the latter finally.[3]

As a matter of fact, the analysis of 'monetary circulation' advocated by monetary circuit theorists is not yet up to the task of explaining the nature of money, as it is based on the simplistic view that the 'flow of money' is a stock moving around within the economic system (as stated by Robertson (1937, p. 29) when he coined the expression of 'money on the wing' recalled above). To be sure, when 'circuitists' maintain that the monetary circuit has a positive duration in time, because '[c]redit money is created whenever an agent spends money granted to him by a bank and is destroyed whenever a bank credit is repaid' (Graziani, 2003, p. 25), they are in fact referring to the circuit of bank *credit*,[4] that is, the period of time separating the formation of income on the factor market from its final expenditure on the market for produced goods and services. In Table 3.1, income is the result of the payment entered in the bank's ledger, when the payer is a firm and the payee one or more wage earner(s). Income is notably formed through the payment of factor costs on the labour market, as this payment creates a bank deposit that is new as well as net for the economy as a whole. Similarly, income is destroyed when deposit holders spend their deposits for the purchase of produced output, whose factor costs the relevant firms recover on the product market and are thereby able to reimburse the bank that granted a credit line to them for the payment of the corresponding wage bills.

We thus note that income has a positive duration in time, and that it exists in the form of a bank deposit (savings) until it is finally spent on the product market:

> Income, in fact, is not an object in itself, but a relationship between a positive bank deposit held by the public [that is, wage earners] and the object of the equivalent negative bank deposit held by firms [that is to say, produced output waiting to be sold and temporarily stored in the firms' inventories against the same firms' debt to the banking system]. (Cencini, 1997, p. 275)

## Income and output as identical macroeconomic magnitudes

On the ground of the theory of money emissions condensed in the previous section, it is possible to show that income and output are two identically equivalent magnitudes, thus vindicating Keynes's (1936, p. 63) analysis, and that both magnitudes exist as a result of Keynes's (1936, Ch. 3) principle of effective demand. This principle makes it possible to show that the equality between global supply and global demand obtains irrespective of the level of employment, so that involuntary unemployment and the identity between income and output are not incompatible with each other. To be sure, the principle of effective demand can be interpreted in two ways, notably, as indicating (1) 'the present value of the expected sale proceeds' (Keynes, 1973, p. 425), or (2) the amount of global demand for each level of produced output (see Keynes, 1936, p. 25). In the first case, effective demand relates to the *ex ante* relation between planned production and expected sales. In this case, supply and demand are therefore also expected (purely virtual magnitudes), and no functional relation can be established between them. Indeed, before production occurs, no agent can express a demand, because no income is available to this effect. Interpreted in this way, the principle of effective demand means that entrepreneurs' decisions are influenced by their expectations, or what Keynes dubbed 'animal spirits'. The second interpretation of the principle of effective demand, however, is even more far-reaching, because it refers to actual or realized magnitudes. As current income is generated by current production, and since the amount of current income determines demand, *ex post* the principle of effective demand establishes the necessary equality (to wit, the identity) of supply and demand on the market for produced goods and services (Gnos, 1998, p. 41). 'Effective demand is the point of intersection of two curves; it is thus as much a supply as a demand, indifferently one or the other, *identically*' (Schmitt, 1988, p. 183).[5]

To be sure, current output (supply) and current income (demand) are the results of the same action: the payment of actual production costs by firms through banks (see Gnos, 1998, p. 45). As the twin outcomes of current production, global supply and demand co-determine their own identity: 'the income derived in the aggregate by all the elements in the community concerned in a productive activity necessarily has a value exactly equal to the *value* of the output' (Keynes, 1936, p. 20). Keynes's statement cannot be clearer than that: the macroeconomic identity between global supply and global demand is the unavoidable result of current production, and indeed expresses the fact that production generates the amount of money income necessary and sufficient for the final purchase of current output. Understood in this way, the Keynes (1936, p. 63) identity $Y \equiv C + I$ means therefore that, whatever the expectations of entrepreneurs and whatever the decisions taken by consumers as well as by investors, actual supply (produced output) cannot differ from actual demand (current income) – although this does not mean that this modern interpretation of Say's Law is the guarantee of full employment (see Gnos, 1998, pp. 45–6, and Rossi, 2001, pp. 193–4, for analytical elaboration on this, which we will come back to in the next section).[6]

This conclusion is corroborated by Keynes's (1936, p. 63) second identity, that is, $S \equiv I$. Indeed, the theory of money emissions provides the conceptual framework necessary to understand that $S$ and $I$ are always and everywhere two identically equivalent figures, independent of the actual level of total income produced (Schmitt, 1972, pp. 164–5; Cencini, 2001, pp. 158–60). As Cencini (1997, p. 276) observes, '[s]aving does not destroy income so it cannot be the source of a positive discrepancy between global supply and global demand'. In reality, as noted already, what monetary circuit theorists called 'hoarded savings' – which in their view hinder the closure of the monetary circuit – are immediately lent by banks to those firms that are unable to recover their costs of production on product or financial markets. If so, then these savings are actually borrowed by firms in order to invest them in purchasing themselves the unsold output, which they deposit in their inventories and seek to sell later on, that is, when the deposit holders (saving households) decide to spend their savings and thereby transform them in 'use value' – that is to say, a basket of physical goods or services they want to consume. After all, national accountants correctly range any inventory variations in the economic category of investment, which confirms that $S$ is always and everywhere identical to $I$ – although of course this concerns actual magnitudes and not necessarily expected figures. (See Schmitt, 1972, for an analysis of the importance of virtual magnitudes for income determination.)

Now, as monetary circuit theorists have pointed out in the footsteps of Keynes (1936, pp. 213–14), labour is the only macroeconomic factor of production (see Graziani, 1990, p. 12). Indeed, it is through the payment of current wage bills that physical output is given its economic form and that a positive income appears in the whole economy, the two magnitudes (economic output and income) being identically equivalent, as pointed out already. Income is the result of production activities to which the banking system gives a monetary (to wit, a numerical) form, in order to commensurate the newly produced physical goods and services and thereby to pay the relevant production factors, that is, wage earners. 'Banks, therefore, do not create value as they issue money, and their newly issued money takes on a real value only if it is associated with new production' (Bossone, 2001, p. 870, fn. 19). It is production that makes it possible for income to exist. Yet, without banks, no income would be produced, because no credit line would be available in order for firms to pay out any amount of wages. In reality, as a purely numerical 'vehicle', money never enters a net sale or a net purchase: in every payment, each of the two non-bank agents involved is simultaneously a purchaser and a seller on the labour, product, or financial markets considered 'as a whole' (to put it in Keynes's words). To be sure, for every economic agent the total sum of expenditures is always and necessarily identical to the total amount of earnings over any given period of time, since there can never exist either a net purchase or a net sale for any agents in the whole economy: an agent's net purchase on the market for produced goods, for instance, is inevitably financed by a net sale of financial assets by the same agent, because when an agent disposes of a bank deposit – either owned or borrowed by him/her – to purchase physical goods or services, he/she surrenders in reality a financial claim over produced output (in the form of a bank deposit). 'Since money flows back instantaneously to its point of emission, it is impossible for any economic agent to be credited without being immediately debited for the same amount' (Cencini, 2001, pp. 57–8). This means that every seller (who is credited by a bank) is also a purchaser (who is debited by a bank), and vice versa, even though, of course, the sale and the purchase do not occur on the same market. Owing to the novelty of this analysis, it may be helpful to expand on that.

Consider two economic agents, I and II, the first of them selling an item, *i*, and the other buying it. As the theory of money emission shows (see Cencini, 2005, pp. 286–90), both I and II are simultaneously purchasers and sellers, if one considers all markets together. Let us start with agent I, who sells item *i* on the goods market. When a bank pays I on behalf of II, at the very instant when I is credited by the bank, he/she is also debited by the same bank, as the deposit of a money income defines the purchase of an equivalent financial claim to it. To be sure, the object of the financial claim purchased by I is a sum of money income deposited with the bank, so that his/her sale of item *i* on the product market is immediately balanced by his/her purchase of an asset on the financial market. The same conclusion may be reached following a different reasoning, notably, taking into account the distinction between bank money (a flow) and bank deposits (stocks of purchasing power) pointed out already: every time that an agent is paid, this agent is the beneficiary of a number of money units that he/she instantaneously and mechanically spends in purchasing a deposit in the bank carrying out the payment (see Rossi, 2003, for analytical elaboration on this line of thought).

With respect to agent II, the analysis runs along the same lines. In order for II to finance his/her purchase, he/she must either earn or borrow an income. If so, then the purchase he/she carries out on the market for produced goods and services is always balanced by an equivalent sale he/she makes on the labour or financial market. 'The necessity of financing a purchase through an equivalent sale is confirmed twice: first, when [II] obtains a positive income by selling his activity on the labour market or by selling a financial security to his bank, and, second, when he transfers his income to [agent I]' (Cencini, 2001, p. 58). Indeed, if one supposes that II borrows the income required for the settlement of his/her purchase on the goods market, he/she obtains a bank deposit in exchange for a claim over his/her future income. If so, agent II sells a claim to the bank and, simultaneously, purchases a claim to a bank deposit: he/she is at the same instant a seller and a purchaser on the financial market. Similarly, when II instructs the bank to transfer his/her income to agent I in payment for the good the former bought from the latter, agent II is a purchaser on the product market and a seller on the financial market.

What Cencini (2005, p. 286) defines as 'the identity between each agent's sales and purchases' is a macroeconomic law that holds independently of any agents' forms of behaviour, which also means that the agents' 'liquidity preference' can never give rise to a discrepancy in this relationship (see above).

> [I]f money is an instantaneous and circular flow, this necessarily implies that both [I] and [II] are simultaneously credited and debited for the same amount of money. This is indeed what happens when the bank pays [I] on behalf of [II]: the bank credits [II] with a sum of money that is immediately credited to [I] who, instantaneously, deposits it back to the bank. Now, if [I] and [II] are simultaneously credited and debited for the same amount of money by the bank, it immediately follows that they are both sellers and purchasers alike. (Cencini, 2005, p. 287)

The instantaneous circular flow defining money induces the necessary equality between each agent's sales and purchases considered on all markets altogether, that is, the factor, product, and financial markets existing within any monetary economy of production.

Indeed, the instantaneous flow of money necessary to carry out the payment order that agent II addresses to the bank is associated with an income, which means that banks are both monetary and financial intermediaries. The simultaneous presence of a monetary and a financial circuit is verified in every payment. Consider our simple example again. The buyer on the product market (agent II) finances his/her purchase through a sale of claims (on his/her bank deposits) on the financial market. In order to be entitled to a bank deposit, however, agent II must be a seller on the labour and/or on the financial markets. The identity of the sales and purchases of agent II is therefore verified when he/she purchases item *i* on the market for produced goods as well as when he/she sold his/her labour services or financial claims. Whilst his/her sale of labour services and/or securities is immediately matched by an equivalent purchase of a bank deposit, his/her purchase of item *i* on the product market is balanced by his/her sale of a financial claim to the same bank deposit. If this mechanics did not apply in reality, no monetary circuit would ever exist actually, which also means that money itself would not exist and that production would remain incommensurate as well as incommensurable in economic terms.

Let us turn now to some macroeconomic pathologies that may (and do) exist in spite of the macroeconomic identities pointed out in this section.

## Fixed-capital accumulation and involuntary unemployment

In his *Encyclopedia of Political Economy* article on the French circuit school, Realfonzo (1999, p. 377) notes that 'Schmitt puts forward a new interpretation of Say's Law', in so far as this concerns the logical identity of each agent's sales and purchases explained in the previous section. Indeed, a modern monetary interpretation of Say's Law shows that the latter is in fact a sales–purchases identity (see Schmitt, 1975). It is wrong, however, to claim that the theory of money emissions applies to a 'real-wage' economy and that it maintains that crises are outside the field of economic analysis (Lavoie, 1987, p. 87).[7] In fact, it is possible to observe a 'Say's Law economy' affected by unemployment. Recall in this respect the explanation of the identity between savings and investment provided in the previous section: those goods that are not purchased by consumers on the product market are necessarily bought by producers, because any firm must cover its costs of production and thus reimburse bank debt – even though this may imply incurring a loss rather than a profit. Hence, although the *consumers'* aggregate demand can differ from aggregate supply, global demand is always identical to global supply – as we noticed in discussing the principle of effective demand on the ground of Keynes's (1936) identities (see previous section).

Indeed, Keynes's identity between global supply and global demand makes it possible to show that a numerical difference between these two terms arises when fixed-capital accumulation and amortization are carried out within a system of banks' bookkeeping in which no distinction has yet been made between money, income, and fixed capital. Let us just give the flavour of this analysis, on which we cannot expand here owing to space constraints (see De Gottardi, 2000, and Bradley, 2003, for elaboration on that).

As monetary circuit theorists explain, the distribution of income between (real) wages and profits is strictly connected to the decisions of producers and to the subdivision of production between consumption goods and capital accumulation: 'firms can decide the activity levels and the nature of production (consumption or investment goods), while wage earners, whatever the level of their money wage, can only buy real consumer goods in the amount made available by producers' (Graziani, 2003, p. 24). Through the investment of profits, part of current income is not consumed and gives rise to fixed capital, that is, machines and equipment. If so, then the accumulation of fixed capital implies a sacrifice by society taken as a whole (macroeconomic saving). Indeed, when forming their profit, firms capture a fraction of wage earners' income, which gives rise to 'forced' saving and a stock of unsold products. This is the 'initial' accumulation of capital that fuels the final investment operation. Wage earners in the investment goods sector are indeed paid out of the profit formed in the consumption goods sector. In so doing, firms purchase the investment goods directly on the factor market and for their own account, and these goods are immediately fixed within firms in the form of capital goods.

Now, having been thus transformed into fixed capital, invested profits should no longer be available on the financial market. This, however, is not what happens in the present system of payments (see Rossi, 2007, Ch. 5): lacking a fixed-capital department where they would be recorded into by banks, invested profits are recorded on the liabilities side of banks' balance sheets as deposits. More precisely, once invested, profit disappears as such: having spent it, firms are no longer the holders of a positive income. Yet, what is destroyed as profit reappears as a bank deposit of wage earners in the investment goods sector, and feeds an equivalent demand on the product market. Clearly, the monetary–structural pathology of the present payments system lies in the fact that invested profits are *expended* instead of being *transformed* into fixed capital literally: despite having been spent by businesses, the bank deposits corresponding to invested profits reappear in the payment of wages, which elicits an inflationary gap between global demand and global supply in the whole economy. Indeed, when new fixed-capital goods are produced, their *final* purchase by firms on the *factor* market entails excess demand leading to an inflationary rise in prices on the market for consumption goods.

Yet, when firms invest their profits into a new production of consumption goods instead of producing investment goods for fixed-capital accumulation, another macroeconomic pathology appears, the supply on the consumption goods market being pathologically increased by those new wage goods already purchased by firms on the labour market. Indeed, as Schmitt (1984, p. 238, our translation) notes, '[t]o the extent that inflationary profits are spent in the production of consumption goods, these goods are offered on the consumption goods market, where no income is available for their purchase'. Although they have already been purchased on the factor market, wage goods must be sold on the consumption goods market necessarily. However, 'the national economy provides only *once* the necessary purchasing power' (Schmitt, 1984, p. 238, our translation). Hence, global supply exceeds global demand in the whole economy, eliciting a deflationary gap that is the mark of involuntary unemployment. Unemployment is thus a macroeconomic disorder induced by a pathological process of fixed-capital accumulation, spurred by a discrepancy between the actual structure of the banks' bookkeeping and the essence of bank money (Cencini, 2001). More precisely, the working of our banking systems is such that pathological fixed-capital accumulation gives rise to an output instantaneously withdrawn from the set of saleable commodities, although the corresponding nominal wage bill adds to the total sum of newly formed money income (Rossi, 2001, Ch. 6). Capital accumulation in a disorderly working payments system such as ours eventually gives rise to inflation and unemployment as the twin macroeconomic outcomes of a discrepancy between logical principles and actual practice concerning our monetary economies of production (see Cencini, 2005, Ch. 8). These disorders have thereby a common cause, which is actually independent of any form of agents' behaviour.

## Conclusion

The theory of money emissions is fundamentally different from monetary circuit theory, as the latter theory is still based on the vision that money is a stock flowing around in an economic system in which 'the vast majority of transactions involve money on one side' (McCallum, 2004, pp. 81–2). Indeed, monetary 'circuitists' are still trapped in a vision that has not severed its neoclassical bondage, and is thereby a victim of the Walras (1909/1990) close analogy between economics and mechanics (that is, physics):

> When it is agreed that money is book-entry money, there is no room left for physical concepts such as quantity, mass or velocity. A numerical vehicle [that is, money] has no mass and its circulation cannot be conceived as that of a physical object. The laws governing the monetary circuit have nothing to do with those of physics. (Cencini, 1997, pp. 276–7)

Let us hope that this chapter has made it clear how to dispose of the bondage that so far impedes monetary circuit theory from constituting a valid alternative to orthodox monetary economics.

## Acknowledgements

An earlier draft of this chapter was presented at the first international conference on monetary circuit theory and post-Keynesian monetary economics, held at the Pierre-Mendès-France University in Grenoble, France, on 24 April 2007. The author would like to thank Riccardo Bellofiore, Guglielmo Forges Davanzati, Jesper Jespersen, Louis-Philippe Rochon, and Catherine Sifakis for their comments on that occasion. The usual disclaimer applies.

## Notes

1. Note in this respect the distinction between the purchasing power of *money* – which results from production – and the purchasing power of *wage earners*, which, as argued by monetary circuit theorists, depends on the firms' mark-up of retail prices over factor costs (see Realfonzo, 2006, p. 115).
2. When the Italian theory of the monetary circuit was set up by Graziani in the 1970s, the relevant problem was not that the monetary circuit may not be closed, but that it may not be opened, that is to say, that the banking system was (is) unwilling to grant credit lines to (creditworthy) borrowers

(such as firms). We thank Riccardo Bellofiore for pointing this out in personal conversation.

3. On the concepts of 'initial' and 'final' finance, see Lavoie (1987, p. 69) and Graziani (1990, pp. 14–16), who elaborates on Keynes's (1937/1973) 'finance motive'. On the notion of payment finality, suffice it here to recall Goodhart's (1989, p. 26) explanation that the payment is final (as opposed to merely promised) when 'a seller of a good, or service, or another asset, receives something of equal value from the purchaser, which leaves the seller with no further claim on the buyer'. See Rossi (2007) for further elaboration.
4. Needless to note, this circuit concerns a credit that a bank may grant to a firm for the payment of factor costs. The case of a bank credit to households, or to the state, would be slightly different to analyse with this paradigm, but we leave this aside here, as this is not germane to the point at stake. The analysis of banks' purchases of securities on the financial market (be it for pure speculation or for portfolio diversification purposes) is also analogous to the analysis of bank credit to businesses, although it is slightly more complex. See Rossi (2007, Chs 2–3) for elaboration on that.
5. This is a point on which Chick (1983, p. 65) as well as Lavoie (1985b, pp. 135–7) agree.
6. 'The *actually realised* results of the production and sale of output will only be relevant to employment in so far as they cause a modification of subsequent expectations' (Keynes, 1936, p. 47).
7. On the distinction between a 'real-wage' economy and a 'money-wage' economy (that is, a monetary economy of production), particularly in connection with Say's Law, see Rotheim (1981, pp. 575–84).

## References

Bibow, J. (2009), *Keynes on Monetary Policy, Finance and Uncertainty: Liquidity Preference Theory and the Global Financial Crisis* (London: Routledge).

Bossone, B. (2001), 'Circuit theory of banking and finance', *Journal of Banking and Finance*, 25 (5), 857–90.

Bradley, X. (2003), 'Involuntary unemployment and investment', in L.-P. Rochon and S. Rossi (eds), *Modern Theories of Money: the Nature and Role of Money in Capitalist Economies* (Cheltenham: Edward Elgar).

Cencini, A. (1985a), 'La teoria quantica della produzione', *Economia Politica*, 2 (2), 215–43.

Cencini, A. (1985b), 'Replica al commento di Augusto Graziani', *Studi Economici*, 40 (25), 143–9.

Cencini, A. (1988), *Money, Income and Time: a Quantum-Theoretical Approach* (London: Pinter Publishers).

Cencini, A. (1997), 'Book review of Graziani (1994b)', *Structural Change and Economic Dynamics*, 8 (2), 272–7.

Cencini, A. (2001), *Monetary Macroeconomics: a New Approach* (London: Routledge).

Cencini, A. (2005), *Macroeconomic Foundations of Macroeconomics* (London: Routledge).

Chick, V. (1983), *Macroeconomics after Keynes: a Reconsideration of the General Theory* (Oxford: Philip Allan).
Chick, V. (2000), 'Money and effective demand', in J. Smithin (ed.), *What is Money?* (London: Routledge).
Dalziel, P. (2001), *Money, Credit and Price Stability* (London: Routledge).
Deleplace, G. and Nell, E.J. (1996), 'Introduction: monetary circulation and effective demand', in G. Deleplace and E.J. Nell (eds), *Money in Motion: the Post Keynesian and Circulation Approaches* (London: Macmillan).
De Gottardi, C. (2000), *Offre et demande: équilibre ou identité?* (Fribourg: Fribourg University Press).
Gnos, C. (1998), 'The Keynesian identity of income and output', in P. Fontaine and A. Jolink (eds), *Historical Perspectives on Macroeconomics: Sixty Years after the General Theory* (London: Routledge).
Gnos, C. (2006), 'French circuit theory', in P. Arestis and M. Sawyer (eds), *A Handbook of Alternative Monetary Economics* (Cheltenham: Edward Elgar).
Gnos, C. and Rasera, J.-B. (1985), 'Circuit et circulation: une fausse analogie', *Cahiers de la Revue d'Économie Politique*, special issue, 41–57.
Goodhart, C.A.E. (1989), *Money, Information and Uncertainty*, 2nd edn (London: Macmillan) (first published 1975).
Graziani, A. (1985), 'Commento ad Alvaro Cencini', *Studi Economici*, 40 (25), 131–42.
Graziani, A. (1987), 'Keynes' finance motive', *Économies et Sociétés* (Série Monnaie et Production, 4), 21 (9), 23–42.
Graziani, A. (1990), 'The theory of the monetary circuit', *Économies et Sociétés* (Série Monnaie et Production, 7), 24 (6), 7–36.
Graziani, A. (1994a), 'Monetary circuits', in P. Arestis and M. Sawyer (eds), *The Elgar Companion to Radical Political Economy* (Aldershot: Edward Elgar).
Graziani, A. (1994b), *La teoria monetaria della produzione* (Arezzo: Banca Popolare dell'Etruria e del Lazio).
Graziani, A. (2003), *The Monetary Theory of Production* (Cambridge: Cambridge University Press).
Hicks, J.R. (1967), *Critical Essays in Monetary Theory* (Oxford: Clarendon Press).
Keynes, J.M. (1930), *A Treatise on Money* (London: Macmillan).
Keynes, J.M. (1933/1973), 'The distinction between a co-operative economy and an entrepreneur economy', draft of *The General Theory*, Chapter 2, in *The Collected Writings of John Maynard Keynes* (vol. XXIX *The General Theory and After: a Supplement*) (London: Macmillan).
Keynes, J.M. (1936), *The General Theory of Employment, Interest and Money* (London: Macmillan).
Keynes, J.M. (1937/1973), 'The "ex ante" theory of the rate of interest', *Economic Journal*, 47 (188), 663–9. Reprinted in *The Collected Writings of John Maynard Keynes* (vol. XIV *The General Theory and After: Part II, Defence and Development*) (London: Macmillan).
Keynes, J.M. (1973), *The Collected Writings of John Maynard Keynes*, vol. XIII *The General Theory and After: Part I, Preparation* (London: Macmillan).
Lavoie, M. (1984a), 'Un modèle post-keynésien d'économie monétaire fondé sur la théorie du circuit', *Économies et Sociétés* (Série Monnaie et Production, 1), 18 (4), 233–58.

Lavoie, M. (1984b), 'The endogenous flow of credit and the post Keynesian theory of money', *Journal of Economic Issues*, 18 (3), 771–97.

Lavoie, M. (1985a), 'Credit and money: the dynamic circuit, overdraft economics, and post-Keynesian economics', in M. Jarsulic (ed.), *Money and Macro Policy* (Boston: Kluwer-Nijhoff).

Lavoie, M. (1985b), 'La *Théorie générale* et l'inflation de sous-emploi', in F. Poulon (ed.), *Les écrits de Keynes* (Paris: Dunod).

Lavoie, M. (1987), 'Monnaie et production: une synthèse de la théorie du circuit', *Économies et Sociétés* (Série Monnaie et Production, 4), 21 (9), 65–101.

Lavoie, M. (1992), 'Jacques Le Bourva's theory of endogenous credit-money', *Review of Political Economy*, 4 (4), 436–46.

Le Bourva, J. (1962), 'Création de la monnaie et multiplicateur du crédit', *Revue Économique*, 13 (1), 29–56.

McCallum, B.T. (2004), 'Monetary policy in economies with little or no money', *Pacific Economic Review*, 9 (2), 81–92.

Parguez, A. (1975), *Monnaie et macroéconomie: théorie de la monnaie en déséquilibre* (Paris: Economica).

Parguez, A. (1982), 'La monnaie dans le circuit ou le voile déchiré', *Économie Appliquée*, 35 (3), 231–65.

Parguez, A. (1984), 'La dynamique de la monnaie', *Économies et Sociétés* (Série Monnaie et Production, 1), 18 (4), 83–118.

Parguez, A. (1986), 'Au cœur du circuit ou quelques réponses aux énigmes du circuit', *Économies et Sociétés* (Série Monnaie et Production, 3), 20 (8–9), 23–39.

Parguez, A. (1987), 'La crise dans le circuit, ou l'intégration de la finance et de la production', *Économie Appliquée*, 40 (4), 755–70.

Parguez, A. and Seccareccia, M. (2000), 'The credit theory of money: the monetary circuit approach', in J. Smithin (ed.), *What is Money?* (London: Routledge).

Realfonzo, R. (1999), 'French circuit school', in P.A. O'Hara (ed.), *Encyclopedia of Political Economy*, vol. 1 (London: Routledge).

Realfonzo, R. (2006), 'The Italian circuitist approach', in P. Arestis and M. Sawyer (eds), *A Handbook of Alternative Monetary Economics* (Cheltenham: Edward Elgar).

Robertson, D.H. (1937), *Money* (Cambridge: Cambridge University Press).

Rochon, L.-P. (1999a), *Credit, Money and Production: an Alternative Post-Keynesian Approach* (Cheltenham: Edward Elgar).

Rochon, L.-P. (1999b), 'The creation and circulation of endogenous money: a circuit dynamique approach', *Journal of Economic Issues*, 33 (1), 1–21.

Rochon, L.-P. (2000), 'The creation and circulation of endogenous money: a reply to Pressman', *Journal of Economic Issues*, 34 (4), 973–9.

Rossi, S. (1998), 'Endogenous money and banking activity: some notes on the workings of modern payment systems', *Studi Economici*, 66 (3), 23–56.

Rossi, S. (2001), *Money and Inflation: a New Macroeconomic Analysis* (Cheltenham: Edward Elgar).

Rossi, S. (2003), 'Money and banking in a monetary theory of production', in L.-P. Rochon and S. Rossi (eds), *Modern Theories of Money: the Nature and Role of Money in Capitalist Economies* (Cheltenham: Edward Elgar).

Rossi, S. (2005), 'Central banking in a monetary theory of production: the economics of payment finality from a circular-flow perspective', in G. Fontana and R. Realfonzo (eds), *The Monetary Theory of Production: Tradition and Perspectives* (Basingstoke: Palgrave Macmillan).

Rossi, S. (2006), 'The theory of money emissions', in P. Arestis and M. Sawyer (eds), *A Handbook of Alternative Monetary Economics* (Cheltenham: Edward Elgar).
Rossi, S. (2007), *Money and Payments in Theory and Practice* (London: Routledge).
Rossi, S. (2008), 'Mainstream economics and the macroeconomic foundations of macroeconomics: an appraisal of the theoretical origins of actual monetary-policy shortcomings', paper presented at the 12th international conference of the Research Network on Macroeconomics and Macroeconomic Policies, Berlin, 31 October–1 November 2008.
Rotheim, R.J. (1981), 'Keynes' monetary theory of value (1933)', *Journal of Post Keynesian Economics*, 3 (4), 568–85.
Schmitt, B. (1960), *La formation du pouvoir d'achat* (Paris: Sirey).
Schmitt, B. (1972), *Macroeconomic Theory: a Fundamental Revision* (Albeuve: Castella).
Schmitt, B. (1975), *Théorie unitaire de la monnaie, nationale et internationale* (Albeuve: Castella).
Schmitt, B. (1982), 'Time as quantum', in M. Baranzini (ed.), *Advances in Economic Theory* (Oxford: Basil Blackwell).
Schmitt, B. (1984), *Inflation, chômage et malformations du capital: macroéconomie quantique* (Paris and Albeuve: Economica and Castella).
Schmitt, B. (1986), 'The process of formation of economics in relation to other sciences', in M. Baranzini and R. Scazzieri (eds), *Foundations of Economics: Structures of Inquiry and Economic Theory* (Oxford: Basil Blackwell).
Schmitt, B. (1988), 'The identity of aggregate supply and demand in time', in A. Barrère (ed.), *The Foundations of Keynesian Analysis* (London: Macmillan).
Schmitt, B. (1996), 'Unemployment: is there a principal cause?', in A. Cencini and M. Baranzini (eds), *Inflation and Unemployment: Contributions to a New Macroeconomic Approach* (London: Routledge).
Schumpeter, J.A. (1954), *History of Economic Analysis* (London: George Allen & Unwin).
Seccareccia, M. (1996), 'Post Keynesian fundism and monetary circulation', in G. Deleplace and E.J. Nell (eds), *Money in Motion: the Post Keynesian and Circulation Approaches* (London: Macmillan).
Walras, L. (1909/1990), 'Economics and mechanics', in W.J. Samuels (ed.), *Economics as Discourse: an Analysis of the Language of Economists* (Dordrecht: Kluwer).

# 4

# The Existence of Profits within the Monetary Circuit: Some Unanswered Questions Revisited

*Louis-Philippe Rochon*

## Introduction

In previous work (Rochon, 2005), I examined the problem pertaining to the monetary realization of profits, arguing that, at the macroeconomic level, profits arise as firms are able to finance part of their investment through bank lending, and can repay the totality of the bank loan over several periods of production. This solution avoided the so-called 'opening-up' fallacy, to wit, relying on some external explanation or sector in order to generate macroeconomic profits.

Since then, there have been a number of articles that have been written on this topic, many of which specifically commented on Rochon (2005). While not overly critical of my views, they nonetheless raised some interesting arguments. This book on monetary circuit theory offers an excellent opportunity to revisit the problem of macroeconomic profits, to comment on some recent alleged solutions, and to further my own approach to, and solution of, the realization of monetary profits at a macroeconomic level.

Before proceeding, however, let us emphasize an important argument: in the real world, all proposed solutions contribute to making profits. This point is not dispelled. Indeed, government expenditures, overlapping circuits, and the external sector all contribute to the realization of corporate profits. The point addressed in Rochon (2005) was whether macroeconomic profits can be explained within a single monetary circuit of production. This is the challenge circuitists must address, in order to provide a logical answer to it.

This chapter is not about the theory of the monetary circuit as such, which has been discussed elsewhere (see for instance Parguez, 1980; Rochon, 1999; Graziani, 2003). Rather, in this chapter we will only consider the realization of monetary profits. In this sense, this chapter will abstain from discussing the intricacies of the monetary circuit.

The next section offers a quick overview of the existing literature, but will specifically address three papers written by Renaud (2000), Zezza (2003, 2004), and Febrero (2008). In that section I also further discuss my own solution, which is to allow investment to be financed by bank credit and reimbursed over several periods, thereby allowing for the existence of monetary profits. In the last section, I will then formalize the discussion of the issue at stake, and present an algebraic analysis of it.

## The realization of profits and the macroeconomic conundrum

The theory of the monetary circuit presents us with an analysis that focuses on the sequential approach to money and macroeconomics. In a sense, it organizes our thoughts around the complexities of causal relationships, and allows us to clearly see the relevant features of a monetary capitalist economy of production. It implies a specific sequence of irreversible events, which begins with the creation of money and ends with its destruction.

Within the logic of these causal relationships, the existence or monetization of macroeconomic profits is a puzzle that has raised serious considerations, and one that many economists have attempted to resolve. Unfortunately, there are as many solutions as there are economists, and the various solutions explore different aspects of the theory of the circuit of production.

The central question, however, remains the same: in a monetary circuit, how does $M$ become $M'$? After all, in an endogenous money framework, if firms borrow $M$ from the banking system in order to pay wages and other production costs, how can they recover more money than they first injected into the circuit? Indeed, at best, firms can only take back what they first injected, such that profits and even the payment of interest on the initial loan seem to be out of the reach of firms. Of course, individual firms can earn profits such that $M$ can be $M'$ at the microeconomic level, but at the macroeconomic level, where does this extra money come from? As Febrero (2008, p. 111) argues, 'if the maximum amount of money that firms can get is limited to production costs, how can profits (and interest on debt) be monetized?' Schumpeter (1934, p. 189) was also aware of this problem: 'it is impossible with a given sum of money to obtain a greater money sum'.

It is precisely because the money supply is endogenous that the problem arises. In an exogenous-money world, either the money supply can always increase, such that *M* can become whatever amount the central bank chooses, or the question becomes irrelevant. Irrespective, in an endogenous-money world, the creation of money is tied to the production process. Indeed, there can be no discussion of production without a parallel discussion of credit and money, and the banking system. The real and the monetary sides of the economic system are intrinsically linked together within the monetary circuit approach, as they are in post-Keynesian theory. This is precisely what separates heterodox economists, broadly speaking, from the mainstream. This link between the real and the monetary sides of the economy explains why the banking system is at the heart of the monetary circuit. It is through the granting of loans to the private sector that banks validate the production process.

## Money creation

In previous work (Rochon, 1999), I analysed the circuit in terms of specific stages, of which the essential arguments are presented below. As stated above, the circuit begins with the creation of money and income. In this sense, money is the result of a flow, and the monetary circuit specifically studies how money flows into, within, and out of the sphere of production.

Money creation begins with the granting of credit to private agents (firms) who need access to banks in order to undertake production and pay wages. This applies equally to firms in the consumption-goods sector as in the investment-goods sector. According to Graziani (1984, p. 9), 'the economic process gets started as the banking sector grants credit to firms'. What is of particular importance here is that credit is used to cover the production costs of all goods produced, consumption as well as investment goods: 'total production costs, namely the costs of producing both consumption and capital goods' (Graziani, 1984, p. 9).

This analysis is consistent with Keynes's 'finance motive' (Graziani, 1984; Rochon, 1999), which is interpreted not as a motive for holding cash, but rather as a motive to demand bank credit for the purpose of production.

In this initial stage, therefore, firms decide on their production levels, which are heavily influenced by what post-Keynesians call 'radical uncertainty': because firms must sell their production, they are sensitive to their expectations of future levels of effective demand and how this influences their expectations of future sales proceeds. Once these production decisions have been taken, firms can then set employment targets, wage and price levels.

During this initial phase, what Graziani (2003) has called the efflux period, in a simple circuit, firms must have access to a wage fund before production begins, workers must be paid in money, and inputs must be purchased in money. This is a fundamental element of the monetary circuit: there can be no production without bank credit, and money is integrated into the economic system at the very moment of production. More specifically, money flows into circulation along with the payment of wages: once credit is obtained and wages are paid, firms transfer money from their bank account to that of workers; money is created *ex nihilo* and released into circulation. 'The decision of a bank to grant a loan gives rise to the simultaneous appearance of a deposit [...]. Banks [...] do not, and could not, collect deposits without having previously granted loans' (Graziani, 1992, p. 218).

The above description makes clear the unique and important relationship between the existence of debt and the creation of money. As Seccareccia (1988, p. 51) points out, production is a process of debt creation. Indeed, as Graziani (1996, p. 143) argues, as soon as wages are paid, 'a triangular debt–credit situation, typical of any monetary economy, is thus created', and a hierarchy of debts arise (see Gnos and Rasera, 1985). Hence, money is created solely because some agents have agreed to enter into a debt relationship with a bank. Money becomes the bookkeeping record of this debt. In fact, there can be no creation of money without the creation of debt; this is what I have called elsewhere the revolutionary theory of endogenous money (Rochon, 1999; Rochon and Rossi, 2009). It does not rely on central bank operations or some stage of development of the banking system, or again on liability management, as has been suggested by some structuralists.[1]

It is in this sense that post-Keynesians and circuitists have argued that money is credit-driven and demand-determined, as Moore (1988) put it over two decades ago. Yet, there has been much confusion about bank credit and whether banks simply give credit to all who demand it. This confusion was one of the arguments at the heart of the debate between horizontalists and structuralists, although I believe it has been resolved today. Horizontalists, going back at least to Moore (1988), have always argued that banks do not grant credit to everyone; in fact, banks are not obligated to grant credit to all those who ask for it. Indeed, banks will refuse credit to those they do not deem creditworthy. In this sense, there will always be, as Keynes tells us, a 'fringe of unsatisfied customers'.

This is because banks, just like firms and other agents in the circuit, operate under a climate of radical uncertainty: the future is unknown and unknowable. It is not possible to know what the future holds, and acquiring more information will not give us more or better knowledge about the future. And since economic events unfold in a sequence over historical time, where the past is known and cannot be changed, the future is a necessary component of the circuit, and uncertainty will have important consequences on the functioning of the circuit.

In this sense, any decision by banks to extend credit must be weighed against the possibility that firms will be unable to pay back their loan. Firms earn revenues from selling goods to consumers, but a general decrease in economic activity, a rise in the rate of interest, or an increase in unemployment will frustrate firms' ability to raise sufficient revenue to meet their contractual obligations with the banks. Both firms and banks therefore place 'bets' on the future ability of firms to raise revenue, that is, on the future level of effective demand (Parguez, 1980).

Uncertainty is therefore a central component of the monetary circuit. It affects all agents similarly, and how agents react to uncertainty can certainly alter the dynamics of the monetary circuit. Agents react to uncertainty with 'bursts of optimism and pessimism'. When banks are pessimistic, they raise the requirements to obtain a loan, that is, they adopt more stringent criteria for evaluating the creditworthiness of firms. It becomes more difficult to obtain a loan. Similarly, when growth and effective demand are strong, optimism about the future is equally strong, such that banks will generally be more willing to lend to firms (Rochon, 2006).

Irrespective of periods of optimism or pessimism, money is introduced into the circuit along with the payment of wages and the creation of income. In this sense, there is a parallel between the creations of money and income. Indeed, consistent with money's endogeneity, the creation of money results from a double bookkeeping entry. Banks grant credit-worthy firms a credit in order to satisfy the needs of production, which is entered on the asset side of the bank's balance sheet. Simultaneously, however, on the liability side of it, an equivalent entry is recorded as a bank deposit (or a line of credit). Firms then draw on their lines of credit largely to remunerate workers. Money results from a flow.

If money exists because firms agree to enter into a debt relationship with banks, firms must also reimburse banks and extinguish their debt, at which point money is destroyed. This arises because firms are able to sell their product, generating income from which they can meet their contractual agreement with the banking system. The reflux phase, as

Graziani (2003) calls it, can arise from two distinct sources: consumption and saving. Indeed, when households consume goods, money flows back to firms, with which they are thus able to reimburse banks and cancel their debt. Yet, the same arises when households purchase new securities on financial markets: money flows back to firms. Firms can then recapture part of what they initially injected into circulation, either from consumption or financial savings, whichever does not matter, as Keynes makes clear in his post-*General Theory* articles.

A number of conclusions arise. First, hoarded savings, that is, the demand for money balances held in bank accounts, threaten the closure of the circuit. Only when we assume no household savings can the circuit close. Otherwise, and more realistically, when we assume that households' demand for money is positive, there will be a final outstanding debt toward the banking system equivalent to household saving. In this sense, the monetary circuit is characterized by permanent outstanding debt toward the banking system.

Secondly, the role of the financial market is not to channel saving toward investment, but rather to reimburse firms for their production costs. Indeed, as Graziani (1992, p. 218) explains, 'clearly at this point the role of financial markets is not one of collecting savings in order to finance investment, but rather one of making it possible for firms to repay their bank debts'.

Yet, a logical problem arises: if firms borrow, say, to cover their wage bill, at best, assuming no household savings, they can extract only what they initially injected through the payment of wages. In other words, as stated above, if they borrow $M$, at best they can reimburse $M$, and even less if households save. But in order for firms to earn a profit, the market exchange must somehow generate $M'$, at least to cover firms' interest payments on existing debt, and conceivably more. According to Zazzaro (2003, p. 233), '[i]f in an economic system (closed to external exchange) the only money existing is what the banks create in financing production, the amount of money that firms may recover by selling their products is at the most equal to the amount by which they have been financed by banks'.

This is a central question of the theory of the monetary circuit, and the failure to find a consensus reveals the degree of confusion on this matter. Indeed, it remains probably the only issue on which there is considerable disagreement, at least on the surface. In the chapter I wrote for the book collecting the proceedings of a conference in honour of Augusto Graziani (Rochon, 2005), I discussed a number of possible solutions, which I further develop in the remainder of this chapter.

**Resolving the profit dilemma**

Over the years, many solutions have been proposed from different perspectives. Indeed, as we will see below, many circuitists offer solutions that are more microeconomic in nature, a rather strange approach given that the problem of profits is essentially a macroeconomic problem. Nevertheless, let us review many of the solutions offered to date.

The first of these possible solutions relies on 'opening up' the circuit, and to include some external injection of money, such as through the existence of state and fiscal policy, or through the existence of a foreign sector. While there is no doubt that fiscal deficits lead to increased private sector profits, or that exports add to the profit process, reliance on opening up the circuit to external explanations means that a self-contained circuit is considered unable to explain the realization of profits. This was one of my most fundamental objections to many of these explanations. Profits must be logically explained within a single, self-contained, closed circuit. Since the realization of monetary profits, within an overall endogenous-money framework, is explained by the production process, then the production process alone should logically be able to explain the existence of profits.

Moreover, in this specific circumstance of relying on a government sector, profits depend on the permanent existence of fiscal deficits (that is, governments must adopt expansive fiscal policies and accept deficits in every period of production) or, in the case of an open economy, on a permanent trade surplus:

> *A fortiori*, governments can be assumed to run permanently budget deficits and/or follow a mercantilist policy of engendering persistent trade surpluses, thus creating the additional amount of credit money that can give rise to a flow of money revenues also in the investment goods sector. [...] Though empirically relevant, these would be merely *ad hoc* solutions to a structural problem of generating a monetary flow to the investment goods sector in an endogenous credit money world. (Seccareccia, 1996, p. 405)

This may be good Keynesian fiscal policy, but it does impose a stringent condition on the monetary circuit for generating monetary profits.

A second approach consists of borrowing the profits that firms will be making in advance of the production process and injecting them into circulation; presumably, such profits would be built into wages. This solution has been proposed, among others, by Renaud (2000) and Rossi (2001). According to Renaud (2000, p. 293), 'the endogenous realization of money profits in the monetary production economy is possible if business firms have the ability to spend in the present [...] the anticipated profits included in their supply price'.

I can think of two criticisms that can be raised against this solution. First, it assumes that firms spend their incomes before the beginning of the circuit and before indeed the realization of their profits. But profits are formed in the goods market after production. Firms do not know, and cannot know, *ex ante* the value of their profits. Secondly, it also raises the question of the role of banks: they lend in the hope that firms will generate profits. Indeed, why would banks lend to firms their profits before the latter are earned? This appears to be a somewhat risky behaviour especially in times of economic slowdown. Thirdly, this solution assumes the existence of profits and does not explain how they are formed. According to Gnos (2003, pp. 333–4), '[u]nfortunately, the question [of the realization of profits] cannot be settled in this way. [...] This is not sufficient to solve the problem under discussion: being anticipated, the formation of profits is not explained but presupposed.'

A third possible solution consists in assuming the existence of a number of overlapping monetary circuits. This solution is shared by many circuitists and some post-Keynesians as well (see Smithin, 1997, for instance). The idea is that, in the real world, economies do not operate as neatly as suggested by circuit theory, in the sense that not all firms borrow and reimburse their debt at the same time. Consider for instance Gnos (2003, pp. 332–4), who argues that

> [t]he reality is that the start of production entails the superposition of different phases of the circuit (and so individual circuits). [...] Whatever the period of time we consider [...] firms again and again pay wages and sell goods, production processes overlapping one another, so that firms have no difficulty gaining profits out of wages provided buyers are prepared to purchase goods at prices exceeding factor costs.

If there are several circuits overlapping each other, then there is always more money being injected at any one time than is being extinguished through the repayment of bank debt, and there is no need to assume that firms borrow profits from banks. It is therefore not a question of how $M$ becomes $M'$: firms always borrow $M$, but since there are many circuits overlapping each other, there is always $M'$ in existence at any one time. In this sense, firms within one circuit get their profits from wage-consumption in another. According to Gnos (2003, pp. 332–4), '[t]he start of production entails the superposition of different phases of the circuit (and so different individual circuits). [. . .] There is no need then to look for any additional quantity of money.'

It is undoubtedly true that in the real world the market is characterized by overlapping or dynamic circuits, but this undermines the very thing that we are trying to explain: the generation of profits within a single monetary circuit. In fact, this solution requires at least two circuits to explain profits. As Febrero (2008, p. 117) correctly points out, 'the problem with this solution is that it implicitly accepts that profits cannot be monetized and the circuit cannot be closed without resort to additional circuits'.

A similar solution is proposed by Zazzaro (2003, p. 234), who adopts a Schumpeterian view, where the real world is characterized by a dynamic market in which 'the economy undergoes an endless process of change that involves the entry of new firms, the start-up of new initiatives and failures of others'. This solution, however, suffers from the same criticism as pointed out above.

A fourth explanation would see the linearization of production (Febrero, 2008) within the investment-goods sector, that is, dividing it into subsectors, where one subsector would sell capital goods to the consumption-goods sector, the proceeds from which would be used to purchase capital goods from another subsector, and so on. This process is repeated indefinitely. This solution is proposed notably by Lavoie (1987) and Renaud (2000).

However, in the end, there would still be a subsector that would be unable to acquire capital goods to produce its own output. Nell (2002) resolves this problem by assuming simply that there exists a subsector that does not require the purchase of capital goods: this 'machine-tool' subsector uses its own goods to produce its goods: 'It does not buy capital goods because it does not need them; it uses what it makes' (Nell, 2002, p. 525) – the production of commodities by means of its own commodities!

There are many problems with this approach. My general criticism of it and of Nell's solution is that it assumes an important asymmetry in the way firms operate within the monetary circuit. Indeed, why do firms within the capital-goods sector need to be subdivided, but not businesses in the consumption-goods sector? Secondly, a machine-tool subsector is surely not very realistic in an advanced production economy. Thirdly, and perhaps more important, this solution assumes that the proceeds from the consumption-goods sector are sufficient to reimburse the debt of all subsectors in the capital-goods sector as well as finance the purchase of capital goods among these subsectors. This is a highly suspicious assumption and probably not very realistic. In the end, however one chooses to subdivide the investment-goods sector, 'there seems always to emerge a group of firms in the investment goods sector who cannot fully validate their output in money terms' (Seccareccia, 1996, p. 406).

Finally, another solution is also proposed by Nell (1996), who suggests that only wages in the investment-goods sector need to be financed by bank credit. This minimalist approach, based on the needs of firms to minimize borrowing costs, can explain the circulation of the economy's entire output. Nell (2002) assumes that firms in the consumption-goods sector need not borrow to finance their production needs: they begin production and pay their workers only when workers in the investment-goods sector spend their income on consumption goods. Moreover, firms within the investment-goods sector extend credit to inter-sector firms. Through increases in velocity and inter-sector credit, $M$ can be turned into $M'$, so that all sectors realize profits in monetary terms.

Unfortunately, this solution presents some important flaws. First, if my interpretation is correct, it assumes that wages in the investment-goods sector are at least equal to those in the consumption-goods sector: otherwise, proceeds from the sale of commodities would not be sufficient to pay their own workers. Secondly, it assumes two important asymmetries. First, it assumes that firms in the investment-goods sector need to pay their workers now (by borrowing), while firms in the consumption-goods sector can somehow wait, implying that capital-goods firms need recourse to the banking sector and bank credit, while consumption-goods firms receive intersectoral credit. Nell (2002, p. 525) recognizes this asymmetry, but argues that 'the apparent asymmetry in monetary arrangements simply reflects a real asymmetry'. I am not sure how real this asymmetry is in the real world, and as Seccareccia (1996, p. 407) argues, '[w]hy should firms in one sector provide private credit for purchases among themselves and, yet, require exchanges in money terms originating from bank credit with firms in the consumption goods sector?' This approach remains difficult to accept logically.

Recently, Febrero (2008) proposed a hybrid of several possible solutions. Yet his approach is difficult to fit within a discussion of the monetary circuit. Recall that one of the most fundamental characteristics of the theory of the monetary circuit is that money enters the economic system along with production (along with the payment of wages); in order to produce, firms must borrow, such that wages are paid as production begins. Yet, Febrero's solution is to separate production from circulation. Indeed, he believes that the main problem with all the solutions of the problem of the monetization of profits, including my own, is that they have too much money because they 'overlap production and circulation' (2008, p. 117). His solution is to separate production from circulation, and suggests that 'money enters the system after one period of production has finished and before the next one starts' (Febrero, 2008, p. 112). Yet, for circuitists, as stated above, money must be introduced along with production, not 'after one period of production'. Production cannot begin without bank credit first being obtained and wages paid out to workers. In this sense, Febrero's solution is not consistent with the theory of the monetary circuit.

Part of this debate focuses precisely on what is being financed by bank credit. While nearly all circuitists and post-Keynesians agree that wages and other costs of production are covered by bank credit, the subject of whether investment is financed by bank credit is at the heart of considerable debate among circuitists.

Graziani (1990, pp. 12–14), for instance, argues that only wages are financed by bank credit. For the author, the question of investment financing arises only at the end of the circuit, allowing for growth in the subsequent period. Investments are financed as 'internal transactions' (Graziani, 1990, p. 12) within the non-financial business sector, that is, through retained earnings and the new issues market (see also Gnos, 2003).

Nell (1998, p. 213; 2004) is even more restrictive, arguing that only a portion of wages is financed by bank credit: as discussed above, wage earners in the capital-goods sector would spend their income purchasing consumption goods, which would be sufficient to ensure the payment of wages in the consumption-goods sector. But, as Febrero (2008, p. 115) states, '[i]n our view, Nell's conclusion that only wages in the capital goods sector are financed with bank credit [. . .] does not hold'.

At the time, I felt that none of these explanations were satisfactory. My main objection to them was that they all relied either on some asymmetrical assumption, that is, some firms behaving differently than others, or on some external assumption, such as the existence of the state or another country's imports. For me, in order for the theory of the monetary circuit to be relevant, it needs to explain profits consistently from within, without relying on some external sector. In other words, can profits be explained within a simple model of a single circuit, with no government and no external sector? As Nell (2002, p. 520) argues cogently, 'it is necessary to show how the system can work without reliance on outside assistance'.

This said, of course, as stated above, I find all these explanations contribute to profits. Indeed, fiscal deficits certainly translate into higher revenues for the private sector; and there can be no doubt that an increase in imports will contribute to profits as well. There is also no doubt that the real world is characterized by new firms entering the market, or simultaneous circuits. My objection was not that these phenomena did not contribute to profits, but that I believed that, at its simplest, the theory of the monetary circuit should be able to account for profits on its own.

## The financing of investment

Given the discussion above, there is therefore a need to find some other way to explain the realization of profits. My own solution was to propose that part of investment expenditures, that is, the purchase of capital goods and not only their production, is financed by bank credit. This position goes against the views of many circuitists. For instance, for Graziani, the question of investment financing arises only at the end of the circuit, allowing for growth in the subsequent period. They are financed as 'internal transactions' (Graziani, 1990, p. 12) within the non-financial business sector, that is, through retained earnings and the new issues market (see also Gnos, 2003). Post-Keynesians also assume that only wages are financed by bank credit, such as Moore (1988), whose theory of endogenous money rests entirely on the financing of wages.

Now, as Seccareccia (1996, p. 402) argues, the 'assumption regarding bank credit going exclusively towards the financing of working capital, is highly questionable'. Indeed, as Seccareccia (1996, 2003) shows, there is plenty of empirical evidence to suggest that at least part of investment is financed by bank credit. This would mean that not only is the production of capital goods financed by bank credit, but so is their purchase. Febrero (2008, p. 119) agrees with this position, arguing that '[i]n our view, and contrary to the "revolving fund argument", long-term bank finance for the purchase of fixed capacity is empirically relevant'.

According to Parguez (1980, 1996), Seccareccia (1988, 1996, 2003), Rochon (1999, 2005), and Parguez and Seccareccia (2000), firms would equally approach banks to cover production and investment needs. In this sense, investment would be covered partly by internal funds (retained earnings from past periods, for instance), and partly by bank credit. In this regard, we must distinguish between two types of credit: short-term credit, granted to firms in order for them to cover the payment of wages, and reimbursed entirely within the period of production, and long-term finance, for the purchase of capital goods, which is reimbursed over several periods of production. Indeed, firms typically take years to reimburse their investment debt.

By including investment finance in the analysis, there is sufficient money to account for the realization of profits. Indeed, all along, post-Keynesians and circuitists were asking the wrong question: it is never about how $M$ becomes $M'$, but rather the other way round: firms borrow $M'$ but only reimburse $M$ within a single period of production.

Zezza has written two articles on the circuit and the monetization of profits, in which he is critical of some of my views (see Zezza, 2003, 2004). For him, '[my] conclusions, as other contributions to this literature, are misguided by not taking into consideration the accounting constraints for the simplified economy being described' (Zezza, 2003, p. 1). Zezza's criticism, therefore, is aimed at much of the literature and not only at my own contribution (Rochon, 2005). This said, Zezza's main objection to my own contribution is that I do not take into sufficient consideration the banking system: 'Rochon [has] ruled out the possibility for bank owners to buy either consumption or investment goods. So it is unclear why there should be any accumulation of wealth in the form of deposits, or why should banks operate at all' (Zezza, 2003, p. 2). Elsewhere, he writes:

> As the accounting is analyzed, it appears that several, if not all, contributors to the TMC [Theory of the Monetary Circuit] fail to take properly into account how banks' profits can be spent in the goods or the financial markets: in several models, interest payments on loans made from firms to banks are not accounted as part of national income, and simply disappear, instead of being a possible source of demand for goods and/or financial assets. (Zezza, 2004, p. 1)

Although Zezza raises an interesting point, his observation is not completely accurate because I do discuss a variation of this solution in Rochon (1999). Admittedly, it is not fully developed, but it is nevertheless discussed. In that work, I discuss the possibility of allowing bank workers (rather than bank owners) to spend their income on consumption goods, and I attribute this conclusion to Robinson (1956). Further, even in Rochon (2005, p. 131), on which paper Zezza was specifically commenting, I argued that '[w]e can resolve part of this dilemma if we assume that the wages and expenditures of the banking industry are injected into circulation, as Robinson (1956) suggested. In this case, since bank profits are merely the interest on loans, firms would be receiving back the interest they paid to banks.' So it is not true that I disregard the banking system, although I do not consider it in full detail. Moreover, Seccareccia (1996) also considers this solution in even greater detail. This approach is also defended by Graziani (2003), when he argues that '[i]n order to get the money needed to satisfy their interest payments, the only thing [firms] can do is to sell part of their product to banks, which is tantamount to saying that interest should be paid in kind' (Graziani, 2003, p. 33).[2]

Zezza does not object to my use of bank credit to finance investment. Indeed, this method is explicit in his own solution. But he concludes that there is no need for firms to reimburse their investment loan over several periods, since there would be sufficient money in the system to reimburse all loans within a single period of production, provided that firms sell their output to the banking system. Zezza rests his own solution on the simple Keynesian idea that consumption does not depend on wages, but rather on income, which arises from all sectors of the economy, including the banking system, that is, bank owners, whose income is $r_L L$, which is the rate of interest charged on loans ($r_L$) multiplied by total loans made to both sectors ($L$).

In the end, Zezza concludes that by including the financing of investment by bank credit, the only impediment to the realization of profits may be the savings accrued as bank deposits. Moreover, if we assume that wage earners and bank owners do not have the same propensity to consume, the conclusion would remain unchanged: savings threaten the closure of the circuit, which is a conclusion typical of the theory of the monetary circuit.

Yet, there are several problems with Zezza's approach. The most important in this respect is the fact that selling goods to the banking system equivalent to interest payments may contribute to some additional income for the consumption and investment-goods sectors, but, at best, only explains how the relevant firms can pay interest on their loans. It does not explain how these firms can generate profits greater than the interest on their loans.

## A numerical explanation of macroeconomic profits

Let us consider a numerical example in order for us to explain the existence of profits at a macroeconomic level.

If we assume that banks only finance wages, then we can show that, at the macroeconomic level, profits cannot exist, as profits in the consumption-goods sector are exactly equal to losses in the investment-goods sector. Indeed, firms producing consumption goods earn profits equal to the wages of the firms producing investment goods, whose losses exactly equal the wages paid to their workers. In this simplest version of the circuit model, profits at the macroeconomic level cannot exist, hence the conundrum. The issue is further compounded if we include the interest firms need to pay on their existing loans.

Of course, at the microeconomic level, profits are not difficult to explain. Indeed, there will always be some firms that will make some level of profits, owing to strong sales, for instance, while other firms will have losses or even declare bankruptcy. As such, firms will compete with each other for household consumption. If we assume workers do not save, consumption will be limited at best to the value of their aggregate wages. Some firms will be better able to attract consumers than others.

To show this, consider the following example, where we assume that households do not save. Further, we assume that the economy is divided into two sectors. The first sector is characterized by firms producing consumption goods, whereas the second is composed of firms producing investment goods. For simplicity, we assume that only firms in the first sector purchase investment goods.

Firms in the consumption-goods sector must borrow to finance wages, $W_C$, as do firms in the investment-goods sector, $W_I$. Workers in both sectors buy consumption goods, and hence the profit function of the consumption-goods sector is

$$\Pi_C = W_C + W_I - W_C = W_I \tag{1}$$

Profits in the investment-goods sector are

$$\Pi_I = -W_I \tag{2}$$

Hence, aggregated profits (that is, $\Pi_C + \Pi_I$) are zero. Even assuming that the profits generated in the consumption-goods sector go toward the purchase of investment goods changes nothing at the aggregate level: it is a mere transfer from one sector to the other. Then where do firms in the investment-goods sector get the necessary funds to close the circuit and pay back the banks?

Now, if we consider interest on bank loans, the situation is worse, and we have the following equations:

$$\Pi_C = W_C + W_I - (W_C + r_L W_C) = W_I - r_L W_C \tag{1'}$$

$$\Pi_I = -(W_I + r_L W_I) \tag{2'}$$

where $r_L$ is the interest rate paid on bank loans. At the aggregate level, we obtain

$$\Pi \quad = -r_L(W_C + W_I) \tag{3}$$

As we can see, by including bank interest, as stated before, aggregate profits become negative. If so, then how can $M$ become $M'$ sufficient to cover interest payments? This is a fundamental challenge for the theory of the monetary circuit. It is not enough to simply account for interest, but firms must also make a profit, over and above interest payments.

We discussed above a number of possibilities, but let us consider here Zezza's (2003) or Robinson's (1956) solution, and open up the system to include banks. One obvious question is whether this solution suffers from the same criticism as above, that is, the fallacy of opening up the circuit to include a third sector. I would argue that it does not, as banks are an integral part of the theory of the monetary circuit. In fact, I would argue, in line with Zezza (2003), that previous attempts at explaining profits that did not include the banking system were deceptively simple. As such, any attempt to explain the monetization of profits must include the banking system in one way or another. This is consistent with the core of the theory of the monetary circuit and endogenous money.

As we can see immediately, however, nothing gets resolved. Indeed, assuming banks do not pay wages or interest on deposits, they can at most spend all their income, $r_L L$. Yet, at best, this simply generates sufficient income to cover interest payments on bank loans:

$$\Pi = r_L L - r_L(W_C + W_I) = 0 \tag{3'}$$

A careful reading of Graziani (1984, p. 33) reveals this clearly: 'In order to get the money needed to satisfy their interest payments, the only thing [firms] can do is to sell part of their product to banks, which is tantamount to saying that interest should be paid in kind.' In the end, merely adding the banking sector is not sufficient to explain profits.

For those advocating opening up the circuit and including a government sector, we get the following equations:

$$\Pi_C = W_C + W_I + G_C - (W_C + r_L W_C) = W_I + G_C - r_L W_C \tag{1''}$$

$$\Pi_I = G_I - (W_I + r_L W_I) \tag{2''}$$

where $G_C$ and $G_I$ are respectively the fiscal expenditures in each sector. Aggregate profits then become:

$$\Pi = G - r_L(W_C + W_I) \tag{3''}$$

Now, profits can be generated, provided of course that $G > r_L(W)$. Yet, in order for this to hold, we need government to run permanent (structural) deficits, otherwise, assuming balanced budgets, $G$ would simply be equal to tax revenue such that injections and withdrawals are the same.

Finally, we can simply assume that investment is partly financed by bank credit, but reimbursed over several periods, which is the solution argued here. There is therefore short-term credit for wages, and long-term credit for investment. As suggested above, adding the banking sector is not sufficient to explain profits, irrespective of how we model banks. Hence, the solution is not simply to add the banking sector. Rather, as we will see, the only remaining, possible, solution is to include the financing of investment.

Profits in the consumption-goods sector can now be represented by the following equation:

$$\Pi_C = W_C + W_I + rL - (W_C + r_L W_C + \varphi L_{IC} + r\varphi L_{IC}) = (1+r)W_I - (1+r)\varphi L_{IC} \tag{1'''}$$

where $W_B$ represents the wages of workers in the banking sector, which are spent on purchasing consumption goods, as in Robinson (1956), Seccareccia (1996), and Rochon (2003); $\varphi$ is the portion of the value of total investment spent by firms in the consumption-goods sector and reimbursed within that circuit, with $\varphi < 1$. Firms must also reimburse interest on that long-term loan.

Of course, we could complicate this analysis in many ways, by incorporating household and rentier savings, or dividends paid on past accumulated capital. Nevertheless, in the end, it changes very little in the fundamental insights of the analysis, and the story remains largely the same. Even by incorporating savings, we know from Graziani (1990, 2003), and indeed from Keynes as well, that household savings, if channelled through the financial markets, play the same role as consumption. In the end, such savings are channelled back to firms, with which they can reimburse banks. Only savings held as liquidity (hoarded savings languishing in bank accounts) remain out of reach of firms: 'If firms are able to attract fully household savings in the capital markets so that the increment in the capital stock would be matched by an equivalent increment in the stock of corporate securities held by the public, firms would still be in a position to retire their debts entirely vis-à-vis the banking system' (Seccareccia, 1996, p. 413). Nevertheless, we abstain from this discussion here.

With respect to the investment-goods sector, profits are represented by the following equation:

$$\Pi_I = L_{IC} + L_{II} - (W_I + \phi L_{II} + r\phi L_{II}) = L_{IC} + L_{II} - (W_I + (1+r)\phi L_{II}) \quad (2''')$$

Firms in this sector receive the totality of the value of the investment purchases from both sectors, but only reimburse a portion of the costs emanating from the investment-goods sector. We assume further that profits from the banking sector are spent purchasing capital goods.

When adding up, we obtain the overall equation for macroeconomic profit:

$$\Pi = (1 - \varphi(1+r))(L_{IC} + L_{II} + rW_1) \quad (3''')$$

Note that now since both wages and investment are financed by bank credit, banks receive interest on both, such that $L = (W_C + W_I + L_{IC} + L_{II})$. Rearranging, and keeping in mind that $rL = r(W_C + W_I + L_{IC} + L_{II})$, we get the following equation:

$$\Pi = (1 - \phi)(1 + r_L)(L_{IC} + L_{II}) - r_D D \quad (3'''')$$

Note that the proportion of total investment that firms pay back to banks within a single period of production is important. Indeed, contrary to Seccareccia (1996), who assumes that all investment is paid back within one period (see also Zezza, 2003), here we note that if $\phi = 1$, profits are negative. Hence, the only way firms can make profits is if they reimburse only a portion of the investment debt within the period of production, as was initially argued by Rochon (2005). This portion will depend on negotiations between banks and firms, and the relative power of banks over firms. Obviously, the greater the value of $\phi$, the lower the macroeconomic profits.

It is worth mentioning that the banking sector's role in determining aggregate profits does not depend on its own profits, although the wages of workers in the banking sector do contribute to the profits of firms in the consumption-goods sector; rather, it depends on the banking sector's ability to impose a higher rate of interest on loans and its power to force firms to reimburse a greater proportion of their long-term loan. The assumption that the banking sector is the solution to the realization of profits is thereby not relevant in this regard.

In the end, profits are primarily determined by the investment decisions of firms. If so, Kalecki's original insight that firms get what they spend is supported here. The value of $\phi$ is therefore important. If banks insist that the totality of capital-goods expenditures be reimbursed within a single period of production, we have negative profits: $\Pi = r(W_I - L)$.

## Conclusion

In this chapter, we revisited some of the issues surrounding the realization of profits, to address in particular the specific comments made on Rochon's (2005) work.

The problem of the reflux is a central issue of the monetary circuit. Not only must the market generate sufficient income, but firms must be able to capture this income in order to reimburse their debt and earn a profit.

Zezza's discussion is interesting, as it focuses on the role of banks and rentier income. Unfortunately, Zezza believes I did not consider this option, which is clearly wrong, as I had specifically addressed the possibility of bank income, as had other circuitists, such as Robinson (1956, pp. 249–50) and Seccareccia (1996). In the end, however, at best, the income from banks is able to account for interest on bank loans, but is not sufficient to generate profits.

It is for this reason that I discussed an alternative and proposed that banks must also finance the purchase of capital goods. This is consistent with Seccareccia (1996). It differs from Seccareccia (1996), however, in the sense that I argue that firms do not necessarily reimburse the purchase of capital goods entirely within a single period of production. This is the only way, I think, that firms are able to generate gross profits sufficient to cover interest on loans and earn net profits.

## Acknowledgements

I would like to thank Sergio Rossi for his comments and criticism. All errors remain my own.

## Notes

1. In this sense, I agree with Lavoie (1996, p. 533) when he writes that 'accommodation or the lack of it, liability management or the lack of it, and financial innovations or the lack of it are second-order phenomena compared to the crucial story that goes from debt creation to the supply of means of payment'.
2. Graziani refers only to the payment of interest, not profits.

## References

Febrero, E. (2008), 'The monetization of profits in a monetary circuit framework', *Review of Political Economy*, 20 (1), 111–25.

Gnos, C. (2003), 'Circuit theory as an explanation of the complex real world', in L.-P. Rochon and S. Rossi (eds), *Modern Theories of Money: the Nature and Role of Money in Capitalist Economies* (Cheltenham: Edward Elgar).

Gnos, C. and Rasera, J.-B. (1985), 'Circuit et circulation: une fausse analogie', *Cahiers de la Revue d'Économie Politique*, special issue, 41–57.

Graziani, A. (1984), 'The debate on Keynes's finance motive', *Economic Notes*, 1 (1), 15–33.

Graziani, A. (1990), 'The theory of the monetary circuit', *Économies et Sociétés* (Série Monnaie et Production, 7), 24 (6), 7–36.

Graziani, A. (1992), 'Augusto Graziani (born 1933)', in P. Arestis and M. Sawyer (eds), *A Biographical Dictionary of Dissenting Economists* (Aldershot: Edward Elgar).

Graziani, A. (1996), 'Money as purchasing power and money as a stock of wealth in Keynesian economic thought', in G. Deleplace and E.J. Nell (eds), *Money in Motion: the Post Keynesian and Circulation Approaches* (London: Macmillan).

Graziani, A. (2003), *The Monetary Theory of Production* (Cambridge: Cambridge University Press).

Lavoie, M. (1987), 'Monnaie et production: une synthèse de la théorie du circuit', *Économies et Sociétés* (Série Monnaie et Production, 4), 21 (9), 65–101.

Lavoie, M. (1996), 'Monetary policy in an economy with endogenous credit money', in G. Deleplace and E.J. Nell (eds), *Money in Motion: the Post Keynesian and Circulation Approaches* (London: Macmillan).

Moore, B.J. (1988), *Horizontalists and Verticalists: the Macroeconomics of Credit Money* (Cambridge: Cambridge University Press).

Nell, E.J. (1996), 'The circuit of money in a production economy', in G. Deleplace and E.J. Nell (eds), *Money in Motion: the Post Keynesian and Circulation Approaches* (London: Macmillan).

Nell, E.J. (1998), *The General Theory of Transformational Growth: Keynes after Sraffa* (Cambridge: Cambridge University Press).

Nell, E.J. (2002), 'On realizing profits in money', *Review of Political Economy*, 14 (4), 519–30.

Nell, E.J. (2004), 'Monetising the classical equations: a theory of circulation', *Cambridge Journal of Economics*, 28 (2), 173–203.

Parguez, A. (1980), 'Profit, épargne, investissement: éléments pour une théorie monétaire du profit', *Économie Appliquée*, 33 (2), 425–55.

Parguez, A. (1996), 'Beyond scarcity: a reappraisal of the theory of the monetary circuit', in G. Deleplace and E.J. Nell (eds), *Money in Motion: the Post Keynesian and Circulation Approaches* (London: Macmillan).

Parguez, A. and Seccareccia, M. (2000), 'The credit theory of money: the monetary circuit approach', in J. Smithin (ed.), *What is Money?* (London: Routledge).

Renaud, J.-F. (2000), 'The problem of the monetary realization of profits in a Post Keynesian sequential financing model: two solutions of the Kaleckian option', *Review of Political Economy*, 12 (3), 285–303.

Robinson, J. (1956), *The Accumulation of Capital* (London: Macmillan).

Rochon, L.-P. (1999), *Credit, Money and Production: an Alternative Post-Keynesian Approach* (Cheltenham: Edward Elgar).

Rochon, L.-P. (2005), 'The existence of monetary profits within the monetary circuit', in G. Fontana and R. Realfonzo (eds), *The Monetary Theory of Production: Tradition and Perspectives* (Basingstoke: Palgrave Macmillan).

Rochon, L.-P. (2006), 'Endogenous money, central banks and the banking system: Basil Moore and the supply of money', in M. Setterfield (ed.), *Complexity, Endogenous Money and Macroeconomic Theory: Essays in Honour of Basil J. Moore* (Cheltenham: Edward Elgar).

Rochon, L.-P. and Rossi, S. (2009), 'Horizontalism and structuralism: a suggested re-interpretation', in B.J. Moore and L.-P. Rochon (eds), *Post-Keynesian Monetary Theory: Reflections and Development* (Cheltenham: Edward Elgar).

Rossi, S. (2001), *Money and Inflation: a New Macroeconomic Analysis* (Cheltenham: Edward Elgar).

Schumpeter, J.A. (1934), *The Theory of Economic Development* (Oxford: Oxford University Press).

Seccareccia, M. (1988), 'Systematic viability and credit crunches: an examination of recent Canadian cyclical fluctuations', *Journal of Economic Issues*, 22 (1), 49–77.

Seccareccia, M. (1996), 'Post-Keynesian fundism and monetary circulation', in G. Deleplace and E.J. Nell (eds), *Money in Motion: the Post Keynesian and Circulation Approaches* (London: Macmillan).

Seccareccia, M. (2003), 'Pricing, investment and the financing of production within the framework of the monetary circuit: some preliminary evidence', in L.-P. Rochon and S. Rossi (eds), *Modern Theories of Money: the Nature and Role of Money in Capitalist Economies* (Cheltenham: Edward Elgar).

Smithin. J. (1997), 'An alternative monetary model of inflation and growth', *Review of Political Economy*, 9 (4), 395–409.

Zazzaro, A. (2003), 'How heterodox is the heterodoxy of monetary circuit theory? The nature of money and the microeconomics of the circuit', in L.-P. Rochon and S. Rossi (eds), *Modern Theories of Money: the Nature and Role of Money in Capitalist Economies* (Cheltenham: Edward Elgar).

Zezza, G. (2003), 'The existence of monetary profits within the monetary circuit: comments on Rochon', comments presented at a conference in honour of Augusto Graziani, Benevento, 5–6 December 2003.

Zezza, G. (2004), 'Some simplified, consistent models of the monetary circuit', Levy Economics Institute Working Papers, no. 405.

# 5
# Saving, Firms' Self-Financing, and Fixed-Capital Formation in the Monetary Circuit

*Jean-Luc Bailly*

## Introduction

Despite their divergences with mainstream neoclassical thought, the immense majority of Keynesians remain strongly influenced by methodological individualism. Their analyses of the formation of macroeconomic magnitudes are still marred by microeconomic presuppositions. Further, there is no denying that Keynesians often sidestep the issue of defining macroeconomic saving, and treat it somewhat hazily as the sum of sometimes voluntary sometimes involuntary individual saving. The upshot is that the relationship between saving and investment is imprecise, indeed even confused.

Keynesians stand by the idea that saving and investment are determined a priori in two unconnected spheres composed of separate, more or less autonomous agents, namely, households and firms. Accordingly, they hold to the principle that the two magnitudes must adjust to one another and are determined within a relationship of cause and effect. Admittedly, they follow Keynes in dismissing the neoclassical claim that saving precedes investment, and that the two are equalized through variations in the interest rate. Considering that in today's monetary production economies there is a hierarchy of agents, Keynesians argue that bank credit enables firms to invest without resorting to households' saving, and that investment creates the saving corresponding to it. Hence, the equality that still holds between the two magnitudes purportedly results from variations in income, and not from any variation in interest rates.

The first section of this chapter sets out to show that the Keynes who founded modern macroeconomics developed a different conception than this of the saving–investment relationship. Notably, when defining income in his *General Theory*, Keynes (1936) emphasizes rather the principle that saving and investment do not adjust one to the other. Keynes (1936) argues that as saving and investment are not defined in separate spheres but within a homogeneous magnitude – national income – they cannot differ in amount. It ensues that the relationship between saving and investment cannot be one of cause and effect. The one cannot be determined independently of the other, and saving and investment are invariably observed to be equal not as a result of any adjustment but because the principle connecting them is one of identity.

The second section of this chapter shows that the primary consequence of the identity between saving and investment is that the formation of fixed capital is a process that does not pertain to the sphere of firms alone. Indeed, net investment directly involves households. This just goes to show the process cannot be financed from bank credit, and fixed capital cannot be formed before the saving that finances it. Thanks to the circuit analysis developed by Schmitt, we can understand that the production of fixed-capital goods is part of a specific circuit embedded in the general circuit of income. Viewed in strictly macroeconomic terms of the identity of saving and investment, the formation of fixed capital can be explained by the complete movement, which is generally termed 'self-financing', of the formation and spending of profit that is not distributed to households as interest or dividends.

## Saving and investment in the circuit of income

By placing money income at the centre of things, Keynes eschews neoclassical methodology, and promotes the general principle that economic magnitudes are not the outcome of the individual behaviour of households on one side and of firms on the other. In the *Treatise on Money* he notably proposes:

> to break away from the traditional method of setting out from the total quantity of money irrespective of the purposes on which it is employed, and to start instead [...] with the flow of the community's earnings or money income, and with its twofold division (1) into the parts which have been *earned* by the production of consumption goods and of investment goods respectively, and (2) into the parts which are *expended* on consumption goods and on savings respectively. (Keynes, 1930, p. 121)

This is one of the essential features marking the truly macroeconomic character of Keynesian theory. National income is determined in the complete movement of its formation in production and of its spending on the various product markets.

When Keynes (1930, p. 90) argues that '[i]ncomes are created partly by entrepreneurs producing for investment and partly by their producing for consumption', he takes the standpoint of entrepreneurs predicting outlets for their products. However, all income is necessarily spent in one way or another, if not on the markets for consumption goods or investment goods, then on the financial market, hence '[t]he decisions to consume and the decisions to invest between them determine incomes' (Keynes, 1936, p. 64).

Income being determined in the single movement of its formation–expenditure, so are its constituents, to wit, consumption, saving, and investment.

### On saving and investment

As our economies have just one production factor – labour – all income is first formed on physical individuals – workers – and macroeconomic saving and investment cannot even be defined independently of the way households as a whole expend their income both by consuming and by saving.

Saving usually designates that part of their income that households do not consume during a given period of time. This does not imply, though, that all saving is voluntary, and that any individual's saving is reflected by an investment of the same amount. This is not because of the behaviour of firms, but because any individual saving does not automatically bring about an increase in net macroeconomic saving. It is an observed fact that a large proportion of household saving is loaned to households for the purpose of consumption. It is self-evident that the saving households lend to each other does not finance any new investment but merely affects the distribution of wealth.

> [N]o one can save without acquiring an asset [...]; and no one can acquire an asset which he did not previously possess, unless either an asset of equal value is newly produced or someone else parts with an asset of that value which he previously had. In the first alternative there is a corresponding new investment: in the second alternative someone else must be dis-saving an equal sum. (Keynes, 1936, pp. 81–2)

Consumed saving is not part of the definition of macroeconomic saving of the current period. So, in breaking free from methodological individualism, we can understand that the saving of *all* households is not the *sum* of individual saving.

On the production side, a firm producing goods intended as capital goods for other firms may perfectly well sell some of its output to households. There is nothing to stop a household from buying a machine tool, say. In this case, one cannot say that the firm that made the machine tool produced investment goods alone; in part it produced consumption goods.[1] From this it follows that any investment operation is defined simultaneously on the side of production of 'capital goods' and on the side of expenditure of the income which, in part, is formed by that production. Investment, then, is a process that hinges both on production and on the purchasing of goods by firms. To be understood in its relationship with saving, investment must be grasped from this dual standpoint.

It is understandable that the objective relationship in macroeconomic terms between saving and investment cannot be established in terms either of firms' expectations alone or of households' willingness to save.

> Our definition of income also leads at once to the definition of *current investment*. For we must mean by this the current addition to the value of the capital equipment which has resulted from the productive activity of the period. This is, clearly, equal to what we have just defined as saving. (Keynes, 1936, p. 62)

Both magnitudes pertaining to the very definition of income, they cannot be handled as if they were formed independently of one another in two separate spheres. Their being determined within current income runs counter to any idea of adjustment, because once we have eliminated the saving that households lend to each other and the goods that are not bought by firms, the terms 'saving' and 'investment' designate the same proportion of current income. The issue of causality of saving and investment does not arise, then, in the terms of the analytical alternative set out by Sawyer (1996, p. 52), namely, that the explanation for causality is allegedly not the same when considering 'separation between those who make savings decisions and those who make investment decisions', and when considering that 'much of savings is undertaken by the same individuals who are making investment decisions'. In fact, both these analyses involve methodological individualism, and fail to grasp the truly macroeconomic character of the issue at stake. In strictly macroeconomic terms, the equality between saving and investment is obviously not a matter of equilibrium:

> Provided it is agreed that income is equal to the value of current output, that current investment is equal to the value of that part of current output which is not consumed, and that saving is equal to the excess of income over consumption – all of which is conformable both to common sense and the traditional usage of the great majority of economists – the equality of saving and investment necessarily follows. (Keynes, 1936, p. 63)

In other words, regardless of the behaviour of households and firms, saving always equals investment, and no gap nor adjustment are to be observed between the two magnitudes in space or time. This conclusion stands as a macroeconomic law and suffers no exception. That firms commonly resort to bank credit in order for them to establish their investment plans does not undermine this principle of identity between macroeconomic saving and investment. On this point Keynes is quite categorical:

> The notion that the creation of credit by the banking system allows investment to take place to which 'no genuine saving' corresponds can only be the result of isolating one of the consequences of the increased bank-credit to the exclusion of the others. (Keynes, 1936, p. 82)

**Investments are savings**

It is true that Keynes did not always strictly adhere to the principle of identity between macroeconomic saving and investment. Proof of this is the exposition of the dynamic multiplier,[2] which, incidentally, acts as an analytical referent for many Keynesians. In his exposition of this mechanism, he emphasizes the idea that the amount of saving by households adapts to the amount of investment because of the variation in income. In short, the dynamic multiplier relies not on the principle that saving and investment are identical but, on the contrary, on the possibility of their being unequal and of their adjusting over time. The process described can occur only because of there being an asymmetry between saving and investment; extra saving by a household would not necessarily cause an increase in investment, while a firm's decision to invest would engender surplus saving by households. As Keynes (1936, p. 117) argues, '[t]he multiplier tells us by how much their employment has to be increased to yield an increase in real income sufficient to induce them to do the necessary extra saving'. Quite clearly, in this passage of his *General Theory*, Keynes remains within the framework of methodological individualism, which may incidentally explain why so many mainstream economists adhere to this model. Even so it is on the basis of this causal schema that post-Keynesians assert that '[t]he driving force of the economy [...] is investment spending' (Lavoie, 2004, p. 20, our translation). This is consistent with Kalecki's assertion that 'it is precisely investment which creates savings [...] because investment always forces savings of the same amount' (Kalecki, 1990, p. 228). This supposes, of course, that investment is an autonomous magnitude, in that it does not depend on current income but rather gives rise to it.

The idea that investment is ultimately financed thanks to household saving is not challenged, of course, which is generally expressed by saying that *ex post* investment is invariably equal to *ex post* saving. The divergences arise in the interpretation of the articulation of the two magnitudes over time. While there is no denying that 'to invest there is no need of prior saving or prior deposits' (Lavoie, 2004, p. 55, our translation), meaning deposits formed in a period prior to the current one, it is not sure that the amount of current investment is determined *ex ante* by firms without any reference to *ex ante*, current voluntary saving of households.[3] It is true that if one considers the assumption that firms and households form two separate sets of agents, there is no reason a priori why voluntary saving should equal investment. However, we can question the distinction between *ex ante* and *ex post* investment in the post-Keynesian tradition. Considering that, because of bank credit, firms are assumed to fulfil their investment plans, one has to accept that *ex post* investment always equals *ex ante* investment.[4]

It is true that in his 1937 papers Keynes shows that thanks to 'finance' firms are sure they can undertake their investment plans, although '"finance" has nothing to do with saving' (Keynes, 1937a, p. 209). A point Keynes (1937b, p. 219) confirms some months later by writing that '"finance" is essentially a revolving fund. It employs no savings. It is, for the community as a whole, only a book-keeping transaction.' It is probably for this reason in particular that post-Keynesians develop the idea that bank credit is a means of 'initial financing' of investment, whereas its final financing, the repayment by firms of their debt to banks, calls for (*ex post*) saving of households in an equivalent amount. However, like Chick, one may question the rationale of such a representation:

> How [...] can we maintain simultaneously that (monetary) investment precedes (monetary) saving, and evaluate the income-creating potential of investment? We can only argue *ex post*: when investment and money income have increased by the same amount, we can infer that the increase in money balances constitute *ex post* saving. (Chick, 2000, p. 133)

In fact, as argued above, in the post-Keynesian model, *ex post* saving supposedly results from an adjustment confirming the *ex ante* investment, which itself is supposedly equal to the *ex post* investment. The assumption of fundamental uncertainty dear to post-Keynesians collapses under its own weight, as the circuit is assumed to be hierarchized; being achieved through 'initial financing', firms' decisions allegedly 'afterwards compel' households. But because of the time lag, it must also be conceded that 'finance' may provisionally replace saving. Now, Keynes claims that such a phenomenon cannot be observed:

> At the 'financial' stage of proceedings no net saving has taken place on anyone's part, just as there has been no net investment. 'Finance' and 'commitments to finance' are mere credit and debit book entries, which allow entrepreneurs to go ahead with assurance. (Keynes, 1937a, p. 209)

The investment *actually made* cannot be any different from the amount of saving used to finance it, and it is actually made only because it is financed by saving. The equality between saving and investment always being observed *ex post* and, let us emphasize it again, *ex post* investment being equal to *ex ante* investment, one can only conclude that *ex ante* investment is equal to *ex post* saving. One might think that it is all a matter of whether there can be a lag between *ex ante* saving and *ex post* saving. But this question is superfluous since, as Keynes writes, 'at the financial stage' the investment has not yet been made: it is virtual and it only comes to be because there is saving corresponding to it. From this it follows that the only logical answer to Chick's question is that there is a feedback effect of macroeconomic saving on *ex ante* investment. This means that *ex ante* investment is no different from *ex ante* saving, and therefore that the identity of saving and investment is confirmed, even when firms resort to bank credit.[5] The amount of investment (*ex ante*) is not left to the free will of firms and of banks: they themselves are constrained by the amount of current income and, following the Keynesian schema, from period to period by the propensity to consume of all households, in other words of macroeconomic *ex ante* saving.

We can gather this from what Keynes in his *General Theory* calls the logical multiplier theory, the terms of which he sets out in a 1936 letter to Robertson as follows:

> If, for example, the public are in the habit of spending nine-tenths of their income on consumption goods, it follows that if entrepreneurs were to produce consumption goods at a cost more than nine times the cost of investment goods they are producing, some part of their output could not be sold at a price which would cover its cost of production. For the consumption goods on the market would have cost more than nine-tenths of aggregate income of the public and would, therefore, be in excess of demand for consumption goods, which, by hypothesis, is only the nine-tenths. Thus entrepreneurs will make a loss, until they contract their output of consumption goods down to an amount at which it no longer exceeds nine times their current output of investment goods. (Keynes, 1973, p. 90)

Keynes (1973, p. 90) goes on making it clear that this 'has nothing to do with velocities of circulation, time-lags, etc. though these things enter detailed, formal analysis of the order of events'. He further specifies in his *General Theory* that 'the logical theory of the multiplier [...] holds good continuously, without time-lag, at all moments of time' (Keynes, 1936, p. 122).

Patently the logical multiplier theory is not a theory of adjustment over time of the components of national income. Here, income is not determined in a hierarchized circuit, and the way households dispose of their income is every bit as decisive as the conditions in which the various categories of goods are produced. *Ex ante* saving (which is *ex post* at the same time) is deduced from the 'habitual' propensity to consume, and the structure of firms' activity in producing goods for consumption on one side and for investment on the other will itself depend on these habits. Even so firms are confronted with a certain level of uncertainty, which means that their plans are not necessarily borne out in the selling-off of their output.

By the principle of the logical multiplier, we can say that if firms have engaged in producing goods intended as equipment goods in an amount greater than current saving, then they have in fact produced consumption goods. As Bradley (1991) shows, the distinction between capital goods and consumption goods cannot be made a priori on the basis of any physical criteria. And if the share of goods intended for investment is greater than the share of income that is saved, or, in other words, if *ex post* saving is below the level of investment firms would have liked, then households' consumption is greater than firms expected. Now, by virtue of the fact that '[t]he decisions to consume and the decisions to invest between them determine incomes' (Keynes, 1936, p. 64), a fraction of goods that were a priori intended for firms' equipment turn out to be consumption goods, as they are purchased by households, and, on the other hand, if the desired investment is less than household saving, goods that were intended a priori for consumption are invested in the form of unsold inventories. 'What was planned as a production of investment goods is in part transformed into a production of (future) consumption goods' (Cencini, 2005, p. 87).

In fact, the *ex post* equality of investment and saving has a feedback effect on the *ex ante* magnitudes, with the result that no lag can be observed either between *ex ante* saving and *ex ante* investment. Either both magnitudes are purely imaginary – and in this case they cannot even be compared as they are non-existent – or they can be observed, which means they have been realized, and so are *ex post*. As Keynes (1937b, p. 219) argues, 'I return to the point that finance is a revolving fund. In the main the flow of new finance required by current *ex ante* investment is provided by finance released by current *ex post* investment.' The equality of saving and investment always holds whatever the standpoint taken. The determination of investment is not dependent on the analysis of economic agents' behaviour but rather on the analysis of the circuit within which the agents' forms of behaviour may interact.

> Assuming that the decisions to invest become effective, they must in doing so either curtail consumption or expand income. Thus the act of investment in itself cannot help causing the residual or margin, which we call saving, to increase by a corresponding amount. (Keynes, 1936, p. 64)

Investment (like saving) is a two-sided operation: the production of goods intended as firms' equipment (formation of income) and the purchase (disposition of income) of investment goods by firms. It follows that saving and investment are not part of a relationship of cause and effect: it is not saving that causes investment any more than it is investment that causes saving. In our economies, one cannot capture any saving that is awaiting investment, nor any investment that is awaiting the saving corresponding to it. Any investment made is identically saving that is made. From a properly macroeconomic standpoint, one cannot distinguish any (*ex ante*) initial financing that might be different from some (*ex post*) final financing of the investment. The same applies to the distinction between *ex ante* saving and *ex post* saving. As the identity of saving and investment does not depend on individual behaviour, it matters little that the saving that finances investment – hence macroeconomic saving – is voluntary or involuntary.

## Fixed-capital formation

As Keynes (1930, pp. 120–1) points out:

> Human effort and human consumption are the ultimate matters from which alone economic transactions are capable of deriving any significance; and all other forms of expenditure only acquire importance from their having some relationship, sooner or later, to the effort of producers or to the expenditure of consumers.

Expressed otherwise, the relationship underpinning a truly macroeconomic analysis of production and consumption may be summarized by the identity $Y \equiv C$. This means that the final purpose of any production is consumption, that consumption is the pretext for all production,[6] and that all income is inevitably destroyed in consumption spending. The first logical consequence of this is that all household saving is ultimately consumed by households.[7] The general circuit of income can therefore be written as Households–Firms–Households (H–F–H).

However, it is true that products formed in the current period are not consumed in the same period. A fraction of them is saved and invested:

> Investment, thus defined, includes, therefore, the increment of capital equipment, whether it consists of fixed capital, working capital or liquid capital; and the significant differences of definition (apart from the distinction between investment and net investment) are due to the exclusion from investment of one or more of these categories. (Keynes, 1936, p. 75)

Generally, investment consists initially in the formation of what might be characterized as time-capital, in that the capital resulting from household saving is in its initial form a postponed consumption, the delayed ultimate expenditure of income. Households cannot accede to the raw materials and semi-finished products of the period but will be able to obtain them later, once these items have been transformed. However, they can never obtain instrumental capital: 'Capital goods are "finished" when they are ready for use [...] by producers as instrumental capital' (Keynes, 1979, p. 88).

As productive structures, firms result from the final immobilization of wealth.[8] Being destroyed in the productive process, fixed equipment does not give rise to any income through its use. This is what Keynes showed when developing the concept of 'user cost',[9] by which he denoted the loss of value of equipment at the same time as the decline in its productive capacity. Wear and tear of capital and its obsolescence are losses that are not found in current income. And so, although it contributes largely to the expansion of production, fixed capital does not impart any value (any income) to the product, because strictly speaking it does not absorb any income (any purchasing power) in its formation. In other words, its formation does not deprive households of any consumption, even if they do not dispose of capital goods. However, the formation of fixed capital is not a matter for firms alone and cannot be reduced to a process of inter-firm exchanges, even if it does not exclude them; but it is part of the relations between firms and households within the general circuit of income. In other words, understanding the process of fixed-capital formation amounts to explaining the mechanisms governing the transformation of a fraction of time-capital (that is, of current saving) into fixed capital.

As pointed out in the first section, net macroeconomic investment cannot be financed by bank credit. 'It is conventionally said that the increase in capital, net investment, has two separate sources, profit (or self-financing) and borrowing on the bond market' (Schmitt, 1984, p. 165, our translation). Clearly, then, it is usually accepted that the formation of fixed capital may be financed either by borrowing from households on the financial market or by self-financing, that is by firms' non-redistributed profit. Let us examine in the first instance financing by borrowing from households.

## Resort to households' saving

In the current period, generally taken as a calendar period, income is defined by the equation $Y = C + I$, meaning that consumption and investment are determined in a single period. For the time being, we also work on the assumption that the economy is divided into two sectors: sector 1 produces consumption goods and invests, and sector 2 produces capital goods that it sells to sector 1. As, for the time being, we exclude profit as a means of financing, it seems logical enough to admit that sector 1 resorts to borrowing from households to finance the increase in its production capacity. To do this it may either issue securities such as bonds, or borrow household saving through the banking system.[10] In either case it contracts a debt that it will have to repay. And so, although it pays sector 2 with the saving collected, sector 1 has still not paid for its capital equipment. This equipment has still not been paid off, as a debt is extant. The operation will not be truly completed until households have been repaid.[11] Let us consider how Walras expresses this situation:

> The capitalist saves in money; he lends this money to the entrepreneur who, when the lease expires, returns the money. This is the operation known as *credit*. It follows that it is product entrepreneurs, and not saving-creating capitalists, who apply for new capital on the market. (Walras, 1952, p. 245, our translation)

As they are the applicants, when they borrow from households, firms anticipate making a profit that will enable them to repay their debt. Thus, the financing of investment by sector 1, and so the net increase in its fixed capital, supposes that this sector makes a net profit with respect to its own output. Failing this, the investment operation would not be completed, and the fixed capital would not be formed in the firms' property. This leads to just one conclusion, which is that the loan by 'capitalists' to firms – whether direct or indirect – is equivalent in fact to an advance of profit: '*All investment has its source in the firm's profit.* [...] If the financing is borrowed, then the firm's profit is "advanced". So investment is the spending of current (already made) profit or the spending of actualized profit' (Schmitt, 1984, p. 166, our translation).

The financing of fixed capital can only be accounted for, then, on the basis of the distribution of current output between households and firms. It is undeniable that the sums composing the profit invested are saving by all households. In forming a profit and in using it to repay their debt to households, firms confirm in some sense the initial loan by households by immobilizing within them a fraction of current output. In addition, the incomes initially issued all being wages, it is certain that the profits invested originate in these same wages, and this is true whatever the nature or shape of the goods to which they correspond.

> In fact one must absolutely adhere to a parallel dictated by logic: as households' incomes are the only source of profits, the output that is transferred to all firms at the time the profit is formed is firstly a sum of money containing wage-goods in the broad sense. (Schmitt, 1997, p. 90, our translation)

Any firm making a profit holds both a stock of goods, to wit, profit goods, and the bank deposit(s) corresponding to them. It can be seen that it would be meaningless to say that firms ultimately spend their profits on the product markets in purchasing the profit goods they hold. Even if one were to evoke the case of a firm holding goods intended for consumption and that spent its profit in purchasing capital goods from a second firm, this would not explain the formation of net fixed capital for the whole economy. The first firm would hold on to its stock of consumption goods, as the second firm would not buy them from it. There would therefore be no exchange between consumption goods and capital goods: the first firm would still hold its stock of unsold products. From this it results that the investment in fixed capital cannot be reduced to inter-firm exchanges, as Poulon (1981) in particular would have it.

For our purposes here, we can say that any net investment is necessarily self-financed. Hence, understanding it involves understanding the formation and spending of non-redistributed profit.

## The circuit of profits

Net macroeconomic investment supposes that the profit financing it is itself net for the economy as a whole. Profit invested by one firm must under no circumstances correspond to a loss by one or more other firms. In short, the financing of a net macroeconomic investment requires the formation and final spending of a net macroeconomic profit. To this is added another logical constraint, namely, that by virtue of the fact that all income is defined in and as a circular flow and is initially formed on a physical person, it is finally destroyed in consumer spending.

> The formation of a profit is the transfer of an income from all households to all firms; all profit originates in households' incomes, which incomes are changed into profit whenever households spend $x + 10$ units of income in purchasing goods whose value is $x$ units. (Schmitt, 1997, pp. 89–90, our translation)

For this reason, income holders cannot immediately consume profit goods which, for that matter, are not offered to them and are stocked in firms. In its first state, this additional capital is not immobilized in firms. For investment actually to occur, the profit goods that are not made over to households must be converted into means of production; and that is done when the non-redistributed profit is spent.

As argued above, taken as a whole, firms cannot spend their profit in purchasing goods they already hold. This has a general consequence, namely, that firms cannot spend it other than with households, and this can only be on the market for production factors, hence in financing production.

As a category of income, profit is caught up in the general H–F–H circuit of income. Being formed in the H–F relationship, it is spent on the market for production factors and is part of the F–H relation. This means that households ultimately dispose of the whole of current period *income*, and that, even so, a fraction of the physical *output* is immobilized in the firms' sphere. This is what we shall explain now.

As with all income, a profit must be formed before it can be spent. Net investment is a process that hinges on two separate operations: (i) the formation of profit on product markets, and (ii) the spending of profit in the purchase of equipment goods. As noted, if firms already held the equipment goods at the time they formed their profits, they could not buy them finally. Net investment, however, presupposes a final purchase by firms, as it is an increase in their own production capacity. Given that it is in the nature of any income to be taken in a circuit, we can conclude that there is a profit circuit embedded in the general H–F–H circuit of income.

Being formed on F as the result of spending by H, but not being destroyed since the corresponding goods are not consumed, and being logically impossible to spend in the sphere of firms, monetary profit is necessarily spent on H,[12] which in turn finally spends it with F. Hence, insomuch as it is income, profit is itself taken in a circuit defined by its formation and spending. Formed by the production activity of H and finally spent by H, it is embedded in the general H–F–H circuit. Resulting from the capture of wages, profit is spent in the formation of wages and, in so doing, firms grab a fraction of the current physical output in the form of capital goods. Considered as such, formed and invested, we notice that the circuit of profits takes the form F–H–F.

The net investment process can be summarized thus: net investment consists in converting captured wage goods (profit goods) into capital goods that are finally integrated in the property of F through that part of

H involved in producing capital goods in sector 2. It is because workers are paid out of profit that one can distinguish sector 2 from sector 1 and describe the former as the sector producing capital goods. Being paid out of profit, sector 2 workers spend their income in the purchase of profit goods stored in sector 1. It is true that households do not procure capital goods, but F–H–F is not for all that an offshoot from the H–F–H circuit; there is no capital circuit limited to inter-firm exchanges.

One distinction that can be made between the two circuits is that whereas in the general H–F–H circuit firms are first intermediaries in household-to-household relations, in the F–H–F circuit of profit, it is households that are the intermediaries. In this circuit, they intervene as production factors engaged in sector 2, and as such they earn wages that they spend and finally destroy by consuming the profit goods of sector 1. On the other hand, firms now have fixed equipment goods that escape from households' purchasing power. It is because the circuit of profit is embedded in the general circuit of income that firms can capture for once and for all a fraction of current output, in other words, that truly macroeconomic saving is formed and that households nevertheless can consume all of the income formed in the economic system.

The articulation of the two circuits follows the principle that income is defined in a circuit that is generated with households and that disappears with households. It confirms the general rule emphasized by Kalecki and that Kaldor puts in the following terms: 'Mr Kalecki's theory of profits [...] can be paraphrased by saying that "capitalists earn what they spend, and workers spend what they earn"' (Kaldor, 1993, p. 93).

On the whole, net investment is a final operation, a definitive saving for the community as a whole, as the goods produced in the capital-goods sector are finally purchased by firms using their own profits, which can be characterized as self-financing.[13] The very existence of the capital-goods production sector results from the fact that firms as a whole convert into capital goods the wage goods[14] contained in their monetary profits by self-financing new production.

## The conversion of wage goods into fixed capital

To say that firms are self-financing is to say they resort to their own resources to finance the increase in their production capacity. That further means they must first form a profit within their own output so as to acquire means of production subsequently. Explaining investment in fixed capital means allowing for the dual temporal and spatial dimensions of the operations on which the circuit of profit articulates: F–H–F. It is a matter of explaining the process by which saved wage goods, which are in firms' hands, to wit, profit goods, are finally converted into capital goods. This conversion occurs through new production in the context of a new division of labour corresponding to the birth of a sector specializing in producing capital goods.

Investment does not correspond then to a phase of pure monetary circulation, as Clerc (2002) claims, but to new production in sector 2. Being spent on the market for production factors, profit comes across as 'a fund from which new wages are drawn' (Schmitt, 1997, p. 90, our translation). Paid out to workers who are busy producing just these capital goods, this wage fund does not provide households with extra purchasing power, though. In their wages, they find the income that was captured by firms in the form of profit. Even so, this spending of profit counts as final financing of investment through self-financing at the same time as the structuring of the economic system into two productive sectors.

> The essential thing is to understand the need to distinguish two periods: one, $P_1$, in which monetary profit is formed, and the other, $P_2$, in which it is spent and converted into investment goods. It would be illogical to mix up the two periods. Whenever the holders of non-wage income are no longer concerned, the set of firms is alone with itself. It results that if spending of profit were maintained in respect of the very output whose sale formed the profit, the formation and spending of profit would create a vicious circle. (Schmitt, 1984, p. 168, our translation)

Apart from involving the organization of industries into two separate production sectors, the explanation of the formation of fixed capital requires understanding that the activity of the two sectors – that producing consumption goods and that producing capital goods – also relates to sequencing in time. The articulation of the two sectors follows from the fact that, like any income, profit must be formed before it can be spent. Profit being formed in the sale of products to households, and so in the consumption-goods sector, there is ground for saying that the capital-goods production sector arises after the consumption-goods sector. This is not a reference to two calendar periods that supposedly concern the economy as a whole, such as a month or a year, but to two, what we might call, 'functional' periods, in the sense that the first corresponds to the formation of profit and the second to its spending.[15] Commonly and for the economy as a whole, the two 'functional' periods are superposed as they are defined by the activity of each firm.

> As compared with diversity of expenditure met simultaneously by firms, the circuit scheme is not a simplified model though. The reality is that the start of production entails the superposition of different phases of the circuit and so different individual circuits. (Gnos, 2003, p. 332)

The segregation by time obeys the same logic as the sequencing of operations that governs the formation of fixed capital. These operations are articulated within a general H–F–H circuit. Households, as the only production factors, ultimately recoup all the consumption goods, but the embedding of the circuit of profit means that fixed capital is definitively immobilized in firms.

Let us run through the sequences again. In period $P_1$, firms have captured a fraction of households' income, which is reflected by the formation of 'forced' monetary saving at the same time as the composition of a stock of unsold products. In some sense, this is the 'initial' accumulation of capital that fuels the final investment operation. What characterizes this saving is that it is a fraction of the own output of firms they wish to invest, and so it does not relate to any debt they may have with individuals, but it does relate nonetheless to a commitment by them to provide increased output to society as a whole in the future.

At the end of period $P_1$, having made a profit, firms have the wherewithal to finance their own investment. However, at this point, households 'pick up the bill', so to speak: they are forced to save a part of their income. They have been unable to consume all of the output. But this is just provisional:

> At the precise moment when households transfer a part of their income to the profit of enterprises, they elicit an equivalent investment in wage goods; at a later date, households recoup their transferred incomes in payment for their production of capital goods. (Schmitt, 1996, p. 92)

In period $P_2$, thanks to the fraction of income they have captured, firms can take on some of the workers for producing capital goods. To simplify matters here, let us assume that firms do not seek to make a profit in $P_2$ to invest in the subsequent period, which means we reason implicitly in a full employment situation. Hence, the activity of the capital-goods sector inevitably requires some 'redeployment' of workers. On this assumption, it may be thought that, in producing equipment goods in $P_2$, firms will employ those workers that produced the equivalent profit goods in $P_1$.

These workers are then paid out of the profit formed in wage funds. In so doing, firms purchase the equipment goods directly and for their own account, and these are immediately constituted in capital goods and immobilized in these firms. The capital goods are not on offer to the workers who made them. The income paid to them is void of any purchasing power with regard to the new output they have produced in the 'capital goods' sector. They cannot buy equipment goods with their wages.

However, thanks to the wage fund that is paid to them, households will be able to procure in $P_2$ the consumption goods, that is, profit goods, stored in $P_1$ and for the exact amount of what they were unable to obtain in period $P_1$. In doing so, they destroy their incomes for good. No profit is made in the operation, and firms now have the capital goods they need, whereas they have sold off their stocks of profit goods. The wage goods captured in the formation of profit are finally converted into capital goods in firms' holdings.

What matters is that the capital goods produced in sector 2 are then definitively fixed in the production process, as households cannot purchase them. It can be seen that the investment is reflected by an increase in firms' productive assets without households losing any consumption power in the end, regardless of their propensity to consume. This explanation seems fully consistent with logical multiplier theory. The decisions to enter into an investment process are, of course, based on firms' expectations in terms of selling off their products to households. Their profits themselves depend on the propensity to consume, which means that the structuring of the economy into two productive sectors satisfies households' consumption habits. In addition, it can be seen that there can be no surplus or shortage of saving in the economy, as it is the unfolding of the investment process that gives rise to its 'own saving'. But it is true, too, that investment can be made only because firms form a profit in selling off their output, in other words thanks to the formation of saving that precedes the production of capital goods. In its final phase, net investment, in the sense of the formation of fixed capital, is made thanks to previous 'functional' saving. It is thanks to this saving, that is to say, non-redistributed profit, and its spending a second time on the labour market, that the economy is structured into two productive sectors.

It is true that Keynes and the post-Keynesians think of investment as a factor that may increase employment. There is no contradiction with the scheme just developed. It may well be imagined that, in period $P_2$, the capital-goods production sector takes on new workers. In this case, it is these latest workers who will be able to procure the stored profit goods; indeed, the increase in employment is reflected by a sharing of consumption goods between sector 1 workers and the new sector 2 workers. In short, whether the economic system is at full employment or not, the process of fixed-capital formation is the same: firms must form a profit in the sale of wage goods to households so as to finance the production of capital goods subsequently.

## Conclusion

The saving–investment relationship is not a simple matter of cause and effect; it is a two-way relationship in a sense. This is because in today's capitalist economies, firms are not simple intermediaries as neoclassical economists claim; they are agents in the full sense. It is true that it is because they decide to invest that firms endeavour to capture a fraction of current output in order to save it. In this sense one might say that investment creates saving. It is no less true either that without the saving of wage goods, investment in fixed equipment could not occur. Hence, one can argue that saving is a material condition for investment. In today's monetary economies of production, household saving is ultimately a staging post in the process of the formation of fixed capital. One can probably speak of 'reciprocal causality'[16] in the sense that the two magnitudes determine one another jointly. Indeed, discussions about the direction of causality between saving and investment arise from failure to see things from different angles.

The formation of fixed capital in today's economies follows a process that leads to firms capturing a fraction of current output. This is why firms are wholly independent economic agents and may have interests that are contradictory to those of households. It is incidentally in demonstrating the deep nature of the investment of profit that Schmitt was able to discover the main cause of inflation and unemployment in our economies. This is how high the stakes are in debating the definition of saving and investment and the relationship between them, not just for the advancement of theory but also in the search for practical responses to these two blights.

## Notes

1. For more on this see Bradley (1991).
2. On criticism of the mechanism, see Schmitt (1971) and Bradley (1994, pp. 93ff.) particularly.

3. The idea of *ex ante* saving leaves no scope for distinguishing between saving that households lend to each other and saving that firms ultimately have available to finance their investment.
4. Any gap between firms' investment wants and the credit granted to them is a matter of the relationship between banks and firms; it is a separate issue from that under discussion here.
5. For more on this see Cencini (2005, pp. 85ff.).
6. See the quantum theory of production and money (Schmitt, 1984).
7. For more on this see Schmitt (1984, pp. 423ff.).
8. Immobilized wealth becomes what accountants call fixed assets and economists call fixed capital.
9. See Keynes (1936, appendix to Ch. 6).
10. 'Finance' has been dealt with earlier on and need not be covered again. Bank loans here are made out of households' income deposited with banks.
11. Remember that the general definition of saving is that it consists in deferred consumption.
12. As argued above, profit cannot be spent by firms on product markets but only on the market for production factors (that is, labour).
13. The funds mobilized are formed by non-redistributed profits.
14. These goods are consumption goods that have not yet been made over to households.
15. With regard to the calendar, the two periods ordinarily overlap, since firms may spend their profits in advance as noted above. This is why the distinction between the two production sectors is usually restricted to a purely spatial dimension.
16. To illustrate this in a wholly different area, we can say that it is the mother who has the child, but vice versa it is because she has a child that a woman is a mother.

## References

Bradley, X. (1991), 'Biens de consommation et biens d'investissement' (PhD dissertation, University of Burgundy at Dijon).

Bradley, X. (1994), 'Le multiplicateur d'investissement et l'épargne des revenus', *Recherches Économiques de Louvain,* 60 (1), 87–105.

Cencini, A. (2005), *Macroeconomic Foundations of Macroeconomics* (London: Routledge).

Chick, V. (2000), 'Money and effective demand', in J. Smithin (ed.), *What is Money?* (London: Routledge).

Clerc, J.M. (2002), 'I ≡ S et le revenu non distribué', *Cahiers Lillois d'Économie et de Sociologie*, 38, 49–68.

Gnos, C. (2003), 'Circuit theory as an explanation of the complex real world', in L.-P. Rochon and S. Rossi (eds), *Modern Theories of Money: the Nature and Role of Money in Capitalist Economies* (Cheltenham: Edward Elgar).

Kaldor, N. (1993), 'Alternative theories of distribution', in C. Panico and N. Salvadori (eds), *Post-Keynesian Theory of Growth and Distribution* (Aldershot: Edward Elgar).

Kalecki, M. (1990), *Collected Works of Michal Kalecki*, vol. 1 (Oxford: Clarendon Press).
Keynes, J.M. (1930), *A Treatise on Money* (London: Macmillan).
Keynes, J.M. (1936), *The General Theory of Employment, Interest and Money* (London: Macmillan).
Keynes, J.M. (1937a/1973), 'Alternative theories of the rate of interest', *Economic Journal*, 47 (186), 241–52. Reprinted in *The Collected Writings of John Maynard Keynes* (vol. XIV *The General Theory and After: Part II, Defence and Development*) (London: Macmillan).
Keynes, J.M. (1937b/1973), 'The "ex ante" theory of the rate of interest', *Economic Journal*, 47 (188), 663–9. Reprinted in *The Collected Writings of John Maynard Keynes* (vol. XIV *The General Theory and After: Part II, Defence and Development*) (London: Macmillan).
Keynes, J.M. (1973), 'Letter to D.H. Robertson', in *The Collected Writings of John Maynard Keynes* (vol. XIV *The General Theory and After: Part II, Defence and Development*) (London: Macmillan).
Keynes, J.M. (1979), 'The distinction between a co-operative economy and an entrepreneur economy', in *The Collected Writings of John Maynard Keynes* (vol. XXIX *The General Theory and After: a Supplement*) (London: Macmillan).
Lavoie, M. (2004), *L'économie postkeynésienne* (Paris: La Découverte).
Poulon, F. (1981), *Macroéconomie approfondie* (Paris: Cujas).
Sawyer, M. (1996), 'Money, finance and interest rates: some post-Keynesian reflections', in P. Arestis (ed.), *Keynes, Money and the Open Economy* (Cheltenham: Edward Elgar).
Schmitt, B. (1971), *L'analyse macro-économique des revenus* (Paris: Dalloz).
Schmitt, B. (1984), *Inflation, chômage et malformations du capital: macroéconomie quantique* (Paris and Albeuve: Economica and Castella).
Schmitt, B. (1996), 'Unemployment: is there a principal cause?', in A. Cencini and M. Baranzini (eds), *Inflation and Unemployment: Contributions to a New Macroeconomic Approach* (London: Routledge).
Schmitt, B. (1997), *Le chômage et son éradication* (Fribourg: Fribourg University Press).
Walras, L. (1952), *Éléments d'économie politique pure* (Paris: Librairie Générale de Droit et Jurisprudence).

# 6
# Finance and the Realization Problem in Rosa Luxemburg: a 'Circuitist' Reappraisal

*Riccardo Bellofiore and Marco Passarella*

## Introduction

The aim of this chapter is to show that Rosa Luxemburg's analysis of capitalist accumulation is framed within a 'circuitist' macroeconomic reading of capitalism as a monetary production economy. The strengths and limits of her approach are to be found elsewhere than suggested by usual criticisms, especially those advocated by Marxist authors. Rosa Luxemburg cannot be reduced to the uncertain theoretical status of an 'under-consumptionist'. On the contrary, she presents a clear (although incomplete) picture of the macro-monetary and sequential working of the capitalist process.

This chapter is organized as follows. The next section examines Luxemburg's comments on how the enlarged reproduction scheme is introduced in volume II of Marx's *Capital*. The third, fourth, and fifth sections summarize, first, the orthodox attack by Bukharin, and then the more sympathetic interpretations provided by Michał Kalecki and Joan Robinson. The sixth and seventh sections emphasize the affinities and differences of Luxemburg's circuitist perspective with the contemporary theory of the monetary circuit. The eighth section concentrates on the problem of the monetization of profits and interests. Some concluding remarks are provided in the last section.

## Luxemburg's criticism

From October 1907 and until October 1914, Luxemburg taught political economy and economic history for the Social Democratic Party School (Krätke, 2009). Luxemburg intended to publish her lectures as a book, and her *Introduction to Political Economy* was actually printed, posthumous and incomplete, by Paul Levi (Luxemburg, 1925). However, when, in early 1912, Luxemburg was completing a first draft of this book, she ran up against a problem with the content of volume II of Marx's *Capital*. That unexpected difficulty had to do with the impossibility of depicting through Marx's schemes capitalist reproduction as a whole, in its concrete relations and objective historical limits. According to Luxemburg, Marx's abstract scheme of enlarged reproduction gives an unrealistic picture of capitalist development, because its economic logic is itself faulty. It is not enough that the surplus value extracted in the immediate production process is 'actualized' in commodity circulation (that is, converted into money). What is needed is that firms expect that they will be able to find outlets in the future, on an increasing scale.

Against this background, the analytical structure of Marx's argument clearly shows its limitations. Marx's schemes merely fix the equilibrium bookkeeping conditions. But the substantial questions, Luxemburg objects, are rather the following: (1) are industrial capitalists able to sell the commodity output on the market against money, at prices including the expected profit? This obviously is the same thing as asking (2) from where comes the monetary effective demand allowing the realization in circulation of the value and surplus value produced in the current period? Of course, this also means asking (3) how can it be taken for granted that industrial capitalists may safely expect growing sales for their future productions, so that there will be systematically an incentive for capitalists to accumulate as time goes by?

According to Luxemburg, the only analytical relevant point of view is that of 'total capital', systematically assumed by Marx in the third volume of *Capital*. Capital 'as a whole' is a 'real' abstraction, not a mere logical assumption. Since total capital is not a fiction, aggregate gross profits must be realized in money form – namely, in gold as money, because Luxemburg, like Marx, adopts a commodity-money perspective. 'Valorization' occurs in the unity of immediate production and circulation, and 'accumulation' requires the prior monetary validation of the output of the valorization process. This 'monetization' of the commodity output refers *ex post* to production, but *ex ante* it refers to the new investment. In this view, a monetary economy is an economy where commodities do not buy commodities, and commodities do not buy money, but only money buys commodities (Patinkin, 1965). Further, it is an economy where there is a cash-in-advance constraint (Clower, 1967). Luxemburg's exploitation is 'demand driven', and the essential 'monetary' nature of capitalism means that both production processes and expenditures (that is, demand) must be financed.

Within a 'pure' and 'closed' capitalist system, there are no money inflows granting the realization of the commodities containing surplus value. It is easy to see why for Luxemburg there is not enough monetary effective demand meeting the total value of the product, if this embodies a surplus value. The point is that finance to production and finance to demand directly or ultimately originate in the capitalist class itself, which is given by industrial capitalists and gold producers. This argument, however, is more transparent in the *Anti-Critique* (Luxemburg, 1921) than in the *Accumulation of Capital* (Luxemburg, 1913), and we will come back to it later on. At this juncture, let us just recall that Luxemburg is stressing that the answer to her problem must be a 'productive' kind of expenditure in the Marxian sense: a demand which is opening new valorization processes. This amounts to saying that the solution must open the way to capitalist investment itself.

This is the reason why an increase in capitalist consumption is not the solution, since it does clash by definition with the productive reinvestment of surplus value. The natural increase in population is not a solution either, since it gives way to a generic increase in consumption needs, but not to a demand backed by new money. The additional expenditure cannot come from 'third' social strata: their consumption is, once again, 'unproductive', and their money income has its source in a deduction from surplus value. An increase in gold production to realize the current level of production is another 'unproductive' way out rejected by Luxemburg. If by chance an increasing share of production turns into investment, this cannot but lead to a paradoxical situation where firms produce capital goods (today) in order to produce even more capital goods (tomorrow). Not only is this doubtful – in order for capitalists to realize the whole surplus value in money, through investments in the current period, there must be the probability of greater money receipts in the future. It is also deceptive, because the capitalist 'circular' process is here depicted as a production for production's sake, not as a production of more money by means of money (as capital).

Given that in a 'pure' and 'closed' capitalist system the capitalist class cannot count on any systematic additional monetary inflow justifying a net addition to employment and means of production, Luxemburg infers that capitalism can exist only in an 'impure' and 'open' setting. It is not only a transitory mode of production; it is also destined to collapse. The inquiry of capitalist development is inseparable from its history, and the latter is marked by the capitalistic compulsion to grab hold of 'external' (that is, non-capitalist) areas. In other words, capitalist nations need to fight not only in order to preserve their domestic markets (protectionism), but also to expand them. Imperialism is the increase of their political and military control over the residual non-capitalist areas. (Net) exports give way also to international loans going from the centre to the periphery. This produces overindebtness, which helps finance the commodity exports of the capitalist countries, but ends in financial instability and crises (Toporowski, 2009).

The only exception to relying upon 'external' demand is that military expenditure may temporarily resolve the difficulty (militarism). Eventually, the never-ending capture of 'external' spaces erodes the basis of the capitalist system, leading to economic breakdown and creating the 'objective' conditions for its overcoming (socialism or barbarism).

## Bukharin: Rosa Luxemburg as under-consumptionist

Luxemburg's work was harshly criticized by social-democratic as well as by Bolshevik authors. A greater attention to Luxemburg was paid by interpreters outside the Marxian camp strictly defined, like Michał Kalecki or Joan Robinson, both stressing the originality of her positions on effective demand in a monetary economy. The debate on Luxemburg as a political economist vanished after the 1970s. The essays in Bellofiore (2009a), however, testify of a renewal of attention to her economic works, mostly by authors influenced by post-Keynesian and monetary circuit perspectives.

The criticisms against Luxemburg usually refer to her *Accumulation of Capital* as a typical 'under-consumption' perspective (see for instance Bukharin, 1924). On the one hand, Luxemburg's emphasis on the necessity for capitalists to 'monetize' the surplus value (that is, to realize it against money) is severely criticized as a crass error. Monetization would just be a 'technical' issue, which has to be ignored in the preliminary abstract analysis of capitalist reproduction. The problem, it is argued, can be easily avoided by supposing an increase of money through gold producers or a higher velocity of circulation of money. The consideration of a plurality of capitalists and the overlapping of different circuits would ensure the metamorphosis of the surplus product from the 'commodity form' into the 'value form', that is, money. On the other hand, the demand that validates potential surplus value comes from the capitalist class itself, in the form of investment expenditure. In this framework, tomorrow's accumulation realizes yesterday's surplus value, without any necessary tendency toward a lack of effective demand and a consequent breakdown of the capitalist system. In this view, Rosa Luxemburg would add nothing but simply reformulate, after

Marx, the under-consumptionist error of Malthus and Sismondi, forgetting that capitalism is 'production for production's sake', not 'production for consumption's sake'.

In the following two sections we shall examine two alternative readings of Luxemburg's theory put forward by Michał Kalecki and Joan Robinson. These two authors are far away from traditional Marxism, and provide an interpretation that links Luxemburg's problem with Keynes's principle of effective demand.

## Kalecki: the 'savings gap'

Luxemburg, taking a 'total capital' point of view, raises the following question: why should one invest if there is no final market in view? Her conclusion that capitalist accumulation is downright impossible depends on the idea that the capitalist class 'as a whole' decides investment expenditures. Kalecki (1967) replies critically that capitalists do many things as a class, but they certainly do not invest as a class. If they really did operate like an individual 'collective capitalist', they would always be able to invest enough to ensure the extended reproduction of the economic system, whatever the total consumption expenditure – as indeed Tugan Baranovski argued. In a setting like this, capitalists always earn enough profits from the capital-goods sector, and may overcome any decline in workers' consumption.

This criticism notwithstanding, Luxemburg's insight about the need to find a market allowing realization of surplus value is a sensible point according to Kalecki. Luxemburg locates these outlets 'outside' the global capitalist system, namely, in the non-capitalist commodified economies. This occurs not only in the underdeveloped, not yet capitalist economies, but also in the non-capitalist sectors of developed capitalist economies. The explanation of this point can be provided on the ground of Kalecki's (1968) reading of the Marxian Equations of Reproduction. Though different from Luxemburg's, Kalecki's interpretation comes down to a very similar conclusion. The schemes anticipate much of modern (Keynesian) economics, that is, Keynes's principle of effective demand and Harrod–Domar's growth theory. The equations show that capitalists can decide how much they invest or consume in the future (and these decisions are in 'real' rather than in monetary terms), but they are not able to decide how much they sell and earn as profits. The issue of the determinants of capitalists' investment was left in the dark both by Marx and Luxemburg. But for sure the schemes show that, although equilibrium is possible in theory, it is not granted and far from being obvious.

The accumulation path is unstable, and there is no reason why, beside the stable rate of growth, the economy should not rather gravitate towards zero net investment, that is, the depreciation rate.

In the long run, then, enlarged capitalist reproduction is possible, as Luxemburg argued, only if there are some 'external markets' that absorb the commodity surplus generated by the ongoing accumulation process. These external markets are, for Kalecki, a needed stabilizing factor. There is an ambiguity in Luxemburg's original mode of thought, because she refers to exports as such. Of course, imports detract from the addition to effective demand, and therefore reduce the number of outlets for surplus production. The 'new' demand for surplus commodities is given only by net exports towards non-capitalist areas. Net exports have to be matched by a corresponding export of capital from the capitalist world towards the non-capitalist world – that is, the capitalist sector has to lend capital to the non-capitalist sector, if it wants to sell its commodities. Such a blunder leads Luxemburg to overestimate the weight of external markets in capitalist development, ignoring the importance of other factors (such as technological innovations). It is true, however – Kalecki stresses – that external markets temporarily allow solution of the contradiction of global capitalism.

Among the 'external' outlets absorbing the commodity surplus and allowing the accumulation process to go on, Luxemburg also includes government purchases, and most of all military expenditure. Again, Kalecki reproaches Luxemburg for considering the whole of government expenditure as an 'external market'. The financing of that expenditure must be accounted for. If it comes from taxes levied on wage earners, there is an equivalent reduction in consumption. On the contrary, government expenditure financed by taxes levied on capitalists, or thanks to loans, contributes to solving the problem of effective demand, since there is no corresponding reduction in investment or consumption. It is as if capital is exported to an internal 'foreign' market, created by government. This is why Kalecki considers government expenditure as 'internal exports', and sees it as an alternative to a trade-balance surplus as a solution to Luxemburg's problem. This Kaleckian mechanism is indeed 'internal' to the economy, but 'external' to the capitalist class as a whole.

This reading of Luxemburg's work was very influential in shaping Kalecki's own view. As early as 1939 Kalecki remarked that Marx did not pay attention to what happens if investment is not sufficient to secure a steady expansion of output. Luxemburg was instead lucid in stressing that, if there are savings from capitalists, their profits can be realized only if they spend a corresponding amount as investment. As a consequence, Kalecki saw in Luxemburg an *ante-litteram* Keynesian:

> Luxemburg considered impossible the persistence of net investment (at least in the long run) in a closed capitalist economy; thus, according to her, it is only the existence of exports to the non-capitalist countries which allows for the expansion of a capitalist system. (Kalecki, 1939, p. 255)

Kalecki (1939, p. 255) concluded on this ground that:

> [t]he theory cannot be accepted as a whole, but the necessity of covering the 'savings gap' by home investment or exports was outlined by her perhaps more clearly than anywhere else before the publication of Mr Keynes's *General Theory*.

Let us turn now to the analysis of Joan Robinson with respect to Luxemburg's work.

## Joan Robinson: the 'inducement to invest'

An even more positive reading of Luxemburg's argument in her *Accumulation of Capital* can be found in Joan Robinson's 'Introduction' to the English translation of that book. Robinson simplifies the main thread of Luxemburg's 1913 book, translating it into Keynesian language (Robinson, 1951). In her view, this should allow us to get over the misunderstandings elicited by Luxemburg's analysis. Luxemburg is not concerned with the equilibrium between investments and savings (which are always equal *ex post*), but rather with the existence of a suitable 'inducement to invest' within capitalism as a closed economy. What motive may capitalists have to enlarge the stock of their capital as a real magnitude? How may they entertain expectations of selling the additional amount of commodities produced by means of the new, additional capital? The answer to these questions may only lie in an 'ever-expanding market', that is to say, capitalists must anticipate an increased demand for commodities. According to Marx, a 'dynamic', Schumpeterian competition process among capitalists to earn a profit from large-scale production forces them to increase their capital and invest. Luxemburg, instead, looks for a prospective demand outside the sphere of production. In this regard, Marxian reproduction schemes provide no help: they give a snapshot of *ex post* monetary magnitudes, and say nothing about *ex ante* demand and profit outlook for capitalists. Of course, if capitalists actually decide to accumulate what they save as a surplus, final commodity demand will absorb total output. But the final question is for Luxemburg a prior one: why should capitalists decide to invest? What motive do they have to increase the stock of capital?

Luxemburg refers to an analytical framework where, with a constant real wage, technical progress translates into an increase in the productive power of labour and a fall in the value of individual commodities. In this setting, the value of labour power becomes smaller period after period. This is nothing but the law of the tendency of the 'relative' wage to fall stressed in her *Introduction to Political Economy*. Joan Robinson forgets to add that this law gives room for an increase in real wages as long as their rate of growth is lower than the growth of the productive power of labour. The rate of surplus value thereby increases. Since the share of surplus (value) in the value added by living labour (to wit, net income) goes up, the amount of real savings is also rising. On these hypotheses, the problem Robinson raises is more serious than in Marx's original schemes, because the equilibrium rate of accumulation is higher than when the rate of exploitation remains constant. Luxemburg also assumes that the 'value composition of capital' – that is, the ratio of constant capital to variable capital – grows over time, as this is in the nature of technical progress assumed by Marx in *Capital*, volume III. This is an assumption that Robinson rightly rejects, because it ignores that technical change may devalue the individual value of the goods that constitute the elements of constant capital, so that productivity may increase together with a falling of the value of capital per person employed. Yet this assumption may be maintained, provided we suppose that technical progress is labour-saving and capital-using.

On these hypotheses, the economic system cannot avoid a disproportionality crisis. The output of the first sector producing capital goods falls short of the needs of constant capital in the whole economic system, while the output of the second sector exceeds consumption coming from the two sectors taken together. This is not surprising, as it is implicit in the logic of the reproduction schemes. In itself, the aforementioned argument is silent about the occurrence of a general overproduction crisis because of a lack of effective demand. Moreover, Luxemburg's analysis is invalidated by 'overdetermination' of the model, as she maintains the assumption that the annual net investment of each sector must be equal to annual savings within the same sector. We may add that this is at odds with Luxemburg's stressing that Marx's correct point of view to rewrite the schemes of reproduction is that of the third volume of

*Capital* – namely, the point of view of 'total capital'. Further, the above assumption is not only absolutely unrealistic; it is also inconsistent with the tendential equalization of profit rates, and with the mobility of capital among sectors as something essential to the nature of capitalism. If we remove this spurious over-determination of the model, it is clear that an equilibrium path may always be written on paper. As long as total investment demand absorbs total savings of both sectors taken together, there is no capitalist breakdown.

'But here we find the clue to the real contradiction. These quantities may conceivably fit, but there is no guarantee that they will' (Robinson, 1951, p. xxxiv). If the propensity to save by the capitalist class exceeds the accumulation rate dictated by technical progress, crisis can be averted only if there is an outlet for investment outside the capitalist system. 'We can substitute for a supposed logical necessity a plausible hypothesis about the nature of the real case' (p. xxxiv). When income distribution and the propensity to save of capitalists generate savings in excess of new investment, there is a chronic excess of the potential supply of real capital over its demand. The system has to fall into a 'chronic depression', as both Keynes and Hansen suggested. Capitalism can ward off the crisis only by incessantly conquering non-capitalist areas, overcoming the contradictions inherent in the lack of demand.

## The *Anti-Critique*: the circuit of money and the issue of finance

Both Kalecki and Robinson read Luxemburg through the spectacles of the principle of effective demand. Their interpretation is much richer than those provided by both orthodox and heterodox Marxists. They highlight how the deficiency of demand is for Luxemburg a structural feature constraining the accumulation of capital in a closed capitalist system without the state. However, both authors see in (net) exports nothing but the solution to the difficulty of realizing current surplus value, and both divorce her problem from her adherence to the Marxian labour theory of value. Kalecki adds that 'internal exports' – that is, government expenditure not financed by taxes levied on workers – may substitute for foreign outlets as a solution.

In this way, two aspects of Luxemburg's argument are lost. The first is that the lack of effective demand originates exactly from the tendential fall in relative wages, which is nothing but the other side of the coin represented by relative surplus value extraction. It is the latter that opens the way, at the same time, to the savings gap and the increasing likelihood of the eruption of disproportionalities. The second aspect is that the solution Luxemburg seeks for the contradiction she detected must be represented by a 'productive' expenditure, that is, in something which is in itself an increase in capitalist investment (Bellofiore, 2009b; see also Bellofiore, 2004).

There is another point missing in the way Michał Kalecki and Joan Robinson approach Luxemburg's work. They seem completely unaware that Luxemburg is a forerunner of what nowadays is known as the theory of the monetary circuit (see Graziani, 2003, but also Deleplace and Nell, 1996; Rochon and Rossi, 2003). The point is mostly implicit in the *Accumulation of Capital* – the book Kalecki and Robinson commented upon. This point is however quite explicit in the *Anti-Critique*, a pamphlet that Luxemburg wrote during her imprisonment and posthumously published in 1921. In the latter book, Luxemburg adopts an entirely macroeconomic, sequential, and monetary view of the economic process, and clarifies her focus on the problem of the 'monetization' of the surplus. In that work, Luxemburg is not merely putting the accent on the increasing chance of an inherent lack of effective demand and on the intrinsic instability of a closed capitalist system. Of course, the share of commodity output containing the latent surplus value extracted in the immediate production process has to be actualized 'against money' before it can be advanced to start a new productive cycle. But Luxemburg is bringing to light a further, connected, and very decisive issue: since the demand for the commodity surplus must be a nominal expenditure flow of the same amount, where does the money backing that demand come from? In the answer, she links the finance to demand to the finance to production. Here we come definitely into 'circuitist' territory.

Luxemburg's socialist critics completely misunderstood this question. Kalecki and Robinson do not confront it altogether. Luxemburg's point is the following. It is the capitalist class itself that sets off the capitalist process as a monetary circuit through injections of purchasing power. Yet this means that what the capitalists get at the end of the circuit, as money 'valorizing' capital, can only be money they themselves brought into the system. Whatever the source of the extra demand for the commodity surplus, it is useless as long as it does not mean an addition of new money 'from outside'. Without this injection the capitalists taken together cannot realize an excess of money receipts over the money they had to advance to finance either production or their expenditure.

On the one hand, as Luxemburg pertinently says, the money circulating among capitalists to replace old capital goods and to buy new capital goods cannot but be an 'internal affair'. By definition, she claims, no money surplus can stem from the capitalists themselves in the aggregate. On the other hand, the source of the money spent by workers (including the newly employed workforce) on consumption goods also flows out from capitalists' pockets. That is why Luxemburg insists again and again that from a macroeconomic point of view the money realizing surplus value can only come from 'external' buyers, who 'receive their means of purchase from an independent source of purchasing power, and do not get it out of the pocket of the capitalist like the workers' (Luxemburg, 1925, p. 57).

Luxemburg maintains that – in the commodity-money setting she shares with Marx – a problem like this cannot be solved by invoking an increase in gold-money output. A new production of gold as money would distract resources away from other capitalist productions to realize surplus value. The new inflow of gold-money would then be obtained through a reduction in the pace of potential capitalist accumulation. What Luxemburg needs as an answer to her question is not simply money 'oiling' the circulation of surplus value, but money that, while monetizing surplus value, is at the same time activating a new capitalistic cycle of accumulation: money as capital. She overlooks the fact that the banking system may multiply the credit available to capitalists on the basis of gold deposits, and increase the velocity of circulation of money. When this happens, capitalists would be able to realize the surplus commodities, although the total stock of gold-money remains unchanged. However, Luxemburg's instinct is right in resisting a solution to her problem via a systematic, continuous exponential rise in the velocity of circulation of money.

## The monetary circuit

Only recently some authors – notably Trigg (2006, 2009) and Bellofiore (2009c) – have rediscovered in Luxemburg this mode of thought, which has remained hidden for almost a century. Trigg investigates mainly the *Accumulation of Capital*, while Bellofiore looks into the *Anti-Critique*: the latter is the text where it is possible to identify a first (though incomplete) scheme of a monetary circuit because of the particular attention devoted by Luxemburg to the inflow and outflow of money. The theory of a monetary circuit in its contemporary version (we refer here mainly to the scheme of thought put forward by Graziani, 2003) provides a picture of the capitalist economy as a monetary sequence of interrelated phases. A comparison with the theory of the monetary circuit can help us to explain both the strengths and weaknesses of Luxemburg's position.

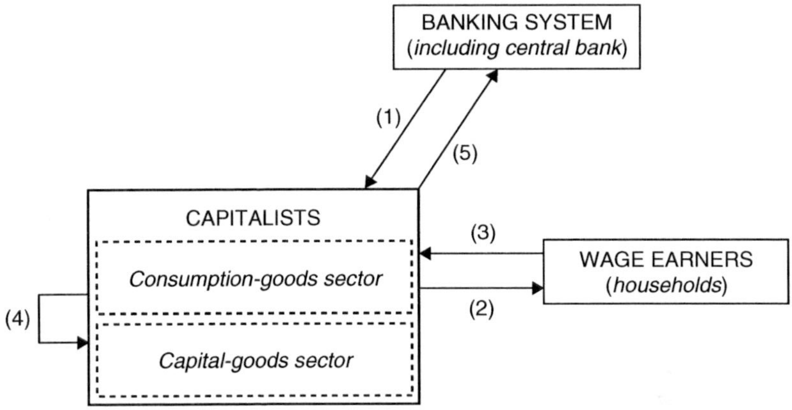


*Figure 6.1* The monetary circuit in a pure credit capitalist economy

Figure 6.1 illustrates the triangular relation in a pure credit economy among bankers, industrial capitalists, and wage earners. The monetary sequence 'opens' with the bankers' decision to grant 'initial finance' to creditworthy industrial capitalists (arrow 1 in Figure 6.1). The latter have to ask banks for (credit-)money, because firms need to hire workers' labour power in order to begin the production process (arrow 2). For industrial capitalists, money represents the purchasing power to obtain workers' labour power, which is the only non-reproducible element of the system. Buying labour power is the only external purchase for the capitalist class as a whole, without which capitalist production could not even begin. In the simplest monetary circuit version, when production is over, wage earners cannot but spend the whole of their income in consumption goods, so that industrial capitalists recoup their 'final finance' (arrow 3). If we imagine a two-sector economy, and we abstract from capitalists' consumption and workers' savings, the profits of the second sector are spent on purchasing capital goods produced in the first sector (arrow 4). The monetary circuit 'closes' as soon as capitalists pay back to banks their single-period debt, that is, reimburse the principal and pay interest (arrow 5).

In the circuit approach, money is a purely social symbol without any intrinsic value, a mere bookkeeping liability for the issuing bank. Its supply is endogenous. On this point, the difference with respect to Luxemburg's view is clear. For her, money is 'gold', that is, the 'general equivalent', namely, the excluded commodity against which all other commodities have to be exchanged. The stress in the monetary circuit approach shifts from (gold as) the 'general equivalent' in universal commodity exchange to (non-commodity bank-) money as finance activating capitalist production. This difference notwithstanding, Luxemburg's analysis converges with the monetary circuit approach.

Her question is: from where do the money inflows come to finance the aggregate demand, which monetizes the surplus that has been produced thanks to the advance of total money capital, including the money wage bill? Her model is actually the simplest model circuitists have in mind, with only one (crucial) difference: gold producers rather than banks as monetary capitalists. She also assumes a historically determined real wage for the working class, whereas circuit authors assume that a real wage is set by capitalists' autonomous decisions about the structure of output. But this is not a deep divergence. In fact, it is quite easy to consider Luxemburg's (and Marx's) hypothesis on the wage as a (theoretically grounded) special and relevant case of the circuitist perspective.

According to Luxemburg, 'capital accumulation' means not only to produce a growing amount of commodities, but first and foremost to turn them into a growing amount of money. Capitalism is defined as that social situation in which industrial capitalists make more money through the advance of money, and the point of view is truly monetary and macroeconomic. The only source for the injections of money being the capitalist class (industrial capitalists are financed by gold producers), a pure capitalist system is simply impossible. Against those remarking that it is the same investment expenditure which could abstractly provide the demand realizing the already extracted surplus value, Luxemburg's answer is that this implicitly means that the finance to demand comes again from the capitalist class. Capitalists can get a bigger amount of money profits only if they themselves inject new money into the economic system.

One position among the circuit school is the following. If industrial capitalists are considered as a consolidated sector, money as a means of payment is completely unessential for the exchanges between capitalists. Surplus value is embodied in capital (and luxury) goods – namely, in the commodities that are exchanged among capitalists themselves. In this regard money simply acts as a 'lubricant oil', and may be ignored in the analysis without any theoretical misgivings. There is, however, no dichotomy between a real and a monetary sector. Money is not just a unit of account nor a stock of wealth. It is finance: it is the essential means of payment, which alone gives agents the purchasing power in order for them to enter the market. The supply of initial finance is the ingredient of any process of production, the monetary foundation for the autonomous decisions concerning the quantity (level) and quality (composition) of output. These considerations, while they are compatible with Luxemburg's stress on the point of view of 'total capital', show how the problem of the monetization of the surplus that she raises is inappropriate.

It is also apparent that Luxemburg, though clearly providing an argument in terms of a monetary circuit, does not clearly distinguish within the capitalist class between the banking sector (which creates money, but does not produce commodities) and the industrial sector (which produces commodities, but does not create money). All her stress on volume III of Marx's *Capital* notwithstanding, she does not include in her analysis the important developments in the theory of money where Marx examines interest-bearing capital, credit, and fictitious capital.

If we consider the division in the capitalist class between firms as a whole (industrial capitalists) and the banking system (monetary capitalists), the difficulty Luxemburg raises can be translated as follows. Ignoring the payment of interest to banks, in a simple reproduction scheme the same amount of credit money is created and destroyed in each period. In this respect, according to the now well-known definition provided by Keynes, finance is nothing but a 'revolving fund'. As a consequence, at the end of each circuit, industrial capitalists have to settle their single-period (short-term) debt to banks. This seems unproblematic, because in a closed economy, if there are no workers' savings, industrial capitalists receive back all the money they injected into the system. Of course, the problem partially disappears for those who do not consider money as 'currency' that lubricates the intra-capitalist-class exchanges. Other positions within the circuit tradition would take more seriously the problem of the monetary realization of the surplus. It is in this perspective that the Luxemburg–Kalecki view stressing 'net exports' and 'internal exports' can be carried on.

Once the distinction between bankers and industrial capitalists is introduced as a defining feature of the analysis, a variant of Luxemburg's problem cannot be avoided: from where does the money come that allows the payment of money interest by firms to banks on initial finance? How can industrial capitalists pay interest on bank loans, in money, since what they can get from the commodity market is no more than the 'initial' finance they injected into it, an initial finance they obtained from the same banks? Whatever the limits of Luxemburg's approach to the monetary circuit, her dilemmas seem alive and well.

## Profits and interest in a monetary circuit framework

The realization of aggregate profits and the payment of bank interest in money terms represent the most intricate *rebus* for the authors of the monetary circuit (Rochon, 2005, p. 125). The point is that if industrial capitalists use bank loans to finance current production, they cannot recover from the market more money than they injected into the system (even if both workers and capitalists have a unitary propensity to spend). In particular, in a two-sector economy, without either foreign markets or government expenditure, only the consumption-goods sector is able to realize profits in monetary terms, and just in the measure in which wage earners spend their income on consumer goods. In contrast, even if there are no workers' savings and the consumption-goods sector completely turns its profit into (net) investment, the capitalists producing capital goods may at best realize an equilibrium between receipts and expenditures.

However, we know that, at the end of the period, industrial capitalists have to pay money interest on the loans to banks. This means that, with a positive bank rate of interest, capitalists producing capital goods systematically suffer monetary losses. The problem could be solved by explicitly considering banks' own contribution to total expenditure on consumption and investment. In this case, capitalists of both sectors would realize gross monetary profits, allowing capitalists to pay bank interest. There are, however, problems for this quite ad hoc solution. First, if banks appropriate a share of capital goods, the separation between the banking system and the industrial sector, which is a basic feature of the monetary circuit model, disappears. Secondly, even if we consider just the consumption of the bank personnel, the latter cannot purchase goods before obtaining income. In fact, banks cannot lend credit money to themselves: they do not have a right of seigniorage. A more reasonable solution is for banks to buy equities from firms.

Since the early 1980s, several explanations have been advocated to resolve the problem of the existence of profits and interest at the macroeconomic level in a circuit model (for a general overview, see Rochon, 2005). A first possibility is to consider 'total capital' and the involved aggregate theoretical view as a first approximation hypothesis, behind which there is the 'reality' of overlapping monetary circuits. The finance to production of some (subsequent) circuits realizes the surplus-value commodities of other (prior) circuits. The basic (hidden) hypothesis is that money injected as initial finance systematically exceeds money destroyed in settling debts to banks in each period. However, this solution goes against Luxemburg's concept of total capital as a 'real' abstraction. Further, it relies on 'a microeconomic explanation of what is a macroeconomic problem' (Rochon, 2005, p. 133).

A second possibility is to explicitly consider that a share of industrial capitalists suffer losses, which correspond to an equivalent amount of profits for their competitors. This is claimed to be the 'creative destruction' process induced by competition among industrial firms on the commodity market (Messori and Zazzaro, 2005). However, this solution raises two criticisms: first, it dodges Luxemburg's question about the necessity of financing demand; secondly, it involves the 'microfoundation' of a macroeconomic problem as well.

A last possibility is to assume the existence of two parallel circuits, the production circuit and the investment circuit. They are not two different overlapping circuits, but a single circuit that is divided on the basis of the related different transactions (Rochon, 2005, p. 136). Both circuits are necessary to pay back bank loans and to earn profits, but the production circuit ends within the single production cycle, whilst the investment circuit lasts for a number of periods of production. This is a 'technical' solution, where an additional flow of money allows producers of capital goods to realize the share of product incorporating surplus value and hence to pay off bank interest. In this way, against Luxemburg, the economic system is able to achieve a dynamic growth equilibrium and hence to reproduce itself on an enlarged scale.

However, this equilibrium may be shown to be very unstable, assuming that it has been achieved (Desai and Veneziani, 2009, p. 50). It depends upon profit expectations of both banks and firms, so that every single deviation from the balanced-growth path gives rise to an explosive dynamics. In practice, the only temporary and local solution to the realization problem, an alternative to increasing government debt, is net exports, namely, the answer provided by Luxemburg in her analysis of the Marxian reproduction schemes.

## Conclusion

While most of her critics regard capitalism as a great barter economy, where money is an inessential 'veil' over real magnitudes, Rosa Luxemburg constantly asks how money enters the system and where *extra* money realizing surplus value comes from.

Her answer is defective on analytical grounds, and is conditioned by a conception of money reducing it to gold. However, her works contain a clear model of the monetary circuit, where the notion of 'finance' is a basic feature of the analysis. Indeed, Luxemburg adopts an analytical point of view close to those adopted by old (Wicksell, Schumpeter,

Keynes) and contemporary (Schmitt, Parguez, Graziani) authors of the monetary theory of production (see Bellofiore, 1992, 2005).

Paradoxically, exactly what her critics dubbed as crass errors (namely, the emphasis on the monetization of surplus value and on the role of 'external' outlets), appear to be what make Rosa Luxemburg a lucid forerunner of today's theories of money, accumulation, and crisis. Her dead ends are the living questions in the heterodox monetary perspective.

## References

Bellofiore, R. (1992), 'Monetary macroeconomics before the *General Theory*: the circuit theory of money in Wicksell, Schumpeter and Keynes', *Social Concept*, 6 (2), 47–89.

Bellofiore, R. (2004), 'Like a candle burning at both ends: Rosa Luxemburg and the *Critique of Political Economy*', *Research in Political Economy*, 21, 279–98.

Bellofiore, R. (2005), 'Monetary economics after Wicksell: alternative perspectives within the theory of the monetary circuit', in G. Fontana and R. Realfonzo (eds), *The Monetary Theory of Production: Tradition and Perspectives* (Basingstoke: Palgrave Macmillan).

Bellofiore, R. (ed.) (2009a), *Rosa Luxemburg and the Critique of Political Economy* (London: Routledge).

Bellofiore, R. (2009b), 'The monetary circuit of capital in the *Anti-Critique*', in R. Bellofiore (ed.), *Rosa Luxemburg and the Critique of Political Economy* (London: Routledge).

Bellofiore, R. (2009c) 'Introduction: Rosa Luxemburg on capitalist dynamics, distribution, and effective demand crises', in R. Bellofiore (ed.), *Rosa Luxemburg and the Critique of Political Economy* (London: Routledge).

Bukharin, N.I. (1924), *Der Imperialismus und die Akkumulation des Kapitals*, trans. R. Wichman, *Imperialism and the Accumulation of Capital* (New York: Monthly Review Press, 1972).

Clower, R.W. (1967), 'A reconsideration of the microfoundations of monetary theory', *Western Economic Journal*, 6 (1), 1–8.

Deleplace, G. and Nell, E.J. (eds) (1996), *Money in Motion: the Post Keynesian and Circulation Approaches* (Basingstoke: Macmillan).

Desai, M. and Veneziani, R. (2009), 'Rosa Luxemburg's critique of Marx's schemes of reproduction: a re-evaluation and a possible generalization', in R. Bellofiore (ed.), *Rosa Luxemburg and the Critique of Political Economy* (London: Routledge).

Graziani, A. (2003), *The Monetary Theory of Production* (Cambridge: Cambridge University Press).

Kalecki, M. (1939), 'Essays in the theory of economic fluctuations', in J. Osiatynski (ed.), *Collected Works of Michał Kalecki*. Volume I. *Capitalism: Business Cycles and Full Employment* (Oxford: Clarendon Press, 1990).

Kalecki, M. (1967), 'Problem of effective demand with Tugan-Baranowski and Rosa Luxemburg', in J. Osiatynski (ed.), *Collected Works of Michał Kalecki*. Volume II. *Capitalism: Economic Dynamics* (Oxford: Clarendon Press, 1991).

Kalecki, M. (1968), 'The Marxian equations of reproduction and modern economics', in J. Osiatynski (ed.), *Collected Works of Michał Kalecki*. Volume II. *Capitalism: Economic Dynamics* (Oxford: Clarendon Press, 1991).

Krätke, M.R. (2009), 'A very political political economist: Rosa Luxemburg's theory of wages', in R. Bellofiore (ed.), *Rosa Luxemburg and the Critique of Political Economy* (London: Routledge).

Luxemburg, R. (1913), *Die Akkumulation des Kapitals*, trans. A. Schwarzschild, *The Accumulation of Capital* (New York: Monthly Review Press, 1951).

Luxemburg, R. (1921) (written 1915), *Die Akkumulation des Kapitals oder Was die Epigonen aus der Marxschen Theorie gemacht haben. Eine Antikritik*, trans. R. Wichman, *The Accumulation of Capital – an Anti-Critique* (New York: Monthly Review Press, 1972).

Luxemburg, R. (1925), *Einführung in die Nationalökonomie*, in *Gesammelte Werke*, Volume V (Berlin: Dietz Verlag).

Messori, M. and Zazzaro, A. (2005), 'Single-period analysis: financial markets, firms' failures and closure of the monetary circuit', in G. Fontana and R. Realfonzo (eds), *The Monetary Theory of Production: Tradition and Perspectives* (Basingstoke: Palgrave Macmillan).

Patinkin D. (1965), *Money, Interest and Prices*, 2nd edn (New York: Harper and Row).

Robinson, J. (1951), 'Introduction', in R. Luxemburg, *The Accumulation of Capital* (New York: Monthly Review Press).

Rochon, L.-P. (2005), 'The existence of monetary profits within the monetary circuit', in G. Fontana and R. Realfonzo (eds), *The Monetary Theory of Production: Tradition and Perspectives* (Basingstoke: Palgrave Macmillan).

Rochon, L.-P. and Rossi, S. (eds) (2003), *Modern Theories of Money: the Nature and Role of Money in Capitalist Economies* (Cheltenham: Edward Elgar).

Toporowski, J. (2009), 'Rosa Luxemburg and finance', in R. Bellofiore (ed.), *Rosa Luxemburg and the Critique of Political Economy* (London: Routledge).

Trigg, A.B. (2006), *Marxian Reproduction Schema: Money and Aggregate Demand in a Capitalist Economy* (London: Routledge).

Trigg, A.B. (2009), 'Where does the money and demand come from? Rosa Luxemburg and the Marxian reproduction schema', in R. Bellofiore (ed.), *Rosa Luxemburg and the Critique of Political Economy* (London: Routledge).

# 7

# Money, Capital Turnover, and the Leisure Class: Thorstein Veblen's Tips for a Monetary Theory of Production

*Guglielmo Forges Davanzati and Riccardo Realfonzo*

## Introduction

Many contemporary scholars maintain that significant similarities can be traced between Veblen's theoretical framework and Keynes's approach, with particular reference to the so-called monetary theory of production (hereafter MTP). In particular, Vining (1939) argues that Veblen should be counted as one of the authors who 'anticipated' Keynes's theory of effective demand, and his monetary conception of the interest rate. Vianello (1961, p. 252) stresses the shared conviction – on the part of both Veblen and Keynes – that the interest rate is not determined by the supply–demand mechanism, and that its variations play a crucial role in determining economic crises. Dillard (1987) emphasizes that Veblen's dichotomy between industrial and pecuniary employment is a key issue of the MTP and that relevant analogies between Veblen's and Keynes's views of the functioning of monetary economies are to be considered:

> Money is a form of private property that wealth holders in business enterprise economy at times treasure more than income itself. It is a device for limiting losses in a profit-and-loss economy. The moral of Veblen's teaching is that in a pecuniary economy, monetary values dominate industrial values. (Dillard, 1987, p. 1646)

In a similar vein, Parker Foster and Ranson (1987, p. 228) maintain that:

> [t]he conclusion reached by both Veblen and Keynes is that the traditional theory of production is flawed. Production is governed not

by real exchanges but by the institution of money. Production continues only as permitted by the creation of new credit to finance new investment.

In comparing Veblen's and Keynes's thought, Mouhammed (1999, p. 26) stresses that 'Keynes's contribution to the monetary theory of production develops further Veblen's finding'. In particular, he maintains that 'Veblen believes (as Keynes does) that the interest rate and the money supply are used to control the economy by the vested interests' (Mouhammed, 2003, p. 268). He also attributes to Veblen the Keynesian principle of effective demand, arguing that a 'vent for surplus' argument via imperialism is important in Veblen's thought (pp. 273ff.). In line with Dillard (1987) and Parker Foster and Ranson (1987), Mouhammed (2003, p. 279) concludes that Veblen developed a model of the MTP, where, although 'a lucid explanation for the interest rate determination' is not provided, mark-up pricing can be used to determine it within the Veblenian theoretical framework. Rutherford (1980, p. 439) expands this argument by arguing that '[n]o firm can survive in the "credit economy" of the New Order that fails to fully extend its credit; and so become dependent on the banker'. Nayaradou (2005) points out in this respect that – in the Veblenian theoretical framework – '[b]ankers become the guardians of the absentee ownership', and bankers – that is, the 'captains of finance' – finance the production process 'via the *ex nihilo* credit'. In this connection, Wilson (2006, p. 1031) points out that both Veblen and Keynes shared the conviction that 'credit finance constrains investment and the scale of output', and that Veblen 'provided the conceptual basis for a general theory of credit-based market economy'.[1]

The aim of this chapter is to expand the basic Keynesian model of the MTP following Veblen's ideas on the role of the 'leisure class' in governing the dynamics of income distribution (see Veblen, 1975 [1899a]). In particular, we will argue that it is on the basis of the desired level of consumption by the 'leisure class' that banks fix interest rates, while money supply is determined by firms' demand for money, as in the basic MTP schema.[2] Further, the conflict within the firm – between business persons and technicians – also affects real wages via 'industrial sabotage'. This argument leads us to maintain that the path of income distribution – and particularly of real wages – is the outcome of firms' decisions as regards the level of production, of technicians' ability to reduce the duration of the production process, and at the same time of the whole of the leisure class's decisions on the level of consumption. The chapter is structured as follows. The next section focuses on the relationship between profits and capital turnover. The third section explores the theoretical links between consumption by the leisure class and the path of real wages. The last section concludes.

## Industry, capital turnover, and the duration of the monetary circuit

According to Veblen, in contemporary monetary economies the management of the firm's financial structure is separated from the control of the firm's production process. This separation involves the conflict between two opposing instincts, namely, the 'instinct of workmanship', typical of technicians, and the 'rapacity' of business persons.[3] This echoes Veblen's famous dichotomy between 'business' and 'industry' resulting from a historical process, where larger-sized firms required specific attention to their financial aspects, hence enhancing the division of labour within the firm.[4] The functional separation between business and industry gives rise to the potential conflict between those who manage the 'pecuniary side' of the firm ('businessmen')[5] and those who control the production process ('technicians' or 'engineers').[6] Veblen describes this conflict as follows:

> In the normal course of business touching this matter of industrial consolidation [. . .] the captain of industry works against, as well as for, a new and more efficient organization. He inhibits as well as furthers the higher organization of industry. (Veblen, 1965 [1904], p. 39)

However, according to Veblen, businessmen need technicians not only because the latter 'keep the industrial machinery in operation' (Walker, 1977, quoted in Tilman, 2003, vol. II, p. 67)[7] but also because technical improvements can positively affect profits insofar as they reduce capital turnover. Let us concentrate on this second issue. Veblen (1965 [1904], p. 93) maintains that 'there are two chief means of shortening the interval of the turnover, currently resorted to in industrial business': these means boil down to 'the adoption of more efficient, time-saving industrial processes', and advertising.[8] In a long footnote in *The Theory of Business Enterprise*, Veblen (1965 [1904], Ch. 5, fn. 5) clarifies that:

> [t]he turnover will count for more in gross earnings at current rates if instead of his own capital alone the business man also engages whatever funds he can borrow by using his capital as collateral. The turnover counted on capital (value of the industrial equipment)

plus credit, at current rates, will be greater than that counted on the capital alone used without credit extension. The turnover may be expressed as the product of the mass of values employed multiplied by the velocity. Hence, if credit be taken as indeterminate fraction (capital/n) of the capital used as collateral, we may say that

Turnover = (1/time)(capital + capital/n), that is
T = (1/t)(c + c/n) = (c + c/n)/t; t = (c + c/n)/T.

The algebraic statement serves to bring out the equivalence between an acceleration of the rate of turnover and an increase of the volume of business capital.[9]

Veblen's emphasis upon the shortening of the interval of capital turnover is very fruitful and captures a key aspect of the real world. His suggestion can be usefully applied within a Keynesian model of the MTP. This is easily comprehensible not only for the linkages between Veblen and the MTP examined in the previous section, but also because according to the MTP time matters. The relevance of time in monetary economies constitutes a basic assumption of the MTP. According to this approach, the working of the economy must be described as a sequential process, that is, a succession of phases logically and temporally connected. The links among these successive phases form a circuit of money (see Graziani, 2003). The basic model of the MTP involves three macro-agents: banks, firms, and workers. The economic process can be described as the succession of five phases:

1. The production process starts with the bargaining in the credit market between banks and firms. Firms need money in order to buy labour power and to start production; banks supply firms with initial finance;
2. Firms use banks' initial finance to purchase labour power and give each worker the previously agreed money wage;
3. Once firms have acquired a labour force, the production phase starts and firms carry out their production plans;
4. After production, there is the phase of circulation. Firms offer the goods for sale to the workers. If workers' propensity to consume is equal to one, firms get back all of the money they laid out to pay wages, and so they can pay off their debt to the banks (except for interest). If workers' propensity to consume is less than one, firms try to obtain the unspent money by selling securities in the financial market. Hence, firms get the final finance from both the commodity market and the financial market;

5. The monetary circuit is closed by the repayment of the initial finance to banks and, thus, by the destruction of the money originally created (Graziani, 2003; Realfonzo, 2006; Fontana and Realfonzo, 2006).

In this approach income distribution is explained outside the principles of the marginal theory of distribution. In fact, profits are explained on the basis of the firm's power alternatively to determine prices (according to the mark-up principle in non-perfectly competitive markets) or to decide the composition of output (consumption goods, investment goods, luxury goods). On the other hand, financial rent depends on banks' power to determine the rate of money interest. What is more relevant here is that in a sequential economy the 'time dimension' matters. In other words, the total amount of profits and rent has to be weighted with respect to the temporal unit (for example, a calendar year). Of course, the shorter the production process (that is, the duration of the monetary circuit), the higher the amount of profits and financial rent.

Following Veblen's terminology, let us indicate with $T$ firms' revenue per unit of time (that is, what firms obtain by selling their product via the use of time-saving techniques), while $c$ is money capital obtained via self-financing, and $c/n$ is the amount of bank credit. By setting the average exogenous length of the production process ($L$), expressed in terms of money revenue per unit of time and given by 'the time ordinarily allowed in the line of industry in which he is engaged' (Veblen, 1965 [1904], p. 93), extra-total revenues ($\Delta R$) for the individual firm (with respect to its competitors) become:

$$\Delta R = T - L = [(1/t)(c + c/n)] - L \quad (1)$$

Note that in this theoretical framework competition is conceived of as a process devoted to gaining differential advantages. In particular, this process is aimed at obtaining extra profits with respect to the competitors. This implies a different notion from neoclassical (static) competition, where the individual firm's decisions are independent of others' decisions.[10]

As a result, in this circuit view by Veblen, revenues for the individual firm $A$ are higher (and higher than those of its competitors) as is its differential advantage, (i) the longer the ordinary duration of the production process (that is, the lower the revenue per unit of time for its competitors, $L$), (ii) the less time required for the production of its goods, that is, the more efficient (time-saving) the production process, and (iii) the higher the money capital supplied to the firm by banks. Revenues ($R$) increase profits ($P$) on condition that total costs remain unchanged.

Condition (i) presupposes that a 'normal duration' of the monetary circuit exists and is known to the entrepreneur. Further, insofar as this 'normal duration' is determined by the technical choices of competitors, the entrepreneur is forced by competitive pressure to use time-saving techniques. In other words, the higher the intensity of competition, the lower the resulting value of $L$, and the more the individual firm is forced to increase the degree of efficiency in the production process.

Condition (ii) is linked to the possibility, and the advantageousness, for firms to exploit the technical knowledge they possess.[11] Although Veblen does not expand on this argument, which would lead to the idea that the maximum technical improvements ($t$) determine the maximum revenues, via $T$, one can argue that the opposite result may occur. This is because technical improvements imply an increase in output ($Q$) and the consequent decline in prices ($p$), so that $R = pQ$ and the increase in $t$ may have a *negative* effect on $T$ on condition that the elasticity of demand is low enough. In formal terms, since $dQ/dt > 0$ and $dp/dt < 0$, $t$ negatively affects $T$ if, in absolute terms, $dp/dt > dQ/dt$. It may happen that, $t^o$ being the maximum degree of technical improvement generated by technicians, its actual value is $t^* < t^o$: underutilization of capital being the consequence.

The condition (iii) derives from Veblen's view of the division of labour within the firm, in the sense that the typical function of the businessman is to manage the 'pecuniary side' of the firm and, hence, to deal with the banking system. This condition establishes a positive relation between investments and revenues, which can be limited by the value of the interest rate. The rationale for this relation, according to Veblen (1965 [1904], p. 94), is to be traced in the 'trite commonplace that the earnings of any industrial business [are] a function [of] the volume of business'.[12] Veblen (1965 [1904], p. 97) adds that a high interest rate may discourage entrepreneurs' demand for credit, hence reducing the turnover of capital: 'on funds obtained on credit the debtor has to pay interest', and '[t]his sets a somewhat elastic limit to the advantageous use of loan credit in business'. This argument leads to the following result: for a given technology, the increase (decrease) in the interest rate determines a reduction (increase) of $T$. Thus 'earnings' increase as the interest rate declines.

As we have pointed out, Veblen (1965 [1904]) also refers to advertising as a means of increasing $T$. This occurs because the rate of turnover may depend on the 'competitive pushing of sales', by selling before the competitors, and accelerating the sales. In this sense, rapidity (in producing and selling) can be a relevant variable in the competitive struggle. Advertising also plays a significant role in modifying the elasticity of demand. As a result, given the argument above, advertising affects the relationship between $dQ/dt > 0$ and $dp/dt < 0$, thus affecting $t$. The more effective the advertising, the greater the difference between $dp/dt$ and $dQ/dt$, and the greater the difference between $t^*$ and $t^o$. In this sense, advertising contributes to the underutilization of capital. Moreover, advertising is waste, since

> competitive advertising is an unavoidable item in the aggregate costs of industry. It does not add to the serviceability of the output [...]. What it aims at is the sale of the output, and it is for this purpose that it is useful. It gives vendibility, which is useful to the seller, but has no utility to the last buyer. (Veblen, 1965 [1904], p. 59)[13]

## Leisure class, income distribution, and the monetary circuit

In his essay 'On the nature of capital', Veblen (1908, pp. 132ff.) refers to the leisure class as a complex social agent. This class includes 'great financiers', that is, those individuals who operate in the financial market, gaining 'a tax on commonplace business enterprise'. It also includes, in general, those who supply firms with money capital without directly contributing to the production process (in this sense, members of the leisure class can be seen as 'absentee owners').[14] In this picture, the ultimate source of the firm's finance is the banking system, controlled by the leisure class, and the capacity of the banking system to produce money appears to be the key issue: 'Broadly speaking' – Veblen (1905, p. 470) emphasizes – 'banking is profitable chiefly because the banker lends more than that he has or borrows', and 'the banker [can] create a new volume of credit'.[15] This occurs in cases where 'in making a loan on collateral, which is not of the nature of a bill of sale, *the banker*, or any similar concern doing a credit business of this kind, *creates a new volume of credit*' (Veblen, 1905, p. 470, emphasis added). However, the Veblenian leisure class also includes industrial capitalists, that is to say, owners of firms as well as entrepreneurs.

Veblen's approach can be usefully employed within an MTP model. Let us consider the following assumptions:

1. The structure of agents is composed of firms, banks, and workers. The leisure class includes both financial and industrial capitalists. All relevant decisions about the economy are in the hands of the leisure class, in particular of entrepreneurs (the 'technicians') and businessmen.

The former decide quantity and quality of output; the latter fix the rate of interest, and control capital and financial markets. Firms and banks aim to earn profits in real terms;

2. The economy is divided into two sectors, one producing wage goods (sector 1), and the other producing luxury goods (sector 2). Workers consume wage goods; the leisure class consumes luxury goods;
3. Members of the leisure class compete on consumption. Note that this assumption reflects Veblen's position on 'invidious comparison' (see Veblen, 1899b, Ch. 2);
4. The unitary money wage is fixed, deriving from wage bargaining at the beginning of the circuit. Further, we will assume that the unitary wage is the same in both sectors, that workers' propensity to consume equals 1, and that firms can move from one sector to another for the pursuit of the highest level of profit;
5. Banks fix the rate of interest while the quantity of money supply is demand driven. Firms operating in the sector of consumption goods will demand an initial finance equal to $wN1$. Firms operating in the sector of luxury goods will demand an initial finance equal to $wN2 + \beta wN2$ (where $\beta > 0$). The amount $\beta wN2$ will be employed in order to buy luxury goods.

In this theoretical approach, the income of the leisure class depends on the volume of gross profit. Since in the models of the MTP the gross profit depends on the firms' decision about production and on the banks' decision to finance production, it is correct to say that gross profit depends on the leisure class's own decisions. It is obvious that gross profit is equal to the production of luxury goods; the distribution of gross profit between net profit and rent will depend on the level of the rate of interest. However, reinterpreting Kalecki, while workers spend what they earn, the leisure class earns what it spends.

In light of the assumptions above, the sequential process of the economy is captured by the monetary circuit illustrated by Figure 7.1.

Consumption by the leisure class ($C$) implies the demand for sector 2 goods only. If $C_0$ is the minimum amount of consumption of luxury goods, $\gamma$ the intensity of competition on consumption, $n$ the number of individuals belonging to the leisure class, the consumption function is as follows:

$$C = C_0 + \sum_{i=1}^{n} \gamma C_i \tag{2}$$

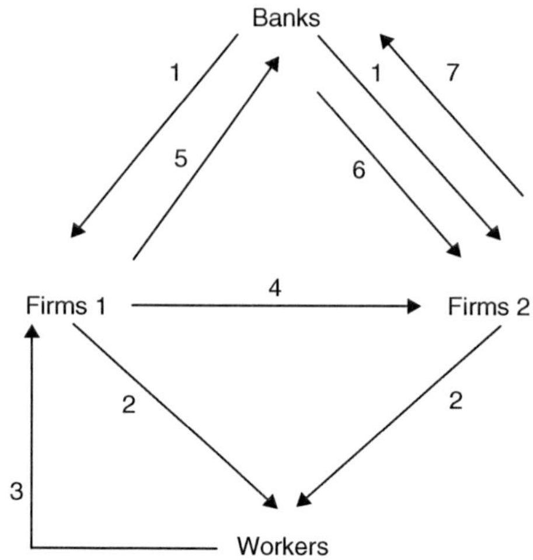


*Figure 7.1* The monetary circuit: (1) initial finance; (2) payment of money wage; (3) purchasing of consumption goods; (4) purchasing of luxury goods (firms 1); (5) reimbursement of bank loans (firms 1); (6) purchasing of luxury goods (banks); (7) purchasing of luxury goods (firms 2) and reimbursement of bank loans (firms 2)

Given the above assumptions, the effect of financial rents on aggregate money profits is the following:

$$P1 = p1Q1 - wN1 - i(wN1) \tag{3}$$

where $p1$ is the unitary price of wage goods, $N1$ the level of employment in sector 1, and $i(wN1)$ is the financial debt in money terms due to firms operating in sector 1 to the banking system. Thus, $P1$ decreases with respect to the interest rate, and (because $p1Q1 = wN1 + wN2$) equation (3) can also be written as follows:

$$P1 = w(N1 + N2) - wN1 - i(wN1) = w(N2 - iN1) \tag{3'}$$

while banks' money rent will be $R = iw(N + \beta N2)$.

It follows that firms of sector 1 are indebted to the banking system when $wN2 < iwN1$. The amount of debt positively depends on $C$ (indeed, the greater the demand and the production of luxury goods, the greater $wN2$ will be).

The price of consumption goods will be as follows:

$$p1 = (w/\pi)(1 + N2/N1) \tag{4}$$

The relation between financial rents and aggregate money profits in sector 2 is given by the following equation:

$$P2 = p2\left(C_0 + \sum_{i=1}^{n} \gamma C_i\right) - wN2 - iwN2 - i\beta wN2 \qquad (5)$$

In particular, the demand of firm 1 for luxury goods is $Y_{f1}^d = w(N2 - iN1)$, while banks' demand for luxury goods is $Y_b^d = iw(N + \beta N2)$, and the demand of firm 2 is $Y_{f2}^d = \beta wN2$.

Aggregate demand for the sector of luxury goods will be $Yd = wN2(1 + i + i\beta + \beta)$, and the price of luxury goods will be

$$p2 = (w/\pi)(1 + i + i\beta + \beta) \qquad (6)$$

where $p2$ is the equilibrium unitary price of luxury goods, $N2$ the level of employment in sector 2, and $i(wN2)$ the share of financial debt for firms in sector 1 due to the banking system. Note that, like the price of consumption goods, the price of luxury goods will always be greater than the cost of production. Equation (6) is a particular version of the mark-up equation, where the unitary cost of production is increased with bank interest and extra spending to buy profit goods on the part of firms.

Money profits of firms operating in the second sector will be equal to $\beta wN2$, while the real profits of the three components of the leisure class – respectively, firms operating in sector 1, banks, and firms operating in sector 2 – will be as follows:

$$P1/p2 = [(N2 - iN1)\pi]/(1 + i + i\beta + \beta) \qquad (7)$$

$$R/p2 = [i\pi(N + \beta N2)]/(1 + i + i\beta + \beta) \qquad (8)$$

$$P2/p2 = (\beta N2\pi)/(1 + i + i\beta + \beta) \qquad (9)$$

Of course, the total real profit for the leisure class will be $\pi N2$, that is to say, the total production of luxury goods. If we indicate with $Nfe$ the level of full employment, it is obvious, in this analytical context, that the production of consumption goods and the production of luxury goods can increase together if $N < Nfe$. Once $N = Nfe$, any increase in the production of luxury goods (that is, any increase in total profits) will necessarily be accompanied by a decrease in the production of wage goods. However, given that

$$w/p = w/[w/\pi(1 + N2/N1)] = \pi N1/N \qquad (10)$$

workers' real wages will decrease any time firms increase the number of workers employed in the luxury-goods sector. In other words, the increase in gross profit is always negatively related to real wages.

A step forward in the analysis could again come from Veblen's insights. Veblen invites us to analyse the effects of competition among members of the leisure class on income distribution. It is well known that – in Veblen's view – consumption by the leisure class is waste (see Veblen, 1899a, b). Veblen's conception of waste can be seen in two different perspectives. First, Veblen's argument is that while workers can improve their conditions of life only by means of 'efficiency and thrift', for members of the leisure class the 'taboo on labour' holds: therefore, they do not contribute to economic growth, mainly because they consume without working. Secondly, consumption by the leisure class is wasteful, because it is competitive: members of the leisure class could obtain a level of comparative consumption that is the same before and after the competition process, while spending resources.

In light of the arguments above, one can conclude that the higher the financial rents-to-wages ratio, the higher the social waste, as 'wasteful consumption' is proportionately higher. Further, the patterns of consumption by the leisure class help to define the specialization of the economy, at least in the sense that producing luxury goods becomes profitable in contexts where the leisure class is sizeable, and its consumption is high:[16] this is what Veblen (1919, p. 328) calls 'the modern use of credit and corporation finance for the collective control of the labor market and the goods market'.

At this stage, one can note *prima facie* that the higher the number of individuals belonging to the leisure class ($n$) and the higher the intensity of competition on consumption ($\gamma$), the greater $i$ and $\beta$, the lower the level of profits in sector 1 and the higher the level of profits in sector 2, for given levels of employment. The following causal chain shows the effects of high rents on wages via profits:

$$\uparrow C \rightarrow \uparrow p2, \uparrow P2 \rightarrow \uparrow m2 \rightarrow \downarrow Q1 \rightarrow \downarrow w/p$$

An increase in consumption by the leisure class ($+i$, $+\beta$) increases the demand for luxury goods, thus pushing firms in sector 2 to increase prices (see equation (6)).[17] This leads to a decrease in both monetary and real profits of firms operating in sector 1 (see equations (3) and (7)) and, as a result, a switch of some of these firms to sector 2 ($m2$ being the number of firms in sector 2). Both the real wage bill and the unitary real wage decline as well.

As Veblen (1965 [1904], p. 252) observes, 'the wasteful expenditures enhance demand, [...] increase profits and raise capitalization'. Note that, in this schema, expenditure by the leisure class increases the price level of both consumption goods and luxury goods, in accordance with Veblen's (1905, p. 471) view that, when banks grant credit, they 'add to the borrower's funds available for purchase, and therefore increase the effective demand for goods, and by so doing help to enhance prices. In such a transaction the banker lends funds which he does not possess.'[18]

Moreover, accumulation of rents could also affect investment. Let us assume that *N*2 workers are employed not only to produce luxury goods but also to produce investment goods. Let us also assume that demand for investment goods – by both firms operating in sector 1 and firms operating in sector 2 – is inversely related to the rate of interest. On these assumptions, it is obvious that an increase in the desired level of consumption by the leisure class (*C*), leading the banking system to increase the interest rate (*i*), will lead to a decrease of investment: productive investment would thus be crowded out by wasteful consumption. These causal links hold on the assumption that firms' expectations are not optimistic enough to keep investment high in response to high interest rates. As a matter of fact, Veblen (1906 [1901], p. 310, emphasis added) insists that:

> [t]he market fluctuations in the amount of capital proceed on variations of confidence on the part of investors, on current belief as to the probable policy or tactics of the guild of politicians, and of the indeterminable, *largely instinctive, shifting movements of public sentiment and apprehension*. So that under modern conditions the magnitude of the business capital and its mutation from day to day are in great measure a question of folk psychology rather than of material fact.

Figure 7.2 illustrates the mechanism of the sequence shown above, with sole reference, for the sake of simplicity, to sector 1.

In panel (a), the credit market is described on the assumption that the interest rate reflects the desired level of consumption by the leisure class (*C*). We assume the money supply curve to be elastic, owing to banks' power of money creation, while the money demand curve (*Md*) is downward sloping, reflecting firms' expectations (as in Veblen's view). An increase in the rate of interest form $i^0$ to $i'$ will determine a shift from $M^0$ to $M'$, given firms' expectations. The *N* curve (in panel b) is drawn on the assumption of a given unitary money wage, which gives rise to different money wage bills (*MWB*) corresponding to different values of *N*. In panel (c), the reduction in *N* implies a reduction in the production of consumption goods (*Q*1) and, hence, in the real wage bill. Panel (c) describes the Veblenian 'production function', namely, a

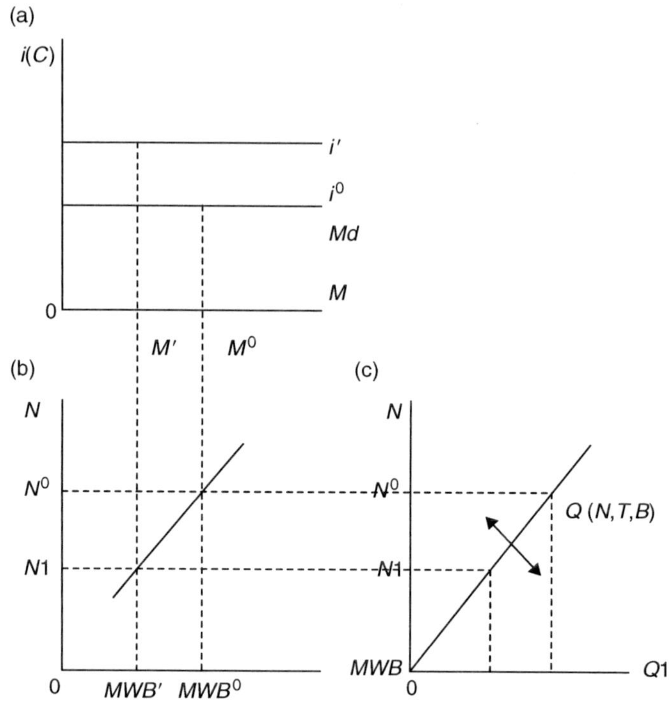


*Figure 7.2* Interest rates and real wages

relationship between $N$ and $Q1$ subject to the contrasting tendencies to expand output owing to the instinct of workmanship ($T$) and to reduce it, via industrial sabotage on the part of businessmen ($B$). It is worth noting that this production function differs from the standard technical relation between inputs and output, as it involves institutional variables, so that the outcome of the conflict between different instincts – 'workmanship' versus 'rapacity', and thus $T$ versus $B$ – ultimately affects it. Hence, the elasticity of the 'production function' indicates the degree of 'industrial sabotage': the steeper the $N$–$Q$ function slope, the less the 'instinct of workmanship' is in operation.[19] As a result, the more sensitive the demand for money is to the interest rate, and the more the interest rate is affected by the desired level of consumption by the leisure class, the more firms operating in sector 1 will move to sector 2, the lower the level of employment in sector 1 and the lower the real wage bill will be. In this sense, conspicuous consumption is waste.[20]

The fall in real wages – following Veblen's argument – clashes with the leisure class aim of preserving the 'institutional inertia condition', that is, a condition where workers do not change their habits of thought and continue being 'docile', giving social and moral recognition to the status of the ruling classes (see Veblen, 2001 [1921]). Veblen is unclear on the determinants of institutional change, and many interpretations have been put forward in this respect. In particular, the recent contribution by Bowles and Park (2005) is worth considering. Assuming that emulative processes are in operation also between classes (that is, the working class emulates the leisure class), Bowles and Park (2005) suppose that the number of working hours increases in proportion to the inequality of income distribution, so that workers react to the increase in conspicuous consumption by trying to increase their wages via a higher supply of labour. We suggest a different interpretation, starting from the emphasis Veblen puts on social conflict, driven by 'popular discontent'. Indeed, workers can react to the fall in wages also via social conflict. In order for social conflict to be in operation, changes in workers' habits of thought must have occurred. Social conflict, in fact, involves a modification of the value judgement attached to the canons of conduct of the ruling classes: waste is not seen as an undisputed moral value, becoming a disvalue, and efficiency becomes a value itself. In the Veblenian theoretical framework, the ultimate cause of social conflict can be traced to a long-run process of changes in habits of thought, above all involving changes in ethical codes by workers. Income distribution, Veblen stresses, is primarily a product of the prevailing canons of morality: 'Principles (habits of thought) countenancing some forms of class or personal preference in the distribution of income are to be found incorporated in the *moral code* of all known civilizations and embodied in some form of institution' (Veblen, 1908, pp. 112–13, emphasis added).

Therefore, one can argue that workers' perception of the 'unfairness' of income distribution – that is to say, when rents and profits are no longer legitimate on moral ground – is the basic motive that leads them to conflictual behaviour. Particularly in *The Vested Interests and the State of the Industrial Arts*, Veblen (1919) approaches the issue in the following terms: 'To the common man who has taken to reckoning in terms of tangible performance, in terms of man power and material resources, [the] returns on investments that rest on productive enterprise as an overhead charge are beginning to look like *unearned income*' (Veblen, 1919, p. 47, emphasis added). When the incomes of the ruling classes are seen as 'unearned', it follows that there is a lack of moral recognition by workers, and the moral basis for social conflict is thus established: 'There has lately been some *irritation* and *faultfinding* with what is called "profiteering" and there may be more or less *uneasy discontent* with what is felt to be an *unduly disproportionate inequality* in the present distribution of income' (Veblen, 2001 [1921], pp. 99–100, emphasis added).

The mechanism described here leads to an evolving process, involving economic and institutional disequilibrium, and it is ultimately generated by a problem of lack of coordination. While the leisure class as a whole is interested in maintaining the existing social order, competition within the leisure class pushes its members to increase consumption, thereby determining a reduction in wages and a possible institutional change, via social conflict.[21] As a result, the higher the degree of competition among the members of the leisure class, the higher the resulting rents-to-wages ratio, and the more inclined workers are to oppose the existing social order, giving rise to institutional change. Institutional change is thus driven by the dynamics of income distribution.

## Conclusion

This chapter proposes an interpretation of Veblen's thought based on the idea that his picture of the functioning of market economies has many similarities with the MTP. We argue that a variant of the MTP can be traced by inserting competitive consumption within its basic schema, and considering that the Veblenian leisure class manages the credit market. The model proposed in this chapter considers the economy as formed by two sectors: one producing wage goods, the other producing luxury goods. Financial rents have a double nature. They are both a cost for firms, in the form of the interest bill, and an item of demand (for luxury goods). We have shown that an increase in financial rents reduces real wages via two mechanisms. First, insofar as the Veblenian firm is a locus of conflict between technicians (interested in maximizing production) and business persons (interested in making money profits via price increases), the increase in demand determines increases in prices and profits in the sector producing luxury goods. This implies a movement of firms towards this sector, and the consequent decline of production of wage goods and real wages. Secondly, consumption by the leisure class has a positive effect on the interest rate, thereby reducing productive investment and wages. Finally, we argued that Veblen's view of the dynamics of institutional change can be interpreted as driven by social conflict, generated by a significant and long-term increase in the financial rents-to-real-wages ratio.

## Acknowledgements

The authors wish to thank John Henry and Antonio Luigi Paolilli for their useful comments on a previous draft of this chapter.

## Notes

1. Note that Veblen wrote only once on Keynes, namely, his review on Keynes's *The Economic Consequence of the Peace* (Veblen, 1920), and that – in so doing – he only dealt with Keynes's *political* (not economic) view. In this essay, Veblen criticizes Keynes's analysis of the post-First World War scenario, by emphasizing his lack of interest in the fact that 'Bolscevism is a menace to absentee ownership'. The important political aspects of the problem, which, according to Veblen, are unclear in Keynes's view, make *The Economic Consequences of the Peace* a 'too superficial review of the case'. In discussing Veblen's theory of the business cycle, and with particular reference to the expansionary periods, Nayaradou (2005, p. 41, italics added) emphasizes that

    > [t]o Veblen, the economy is inherently unstable, because the price system is not able to regulate the capital market or the current market. As prices rise, credit supply should slow down as the real interest rate falls, but none of this happens. On the contrary, *credit supply increases to meet the ever-growing demand for credit.* It becomes more interesting for firms as prices rise, since the cost of borrowing becomes relatively lower than any other form of capital financing.

    A similar mechanism is also considered within the MTP.
2. In a similar vein, Vianello (1961, p. 247) points out that, in Veblen's theoretical framework, 'great interests determine the level of credit'.
3. It is worth noting that instincts – in Veblen's view – do not rest on purely biological grounds, but involve psychological and social aspects. See Asso and Fiorito (2004), Cordes (2005), and Wolozin (2005).
4. 'The pecuniary side of the enterprise came to require more unremitting attention, as the change for gain or loss through business relations simply, aside from mere industrial efficiency, grew greater in number and magnitude. The same circumstances also provoked a spirit of business enterprise, and brought on a systematic investment for gains' (Veblen, 1965 [1904], p. 24).
5. On the terminological distinctions between businessmen, entrepreneurs and captains of industry see, in particular, Veblen (2001 [1921], pp. 20–1).
6. This point is particularly stressed by Rutherford (1984) and more recently by O'Hara (2000). In the same vein, Anderson (1933, quoted in Tilman, 2003, vol. II, p. 20) writes that

    > [t]he purpose of industry is goods for the subsistence and comfort of men. The purpose of business, on the other hand, is to make money profits. So long as markets are expanding, as was the case in the handicraft period, this duality of purpose need cause no harm; but in the modern industrial age markets do not expand at a sufficiently rapid rate. The result is that the duality becomes a conflict.

7. 'The processes of production were continually growing more intensive, diversified, complicated, and more difficult for any layman in technology to comprehend' (Veblen, 2001 [1921], p. 28).
8. 'Improvements of industrial plant and industrial processes' – Veblen (1965 [1904], p. 94) adds – 'having this in view are gaining in importance in the later developments of business, since a closer attention is now given to the time element in investments, and great advances have been made in this direction'.
9. Veblen recalls Jevons's *Theory of Political Economy* on this point and criticizes Sombart's view, in *Kapitalismus*, that 'the use of credit lengthens the time of turnover of capital'. He underlines the difference between his approach and that of Böhm-Bawerk and Fisher as follows:

   > Technological (industrial) procedure, being of the nature of physical causation, is subject to the time relation under which causal sequence runs. This is the basis of such discussions of capital and interest as those of Böhm-Bawerk, and of Fisher. But business traffic, as distinguished from the processes of industry, being not immediately concerned with the technological process, is also not immediately or uniformly subject to the time relation involved in the causal sequence of the technological process. Business traffic is subject to the time relation because and in so far as it depends upon and follows up the processes of production. (Veblen, 1908, p. 124)

   This is to say that the time element is not only involved in the production process but also in the market process, where the latter (that is, the time spent in selling goods) is likely to affect the former (that is, the time spent in producing goods) and vice versa. It could be useful to recall that, in *Capital* (book II, section 2), Marx maintains that the overall length of the cycle of a given capital results from the sum of its time of circulation and its time of production: in this sense, Veblen's view appears similar to that of Marx, on this specific point, insofar as capital turnover also includes the time of circulation. $R$ being one year (as the unit of measurement of the turnover), $r$ the turnover time of a given capital and $n$ the number of its turnovers, the following formula gives Marx's theory of capital turnover, as presented in *Capital*: $n = R/r$.
10. In *The Theory of Business Enterprise*, Veblen (1965 [1904], p. 218, emphasis added) argues that

   > [t]he business man's object is to get the largest aggregate gain from his business. It is manifestly for his interest, as far as may be, to shorten the process out of which his earnings are drawn, or, in other words, to shorten the period in which he turns over his capital. If the turnover consumes less than the time ordinarily allowed in the line of industry in which he is engaged, he gains *more than the current rate of profits in that line of business*, other things equal; whereas he loses if the turnover takes more than the normal time.

   Otherwise, Veblen (1965 [1904], p. 218) often refers to the aim of obtaining 'differential advantage as against other competitors'. Cutrona (2005, pp. 269–74) convincingly remarks that Veblen's theory of the firm overcomes the conceptual problems of the neoclassical approach: 'One of the weaknesses of orthodox theory is the lack of connection between the firm and the macroeconomic setting in which it operates. This connection is established here as a consequence of the assumption that the firm is an institution for the attainment of pecuniary gains' (Cutrona, 2005, p. 269). Cutrona (2005, p. 273) adds that the Veblenian firm is engaged in 'obstructing competitors' strategies', acting in view of the 'movements of competitors'. Thus, 'the entrepreneur behaves strategically' and this view 'anticipates' the theories of 'administrated prices in oligopolistic markets' (Curtona, 2005, p. 276). See also Viano (2005), who explores the relationships between Veblen's reading of Kant and his theory of instincts, with particular reference to businessmen's behaviour.

11. In dealing with Veblen's view of technology, it seems necessary to distinguish between the genesis of technological knowledge and its (capitalistic) use. While the problem addressed here only regards the latter use, it is important to stress that – according to Veblen – technology is a social construct (see Lawson, 2006). As Hodgson (2004, p. 183) argues, '[t]he individual and the social aspects of knowledge are connected, because the social environment and its "common stock" of experience provide the means and stimulus to individual learning'. Mouhammed (2003, p. 151) notes in this respect that

> [t]echnology (the industrial arts or the joint stock of knowledge) is a social ownership of the community and is accumulated over time. However, by private ownership of the means of production capitalists invariably manage to appropriate the benefits of the technological advantages, which should have been imputed to the community. Thus, for Veblen, the neoclassical marginal productivity theory cannot be applied either to the tangible (or the durable part of the capital) or to the intangible part.

Note also that technology affects uncertainty, since agents cannot foresee which alternatives will ultimately be selected in future because selection processes are outside of their control (see Van der Steen, 1999).

12. Veblen attributes this 'trite commonplace' to Alfred Marshall and his *Principles of Economics*.
13. As Arrow (1975, quoted in Tilman, 2003, vol. II, p. 48) emphasizes, '[t]hese expenditures [...] can be regarded as wastes; they yield indeed a competitive advantage but no social advantage'. In view of the arguments above, the potential conflict between technicians and businessmen manifests itself in the underutilization of capital, or, in Veblen's words, in 'perversion': 'The ownership of the capital goods affords a discretionary power of misdirecting in the industrial process and *perverting industrial efficiency*, as well as inhibiting or curtailing industrial processes and their output, while the outcome may still be profitable to the owner of the capital goods' (Veblen, 1908, p. 108, emphasis added). Veblen (1908, p. 107) adds that '[t]he most comprehensive principle involved in [...] business management is that of rising prices, and so increasing the net gains of business, by limiting the supply'.
14. Veblen (1923, p. 2) considers absentee ownership as 'the dominant institution' via 'the use of credit', and 'accountants, advertisers, public servants,

members of parliament, owners of land and capital, banks and sales workers' are the representative members of the leisure class. Moreover, he adds that members of the leisure class can control firms also by means of the ownership of company stocks (as a part of its intangible assets): 'The free income which is capitalized in the intangible assets of the vested interests goes to support the well-to-do investors, who are for this reason called the kept classes, and whose keep consists in an indefinitely extensible consumption of superfluities' (Veblen, 1919, p. 113).

15. Cutrona (2005, p. 270, fn. 18) stresses that – in Veblen's view – 'credit consists in the creation of new purchasing power; that is, it is a pecuniary phenomenon'. Note also that Veblen (1906 [1901], p. 310) maintains that the nature of the interest rate does not rest on clearly defined economic grounds, insofar as 'productivity theories of interest should be as difficult to maintain as productivity theories of the gains of the pecuniary employments, the two resting on the same grounds'.
16. For the sake of simplicity, public expenditure is excluded here. Veblen maintains that the main role of government is to guarantee social order. This occurs mainly via the claim for 'national integrity' and the consequent social cohesion, in the form of what Bush (1987) names 'regressive institutional changes'. As Tsuru (1993, p. 61) clearly emphasizes,

    > Veblen [...] differs from Marx and Engels in thinking that the state does not exclude the underlying population from the governing process for the reason that the business leadership would not be able to govern without 'the advice and consent of the common run'. [...] Veblen was aware of a possible crisis [and] he developed a theory regarding the counter instruments to which the business leadership was expected to resort. Thus came his theory of 'national integrity' (or plain nationalism) into the picture. It had two aspects, namely: (1) equating the interests of business leadership with those of the nation as a whole; and (2) adopting aggressive policies towards the outside world, accompanied by the militarization of society.

    O'Hara (2004, p. 979, emphasis added) convincingly supports the idea that

    > Veblen recognized that politics and economics were two aspects of a unified social whole to be understood together. The state is the guarantor of the existing social order and protects existing property rights and the interest of the leisure class. [...] Veblen made it very clear that the interests of the capitalist absentee owners are the *primary concern* of the government.

17. For the sake of simplicity, the so-called Veblen effect (that is, any increase in $p2$ determines an increase in demand for luxury goods) is not taken into consideration. See, among others, Forges Davanzati (2006, Ch. 3) for the debate on the significance of this effect.
18. More generally, Veblen (1905, p. 461) argues that '[credit and prices] stand in a casual relation to one another, possibly as being the effects of the same causes'. In particular, he argues that – in periods of 'prosperity, or

speculative advance' – it is not the increase in money supply that generates price increases, but the other way round. This is because,

> [n]otoriously, a period of advancing prosperity is a period of relatively high prices, at least in some of the important branches of industry, and usually it is also a period of advancing prices. Extensions of credit, of course, run in terms of money, and are based on the money values (price) of the property submitted as collateral. If the market value of collateral advances, then the amount of the credit which it will support will likewise increase. (Veblen, 1905, p. 462)

19. In particular, the more 'workmanship-type' the firm, the more the 'production function' shifts upwards and, by contrast, the more 'business-type' the firm, the more the 'production function' shifts downwards. For a discussion on this point, and the related issue of the distinction between productive and unproductive labour, see O'Hara (2000).
20. It is worth noting what Keynes (1971 [1930], pp. 111–14) writes on this issue. He defines 'unproductive consumption as consumption which could be forgone by the consumer without reacting on the amount of the productive effort, and "productive consumption" as consumption which could not be forgone without such a reaction'. He maintains that '[f]ull employment of the factors of production requires a redistribution, not a reduction, of the aggregate of consumption', namely, 'by supporting productive consumers instead of unproductive consumers'.
21. Rereading Veblen in light of the theoretical category of social conflict poses the problem of the similarity and the differences between Veblen and Marx. Edgell and Townshend (quoted in Tilman, 2003, vol. I, p. 313) stress that 'Veblen's theory of increasing status competition, expressed in terms of a "struggle to keep up appearances" represents an alternative to Marx's theory of increasing class conflict'. Indeed, and in line with the interpretation proposed here, Veblen's theory of evolutionary change differs from Marx's view in at least two respects: (i) conflict concerns workers versus the leisure class (or even technicians and businessmen), not, as in Marx, labour versus capital; (ii) conflict is driven by changes of habits of thought by workers, also involving value judgements on the existing income distribution, without reference to the material (structural) foundation of Marxian class conflict. See also O'Hara (2000) and Forges Davanzati (2006, Ch. 3).

## References

Arrow, K.J. (1975), 'Thorstein Veblen as an economic theorist', *American Economist*, 19 (1), 5–9.

Asso, P. and Fiorito, F.L. (2004), 'Human nature and economic institutions: instinct psychology, behaviorism, and the development of American institutionalism', *Journal of the History of Economic Thought*, 26 (4), 445–77.

Bowles, S. and Park, Y. (2005), 'Emulation, inequality and work hours: was Thorstein Veblen right?', *Economic Journal*, 115 (507), 394–412.

Bush, P.D. (1987), 'The theory of institutional change', *Journal of Economic Issues*, 21 (3), 125–67.

Cordes, C. (2005), 'Veblen's "instinct of workmanship", its cognitive foundations, and some implications for economic theory', *Journal of Economic Issues*, 39 (1), 1–20.

Cutrona, S. (2005), 'Veblen and the firm', in M.E.L. Guidi and D. Parisi (eds), *The Changing Firm: Contributions from the History of Economic Thought* (Milan: Franco Angeli).

Dillard, D. (1987), 'Money as an institution of capitalism', *Journal of Economic Issues*, 21 (4), 1623–47.

Fontana, G. and Realfonzo, R. (2006), 'The theory of the monetary circuit: a view from fringe', *Storia del pensiero economico*, 2, 105–14.

Forges Davanzati, G. (2006), *Ethical Codes and Income Distribution: a Study of John Bates Clark and Thorstein Veblen* (London: Routledge).

Graziani, A. (2003), *The Monetary Theory of Production* (Cambridge: Cambridge University Press).

Hodgson, G. (2004), *The Evolution of Institutional Economics: Agency, Structure and Darwinism in American Institutionalism* (London: Routledge).

Keynes, J.M. (1971 [1930]), *A Treatise on Money: the Applied Theory of Money* (London: Macmillan).

Lawson, C. (2006), 'Ayres, technology and technical objects' (University of Cambridge: mimeo).

Mouhammed, A.H. (1999), 'Veblen and Keynes on the economic theory of the capitalist economy', *Journal of Institutional and Theoretical Economics*, 155 (4), 25–38.

Mouhammed, A.H. (2003), *An Introduction to Thorstein Veblen's Economic Theory* (Ceredigion: The Edwin Mellen Press).

Nayaradou, M. (2005), 'The influence of firm strategy on business cycle in Veblen's economic theory', *Oeconomicus*, 7 (4), 37–56.

O'Hara, P.A. (2000), *Marx, Veblen, and Contemporary Institutional Political Economy: Principles and Unstable Dynamics of Capitalism* (Cheltenham: Edward Elgar).

O'Hara, P.A. (2004), 'Veblen and Sweezy on monopoly capital, crises, conflict and the State', *Journal of Economic Issues*, 38 (4), 969–87.

Parker Foster, G. and Ranson, B. (1987), 'Thorstein Veblen on money and production', *Economics and Societies*, 67 (9), 221–8.

Realfonzo, R. (2006), 'Italian circuitist approach', in P. Arestis and M. Sawyer (eds), *A Handbook of Alternative Monetary Economics* (Cheltenham: Edward Elgar).

Rutherford, M. (1980), 'Veblen on owners, managers, and the control of industry', *History of Political Economy*, 12 (3), 434–40.

Rutherford, M. (1984), 'Thorstein Veblen and the processes of institutional change', *History of Political Economy*, 16 (3), 331–48.

Tilman, R. (2003), *The Legacy of Thorstein Veblen* (Cheltenham: Edward Elgar).

Tsuru, S. (1993), *Istitutional Economics Revisited* (Cambridge: Cambridge University Press).

Van der Steen, M. (1999), *Evolutionary Systems of Innovation: a Veblen-Oriented Study into the Role of the Government Factor* (Assen: Van Gorcum & Co.).

Veblen, T.B. (1899b), 'Mr. Cummings's strictures on "The theory of the leisure class"', *Journal of Political Economy*, 8 (1), 106–17.

Veblen, T.B. (1905), 'Credit and prices', *Journal of Political Economy*, 13 (3), 460–72.

Veblen, T.B. (1906 [1901]), 'Industrial and pecuniary employments', in *The Place of Science in Modern Civilization and Other Essays* (New York: Russell and Russell).

Veblen, T.B. (1908), 'On the nature of capital: investment, intangible assets, and pecuniary magnate', *Quarterly Journal of Economics*, 23 (4), 104–36.
Veblen, T.B. (1919), *The Vested Interests and the State of the Industrial Arts* (New York: Huebsch).
Veblen, T.B. (1920), 'Review of John Maynard Keynes, *The Economic Consequences of the Peace*', *Political Science Quarterly*, 35 (4), 467–72.
Veblen, T.B. (1923), *Absentee Ownerhip and Business Enterprise in Recent Times: the Case of America* (New York: Huebsch).
Veblen, T.B. (1965 [1904]), *The Theory of Business Enterprise* (New York: Kelley).
Veblen, T.B. (1975 [1899a]), *The Theory of the Leisure Class* (New York: Kelley).
Veblen, T.B. (2001 [1921]), *The Engineers and the Price System* (Kitchener: Batoche Books).
Viano, F.L. (2005), 'Cognitive models and enterprise: Veblen revisited', in M.E.L. Guidi and D. Parisi (eds), *The Changing Firm: Contributions from the History of Economic Thought* (Milan: Franco Angeli).
Vianello, M. (1961), *Thorstein Veblen* (Milan: Edizioni Comunità).
Vining, R. (1939), 'Suggestions of Keynes in the writings of Veblen', *Journal of Political Economy*, 47 (5), 692–704.
Wilson, M.C. (2006), 'Budget constraints and business enterprise: a Veblenian analysis', *Journal of Economic Issues*, 40 (4), 1029–44.
Wolozin, H. (2005), 'Thorstein Veblen and human emotions: an unfulfilled prescience', *Journal of Economic Issues*, 39 (3), 727–40.

# 8

# From Wicksell to Keynes? Some Thoughts on the Role of a Central Bank in the Tradition of Monetary Circuit Theory

*Stefano Figuera*

## Introduction

At the time of writing, 70 years after Hicks (1937) began his reinterpretation of Keynes's theory, a new neoclassical synthesis is taking shape. Keynes's theory is still acknowledged as valid on a short-term basis, while in the long run the conclusions of the neoclassical point of view are deemed correct.

A new interpretation of monetary policy and of the role of the central bank becomes relevant in this context, together with an analysis of the nature of money supply differing from that of the original neoclassical synthesis, as we shall consider in the next section. The approach to monetary questions has changed, as confirmed by the growing reference to Wicksell's theory. In the third section of this chapter we focus our attention on this return to Wicksell and on the hypothesis of a policy of the central bank based on interest rates. We will point out some limitations of this new interpretation. This will provide our starting point for a reinterpretation of those profiles of Keynesian monetary analysis that are still relevant at the time of writing: Keynes's contribution on the nature of money and the determination of interest rates forms a significant part of the fourth section. On these grounds, our attention will focus in the fifth section on contributions stemming from the theory of the monetary circuit and the monetary theory of production. Keynes's monetary theory and these 'heterodox' developments will prove useful in defining a role of the central bank alternative to that of the theoretical mainstream.

## The recent evolution of the neoclassical reinterpretation of Keynes's theory

The recent theoretical debate has led to renewed interest in some macroeconomic questions and to a reconsideration of the monetary nature of the capitalist economy.

Discussion on monetary issues appears to bring together scholars and central bankers in their search for an effective means of controlling some macroeconomic magnitudes. Blinder (1997a) emphasizes that central bankers and scholars in monetary economics may help one another. He underlines the fact that a theoretical 'kernel', which registers a general convergence of opinions, may now be identified (see Blinder, 1997b, p. 241). Despite the undeniable limitations of the IS–LM model – Blinder (1997b) states – this model still continues to represent an important starting point for determining effective economic policies.

The recent re-elaborations of the neoclassical theoretical model leading to the development of the new neoclassical synthesis may be considered in this perspective.

### Stability of the system and exogeneity of the money supply in the first neoclassical synthesis

Let us recall some important aspects of the original neoclassical synthesis. This was the reply to the 'Keynesian revolution' of scholars who wanted to restate the validity of the model of general economic equilibrium in an aggregated form.

The neoclassical version of Keynesian economics confirmed the validity of the neoclassical model, acknowledging that Keynes's theory focused on elements capable of altering the normal development of the economic system.

The original formulation of the neoclassical synthesis states two indispensable conditions for a stable equilibrium of full employment: flexibility of prices and wages, and the exogeneity of the money supply (see Modigliani, 1944). In the IS–LM model, considering a decrease in global demand, a movement of the IS curve to the left leads (following a drop in prices) to an increase in real balances and, given the money supply, to a fall in interest rates and a rise in global demand. According to Patinkin (1948), the real balance effect ensures full employment, assuming flexible prices and a constant money supply.

Several post-Keynesian authors criticized this approach to money supply.[1] Nevertheless their critiques do not appear to have shaken the convictions of the authors of the neoclassical school. Only recently have some of them changed their attitudes, mainly considering that it is impossible to conceive of a quantity of money as an exogenous magnitude.

## The New Neoclassical Synthesis and the hypothesis of endogenous money supply

The New Neoclassical Synthesis (NNS), like its predecessor, proposes to combine Keynesian and neoclassical elements. It ascribes to Keynes's analysis the merit of explaining macroeconomic fluctuation by frictions in prices and wages. In the synthesis initiated by Hicks, this explanation of the frictions was not based on solid theory, but the problem now no longer exists (see Goodfriend and King, 1997). The NNS buries its roots deep in the theory of Real Business Cycle and the New Keynesian Economics, whence it has inherited the hypothesis of imperfect competition and sticky prices (see Goodfriend, 2004, p. 31). It defines monetary policy as a suitable instrument to counteract fluctuations in aggregate demand (Goodfriend and King, 1997, p. 255).

The endogenous nature of money supply can be observed in this context. The central bank is given an important role in stabilizing the economy, controlling inflation no longer by limiting money supply but by controlling interest rates and by a passive adjustment of money supply (see Goodhart, 1989, 1994). This affirms the 'Taylor rule' (Taylor, 1993), and represents a fundamental step in that 'consensus model' which has replaced the neoclassical models in guiding decisions of economic policy (see Meyer, 2001; McCallum, 2001).

> This consensus is typically expressed in terms of a simple three-equation dynamic model:
>
> $$Y_t^g = aY_{t-1}^g + bE_t(Y_{t+1}^g) - c[R_t - E_t(p_{t+1})] + x_t \quad (1)$$
>
> $$p_t = d(Y_t^g) + w_1 p_{t-1} + w_2 E_t(p_{t+1}) + z_t, w1 + w2 = 1 \quad (2)$$
>
> $$R_t = r^* + E_t(p_{t+1}) + fY_{t-1}^g + g(p_{t-1} - p^T), \quad (3)$$
>
> where $Y^g$ equals the output gap (the percentage point difference between actual and potential output), $R$ equals nominal interest rate, $r^*$ equals equilibrium real interest rate, $p$ equals inflation, $p^T$ equals inflation target, $x$ and $z$ are stochastic shocks, and all the coefficients are positive. (Meyer, 2001, p. 2)

Equation (1) is a dynamic version of the IS curve, equation (2) is at the basis of an expectations-augmented Phillips curve, while equation

(3) indicates a monetary policy rule (see Taylor, 1993). This is a different way, compared to the traditional neoclassical synthesis, of considering the money market. The LM curve, as Meyer (2001, p. 3) notes, has been replaced by equation (3).[2]

Taylor (1998) argues that his proposed approach to monetary policy does not represent a complete break with the monetarist tradition; the consensus model too must be viewed in a perspective of substantial continuity. The basic neoclassical framework is thereby preserved, although the monetary policy with regard to price level control is different. The role of monetary policy is of small importance, being neutral in the long run with respect to income and employment. Its only task is to favour the short-term stability of income and the long-term stability of prices (see Arestis and Sawyer, 2003, 2004, and Fontana, 2006, 2007).

This new approach is the result of a process whereby part of the theoretical mainstream has 'metabolized' some unavoidable implications of the monetary nature of capitalist economies, accepted by Keynesian monetary analysis or by its immediate successors.

## A Wicksellian foundation for monetary policy?

Recent considerations on monetary policy refer to Wicksell's theory, which contains the foundations of a monetary policy not based on limiting the quantity of money.

Wicksell's monetary theory has recently provided a point of reference for important exponents of the theoretical mainstream, as well as some central bankers.[3]

### Current reinterpretation of *Geldzins und Güterpreise*

Many authors have recently underlined the need to return to the Wicksellian theory. Some decades ago, Patinkin reassessed this theory within the context of the original neoclassical synthesis (see Patinkin, 1952, p. 839).

Patinkin (1965) reconsidered Wicksell's theory in its original neoclassical context, acknowledging his crucial role in progression towards the integration of monetary theory and value theory. Patinkin (1965, pp. 579–80) saw in Wicksell a forerunner of the theory of the real balance effect. He judged the Wicksellian model of pure credit as secondary compared to that of an exogenous money supply, to emphasize the validity of the real balance effect. Friedman (1968) further underlined the contribution of the great Swedish economist. In his view, the identification of a natural rate of interest proved essential to determine the natural rate of unemployment. Subsequently, Leijonhufvud (1981, p. 2) referred to a 'Wicksell connection', indicating in the Wicksellian theory a common denominator of a large group of scholars.

But Wicksell's monetary theory has been given new and significant relevance especially in recent times (see Fontana, 2006, 2007, and Tamborini, 2006).

Woodford's (2003) important contribution reinterprets Wicksell within the context of the NNS, underlining the identification of a theoretical referee (Wicksell), alternative to the previous one, capable of founding a monetary policy not based on the control of the quantity of money. Woodford's (2003) work, significantly entitled *Interest and Prices* (that is, the title of the English edition of Wicksell's *Geldzins und Güterpreise*), justifies the importance attributed to Wicksell's monetary theory in his own analysis.

> Probably the earliest example of a prescription for monetary policy in terms of an interest-rate rule is due to Wicksell (1898, 1907). Although writing at a time when the leading industrial nations remained committed to the gold standard, with even most scholars assuming the necessity of a commodity standard of one sort or another, Wicksell foresaw the possibility of a pure fiat standard and indeed argued that it was essential for the development of 'a rational monetary system'. (Woodford, 2003, p. 37)

This reinterpretation of Wicksell's work is open to debate: some authors share Woodford's view (McCallum, 2005) while there are also more cautious reactions (Laidler, 2004). To those who criticized Woodford (2003) for offering an incomplete representation of Wicksell's theory, the American economist replied that his sole aim was to define new instruments for economic policy based on Wicksell's work (see Woodford, 2006).

Some aspects of Woodford's construction have been considered insufficiently realistic. According to Goodhart (2004), it is impossible to underestimate the hypothesis assumed of complete financial markets and the elimination of the market for intermediaries and commercial banks. Goodhart (2004, p. 200) concludes that 'Wicksell (and Woodford) are splendid; but modern macro badly needs a proper empirical base!'

If Woodford (2003) attributes particular importance to the endogeneity of money supply, this stems from the fact that money supply aims to satisfy the demand for liquid balances of private citizens, not to finance production.

In our view, Goodhart's assessment of Wicksell may be reconsidered if other important profiles of his monetary theory, which modern interpreters have not considered necessary to highlight, also become an object of study.

## An alternative interpretation of Wicksell's monetary theory

Scholars had already observed how Wicksell's theory represented an evolution in the neoclassical vision, the prelude to important developments (see Graziani, 1981; Chiodi, 1983; Berti, 1987; Realfonzo, 1998). Graziani (1981) underlined the innovative nature of Wicksell's analysis, which remained within the neoclassical school of thought while emphasizing the role played by money in capital accumulation and income distribution.

The focus on the emission of money into the economic system (see Berti, 1987, p. 33) is doubtless an important element. While the neoclassical theory studied changes in price levels, given a quantity of money of unexplained origin, Wicksell examined how the emission of this quantity of money occurred. His representation of the working of the economic system in terms of monetary flows is illuminating. Wicksell's considerations show him to have been moving with considerable autonomy of thought compared to the positions of his time (see Chiodi, 1983, p. 80).

In his illustration of the economic system, one innovative element is the introduction of a new protagonist, that is, the banking system, whose decisional autonomy is underlined and whose decisions are fundamental in determining the functioning of the productive process (see Berti, 1987, pp. 21–2).

Wicksell's analysis of a model of pure credit has not received due attention in some modern interpretations. Such a model is not a mere methodological expedient, however brilliant, to get around the limits dictated by the quantity theory, as Ohlin (1936, p. 14) maintains, but an important theoretical step, and evidence of a new interpretation of the monetary mechanisms regulating the capitalist economy (see Chiodi, 1983, p. 63). In this hypothesis, a circumstance not always grasped in all its significance, money supply is not subject to any limitations except those deriving from money demand (see Wicksell, 1898, p. 248; see also Wicksell, 1897, p. 384).

Woodford's (2003) analysis does not underline these aspects: there is no room in it for financing production; the only demand for money comes from families, who desire a liquid reserve. His proposed reconstruction of the capitalist economy is set in a context of general economic equilibrium. His reference model is that bartering economy on which Wicksell (1898, p. 304) expressed reservations.

The innovation in Wicksellian monetary analysis cannot therefore be considered limited to a different explanation of the inflation phenomenon and a double theory of interest rates (see Schumpeter, 1954, p. 1334).

A central point, moreover, consists in recognizing that the monetary nature of a capitalist economy may be a source of disequilibrium, giving rise to income distribution not depending on a marginalistic logic, but conditioned by the different possibilities of the various categories of economic agents to obtain bank credit. If, as Wicksell affirms, this disequilibrium tends to represent the norm, it implies that in a capitalist economy the traditional explanations with regard to price definition and income distribution must be reconsidered (see Chiodi, 1983, p. 55).

Finally, we must not underestimate Wicksell's ideas regarding the relations of strength between groups of agents. The production process appears as the result of decisions of categories of economic agents who are in different conditions with regard to their possibility to influence income distribution (beyond the marginalistic rules); the decisions of firms and banks, Wicksell (1898, pp. 302–3) concludes, effectively determine income distribution.

While these considerations invite us to use caution in our present reading of Wicksell, they confer a greater value of knowledge on the Wicksellian theoretical construction, causing us to reconsider also Goodhart's (2004, p. 200) assessment quoted above.

Wicksell's acknowledgement of the endogenous nature of money supply therefore represents a crucial moment in his considerations and also a starting point for future developments.

An important analytical step, possibly connected to that of Wicksell, was taken by Schumpeter (1912). In his analysis of economic development Schumpeter assumes that money is no longer an intermediary in exchanges but an indispensable means of payment. Schumpeter may be considered even further than Wicksell from neoclassical logic. He refutes the basis of the latter in his analysis of the system outside equilibrium, but also in a situation of equilibrium. Moreover, as the banking system is involved as creator of the liquidity necessary to realize innovation and form profit, the interest rate no longer appears as the price of saving but as a way for banks to appropriate part of the profits as payment for financing production. The hypothesis of an endogenous money supply and the idea that banks are free to fix the interest rate will condition theoretical developments increasingly after Schumpeter.

But it is with Keynes's theory that the endogenous nature of money supply assumes a different qualification, opening the door for a new interpretation of the role of the banking system.

## Keynes's monetary theory today

The need to return to Keynes's theory to understand how the capitalist economy works has frequently been restated (see Pasinetti, 1997, p. 771). Several elements indicate that a reconsideration of Keynes's monetary theory, in its totality, may prove of great interest in defining the role of monetary and financial institutions.

As we know, many studies of Keynes's monetary analysis have focused on the theory of liquidity preference, leading to drastic cuts in the reflections in general and therefore a reductive view of Keynes's contribution. This has made it easier to 'reinstate' the neoclassical synthesis, but an important theoretical profile in Keynes's work has been lost thereby. It may therefore be worth going back to some aspects of Keynes's reflections on money and credit, starting from the contributions of the first decades of the twentieth century, to give a new interpretation to the role of the central bank.

### Keynes's contributions to the debate on the central bank

The switch of central bankers from monetary targeting to inflation targeting in policies aiming to control inflation has further underlined the problem of the independence of the central bank. McCallum (1995, pp. 210–11) has significantly repeated the need to attribute sufficient importance to this question.

A number of post-Keynesian authors have also addressed this question (Bibow, 2002; Sawyer, 2006), underlining how Keynes stresses the necessity for this institution to remain autonomous. Keynes's contribution on this point is of great interest and needs to be re-examined: *Indian Currency and Finance* (Keynes, 1913) and some other works belonging to the first decades of the twentieth century (Keynes, 1928, 1932), all clearly indicate Keynes's serious concern for a central bank free from economic and political influence.

At the start of the First World War Keynes addressed the question of the convertibility of gold, focusing his attention above all on the Bank of England. In those years he showed his interest for the independence of the British central bank, stating how some decisions taken by Lloyd George to solve the liquidity crisis of banks, such as the measures taken in favour of the Accepting Houses (see Keynes, 1914, pp. 611 and 619), had had inflationary consequences.

In 1914 Keynes began to analyse the importance of gold reserves in money emission, anticipating a position he was to assume later in the *Treatise on Money*.[4]

In 1927 Keynes showed real appreciation for the contribution of McKenna, president of the Midland Bank (one of the 'big five'). He attributed to McKenna the merit of having focused attention on some of the basic principles of monetary policy 'of which the truth is as certain as the day, but to which the City is blind as night' (Keynes, 1931, p. 201).

Unfortunately the British banker had shirked 'half the problem', because he had not taken into account the limits imposed on the Bank of England. Keynes (1931, p. 202) asked himself a rhetorical question: 'Is the Bank of England in its newforged golden fetters as free an agent as Mr McKenna's policy requires?' The central bank therefore needed to act in a situation of autonomy, without external influence, in order to enact the necessary interventions in monetary policy. These conclusions will be set out again clearly in a slightly later work (Keynes, 1932). If it is true that for the Bank of England 'its independence and its prestige are assets' (Keynes, 1932, p. 132), it is also true that it must be subject to clear rules in order to avoid incurring various types of risk (see Bibow, 2002, on this point).

From an analysis of these contributions it emerges that Keynes had set in motion a process to free money emission from both material limits (the gold reserves in the safes) and political limits, an essential condition for elaborating a monetary theory of production. But it is above all the considerations devoted to the genesis of money and the nature of interest rates that prove illuminating and useful in determining the role of the central bank.

## The endogeneity of money supply and the determination of interest rates

The analysis of the monetary nature of the capitalist economy was central in Keynes's considerations with reference both to the crisis and to the working of the system beyond the crisis. His *Treatise on Money* (Keynes, 1930) addresses the problem of money emission by banks, and underlines that a bank may create rights to receive money in exchange for values which it recognizes as such. It also points out that a bank may issue money following the creation of a credit towards itself, observing that, although there is no difference between the two operations from the bookkeeping point of view (in both cases the bank issues money entering the transaction in its accounts), the nature of the loans granted differs greatly.

A fundamental passage in Keynes's considerations on money is represented by the debate on the so-called 'finance motive'. In his articles on the finance motive, Keynes distinguishes clearly between financing production and financing investment. He observes that money issued to finance production is a bookkeeping transaction, deriving from a series of accounts (see Keynes, 1937b, p. 219). The theoretical heritage on Keynes's finance motive consists precisely in having restated the central position of money as a means of financing (see Graziani, 1983, 1985). In this perspective, money appears in its essence as credit, that is, a creation of the banking system, indispensable for firms to start production. The quantity of money that is on the market is therefore endogenously determined, and there is no room for intervention by the central bank.

Analogously, the decision on the interest rate by the central bank appears to be an arbitrary intervention. Keynes's theory offers precise indications with regard to the nature of the 'money market' interest rate, that is, the interest charged for financing production. As clearly stated in the *Treatise*, in the pages devoted to the debate among the 'bankers' (who limited the issue of money by commercial banks) and the 'heretical' economists (who recognized the possibility of an unlimited supply of money), Keynes (1930) appears to share with the latter the opinion that, as money is created by the banking system without resorting to a preexistent saving, this interest rate may be fixed by the banking system at a very low level. If the emission of money is a bookkeeping transaction, nothing should be payable to the banks, except the costs of providing this 'service'.

Several considerations must be made, with reference to Keynes's definition of the interest rate on the financial market and what has been viewed as Keynes's 'variation on a theme of Wicksell', to use Leijonhufvud's (1981) definition. Although Leijonhufvud considers Keynes's contribution as a Wicksell connection, it must be underlined that Keynes (1936, p. 242) stated clearly his disagreement with the hypothesis of a natural rate of interest. Although some parts of his *Treatise on Money* indicate his appreciation of Wicksell's theory of definition of prices, his *General Theory* dissents from the concept of the natural interest rate and clarifies his previous position (see Keynes, 1936, pp. 242–3). In this work Keynes (1936) underlines how interest rates on the financial market may be influenced by the behaviour of agents, whose subjective assessments tend to confirm themselves and influence one another. He specifies that it would be preferable to say

> [t]hat the rate of interest is a highly conventional, rather than a highly psychological, phenomenon. For its actual value is largely governed by the prevailing view as to what its value is expected to be. *Any* level of interest which is accepted with sufficient conviction as *likely* to be durable *will* be durable. (Keynes, 1936, p. 203)[5]

Some months later, Keynes (1937a) repeated that his position on interest rates differed from the neoclassical stance. In fact, he specified to Myrdal that his position was different from Wicksell's (see Keynes, 1937c).

The passage towards a Keynesian perspective appears a fundamental theoretical step to determine the rules to be established as the basis of monetary policy. While for Wicksell the manoeuvring of the interest rate, though difficult to realize, is justified by the need to ensure a balance between savings and investments, this is not true for Keynes.

## Post-Keynesian developments in monetary circuit theory and the monetary theory of production

Keynes's monetary theory was taken into consideration again during the second half of the twentieth century, by authors who, refusing the neo-classical paradigm, initiated an approach which may be generally defined as 'heterodox'. Monetary circuit theory, which developed in France in the wake of Schmitt, and the monetary theory of production, which flourished in Italy thanks to Graziani, may be considered within this context. Both are of great interest for explaining monetary mechanisms and defining the role of the central bank. Important implications stem from the idea adopted by these authors, and successively reanalysed and developed, that money supply is endogenous. This theory is different from those of Kaldor and Minsky.

Both these lines of thought join Schumpeter (1954, p. 352) in warning against 'confusing the historic origin of money [...] and its logical nature', and underline that the latter is 'completely independent of the goods nature of money itself'. A central point in Schumpeter's considerations consists in recognizing money as credit money and the endogenous nature of its supply.[6] Credit money is a *condicio sine qua non* of the capitalist economy.

There is a radical contrast between the neoclassical view and these theories. The latter offer an explanation for the working of a capitalist economy, starting from the refutation of methodological individualism and denying the value of the marginal theory of distribution, to define an economic process in which the division of subjects into macro-groups (banks, firms, and wage earners) is fundamental, and in which money plays an essential role in the allocation of resources. The levels of production, employment, and income distribution are the result of decisions taken by banks and firms, which have a greater amount of freedom than wage earners.

## Money emission and the role of the banking system in a monetary economy of production

Since the early 1960s Schmitt (and others – among them Cencini, Gnos, Rossi, Sadigh – who with him form the 'Dijon School' of the monetary circuit) has been considering a number of aspects of monetary theory proposing a return to the Classics (from Smith to Ricardo, and Marx) and a reconsideration of Keynes's monetary theory, different from that of neoclassical authors (see Schmitt, 1960, 1966a, b, 1975).

For the authors of the Dijon School it is important to consider the capitalist economy in its dimension as a monetary economy of production. To this end it is not sufficient to acknowledge the indispensable nature of money; it is necessary to recognize that prices and money, production and exchange are intimately interwoven, constituting a single whole excluding any dichotomy. The circuit appears as the analytical instrument *par excellence*, best suited to explain the dynamics of monetary flows characterizing the capitalist economy.

The common denominator for all the works of the 'circuitists' is the particular attention devoted to the creation of liquidity, essential to start any production. Their view is based on the functional division in three groups of those economic agents that are involved in production: banks, firms, and wage earners. Money is credit money and of an endogenous nature; its amount is determined by banks to permit firms to realize the volume of production established according to effective demand.[7] The subdivision into a banking sector and a business sector is fundamental in this representation (see Graziani, 1984, p. 10).

Those who agree with monetary circuit theory focus their attention on money as a means of payment and purchasing power. The logical succession of steps (opening of the circuit; production; monetary expenditure; closure of the circuit), and the iterative nature of this model are typical of this approach.

The demand for liquid balances with its traditional motivations is considered secondary, or ignored completely. Schmitt, emblematically, proposes a reassessment in particular of the first seven chapters of the *General Theory*. His view of the crisis differs from the traditional Keynesian view: while the cause of crisis for Keynesian economists is failure to close the circuit, for Schmitt (and the Dijon School) the opening of the circuit necessarily presupposes its closure. There is nothing however to guarantee that the level of income at which the monetary circuit opens (established by firms and ratified by banks) corresponds to full employment. Further, with regard to the way out of a critical situation, the endogenous nature of money excludes the intervention of any automatic stabilizing mechanisms (like the so-called Pigou effect) (see Graziani, 1989, p. 22).

The contribution of Graziani and other authors in his wake to the debate on monetary theory may undoubtedly be situated within the context of the 'heterodox' Keynesian approach, uncontaminated by neoclassical reconsiderations. This theory differs from that of the Dijon School, sharing with the latter only the merit of having given life to a reconsideration of the monetary nature of the capitalist economy and a reassessment of Keynes's monetary theory. The Keynesian elaboration of a monetary theory of production is one of the most significant contributions of Graziani, whose work constitutes a reference point for many researchers, not only in Italy.[8]

Keynes's *Monetary Theory of Production*, which he would have liked to publish after his *Treatise on Money*, aimed to be an analysis of a capitalist economy in its monetary dimension. The title was later used for an article in honour of Spiethoff, in which Keynes (1933) underlined the need for a theory to analyse how money enters the economic system, conditioning its decisional processes and becoming 'one of the operative factors in the situation' (Keynes, 1933, p. 408).

Graziani (1994) gave this same title to the work that synthesizes his theoretical analysis of several decades (see Graziani, 1977, 1980, 1983, 1984, 1989). His contribution is of great importance for understanding the monetary nature of a capitalist economy. This has also contributed to render the name 'monetary theory of production' appropriate for this line of thought.[9]

The succession of steps outlined by Graziani regarding the working of the capitalist economy is analogous to that of the monetary circuit model. In the construction of a monetary theory of production the intervention of money – which stems from a triangular transaction whatever the source of money creation (see Graziani, 1994, p. 68) – makes it possible to go beyond the limits of barter and credit economies, guaranteeing the existence of final payments.

While the automatic closure of the monetary circuit characterizes the analyses of many circuitists, the same cannot be said for the monetary theory of production, where money is also a store of value.[10]

Graziani (1994, p. 80) underlined the 'tendency to ignore the problem of financing' of production in the literature. This attitude represents the common denominator and the intrinsic limitation of monetary theories, also of authors outside the neoclassical school. It is necessary to distinguish three forms of financing (see Graziani, 1996a), namely, financing exchange, financing the economy, and financing investment. The financing of exchange is the initial finance which permits the basic exchange of the capitalist system, between firms and wage earners. The willingness of firms to start a production process constitutes a necessary condition but is not alone sufficient for this to take place: the opening of the circuit (and the formation of money income) occurs when banks decide to finance the business projects submitted to them and issue money thereby.

It would be possible to think that in a monetary theory of production a hierarchy exists in which the banking sector prevails over the business sector. If firms plan their production initiatives correctly, and banks operate rationally – assuming the absence of obstacles to the granting of a loan apart from those deriving from a healthy management of credit – there is however no room for 'dissatisfied borrowers' (whose dissatisfaction is justifiable). If the banks were to exercise their power in a restrictive sense, this would constitute an 'irrational' behaviour.

Besides this, the banking system may be called upon to grant a further loan: that of the 'economy'. This enters into play when a part of the income distributed to wage earners is not spent for the purchase of commodities or securities, so that firms cannot recover on the market the entire initial loan, remaining in debt to the banks. Thanks to this further loan, firms may extinguish the debt originally contracted with the banking system: its amount is equal to the difference between the money previously created and that which has been destroyed (see Graziani, 1996b, p. 32).

Finally, a loan exists whose aim is to ensure to firms a quantity of saving equal to their investment, for which the banking system is not indispensable. The equality between investment and savings is ensured without the intervention of banks, which do not finance investment through their intermediation: the balance between savings and investment is established in any case without the intervention of the banking system.[11]

Let us point out that this is not a return to the neoclassical approach, in which savers are the financers and owners of investment goods. The difference is that, in this case, part of the savings financing investment consists of profits obtained by firms.

We may draw interesting results regarding the determination of interest rates from this analysis of the genesis of money. For the monetary theory of production, as for circuit theory, the interest rate on the financial market is not viewed as a price ensuring equality between savings and investment. The task of the financial rate of interest is to determine the division of savings between securities and bank deposits.

On the monetary rate of interest, the influence of both Schumpeter and Keynes is clear. To define it, given the hypothesis of an endogenous money supply, we must consider the subjects that actually finance production in a capitalist economy. The financing of production is effectively granted by wage earners and nothing is owing to the banking sector, except what is necessary to cover the costs of such a service. The interest exacted by banks for financing production, at this point, assumes the status of an arbitrary debit, if fixed with reference to the interest rate determined on the financial market. In reality, it should be paid out to wage earners as a compensation for having permitted production to begin even before receiving a wage in real terms.[12]

**New tasks for the central bank?**

Recently, as often in the past, many banks have had serious organization problems owing to an overcasual management of credit. The considerations already made several years ago by De Cecco (1986, p. 174, our translation) appear still relevant at the time of writing: 'Linking the creation of money to the creation of credit, the banks have found the philosopher's stone. They can expand the credit as they wish and without limits, unless the sovereign and the citizens find the way to "constitutionalize" their power.'

But what are the instruments to 'constitutionalize' these powers? We believe the answer to this question must take into account what has been argued regarding money creation.

As the monetary theory of production and the theory of the monetary circuit suggest, in a context where money is credit money and endogenous, there is no sense in controlling the amount that the banking system must inject into the economy in order to finance production. As the quantity of money necessary is determined endogenously, the control of this amount appears unfounded and difficult to realize. The ratio between production and its value in monetary terms is established at the time of granting the loan needed to remunerate wage earners (Schmitt, 1975, and Graziani, 1983). Subsequent alterations (through subtractions or injections) of the quantity of money injected into the system have an effect on prices, leading to income redistribution.

The central bank can therefore not be free to modify, albeit in light of certain objectives, the amount of money in circulation; its function must be that of a 'controller'. It should not question the amount of money banks, requested by firms, put into the economic system. On the other hand, it must ensure that the rules governing the granting of credit (and therefore the financing of payments) are respected, to prevent both deflationary and inflationary pressures. To avoid an upward trend in prices, for example, the central bank must prevent the banking system from giving rise to 'gratuitous' creations of money, that is, not to finance (or 'monetize') a specific production, or from lending more than it has recorded as its clients' deposits.

This approach to the role of the central bank may appear a return to the hypothesis of free banking. With respect to the recent formulations of the latter theory (proposed by authors from Klein to Hayek and White), this drastic limiting of the intervention of the central bank has a different theoretical point of reference. In the theory of the monetary circuit, as in the monetary theory of production, the ratio between money and production, as it is generated at the moment of starting production, fixes the quantity of money that is to circulate.

Hayek's hypothesis is different: he considers money as a good like all other goods. It is necessary for money to remain neutral without altering the equilibrium of the system, which is essentially that of a barter economy (see Desai, 1982).

While the merit goes to Hayek for underlining the substantial equivalence between the money emission effected by commercial banks and that of the central bank, he has not abandoned the view of the bank as a simple intermediary: the money that a bank may lend is limited to the savings deposited in it. In this view, banks have the acknowledged task of ensuring a balance between savings and investment through the balance between deposits and loans.

Another point to be reconsidered in light of the above discussion refers to the possibility of a central bank controlling interest rates. We have seen the nature of the 'monetary interest rate' paid for the financing of payments.[13] This must therefore be fixed in order to cover the costs of producing the banking service. It is an amount that certainly cannot be established by the central bank or by monetary authorities.[14] If the interest rate fixed for money emission is such as to permit banks to recover more than the costs of the banking service, this result is detrimental to the profit earned by firms. It is clear that the manner of this sharing-out must be considered beyond the field of intervention of the central bank. It would be very strange, in fact, if the latter should attribute to itself the task of deciding how profits should be shared between banks and firms.[15] The monetary interest rate should be fixed on the basis of the costs incurred by banks in financing production.

The central bank, rather, should avoid the consolidation of monopolistic positions on the banking market, since these may lead to additional costs for firms. It should ensure that the credit market is as competitive as possible, so that the monetary interest rate is as low as possible.

## Conclusion

As we noted in this chapter, the problem of the nature of money supply has been raised by supporters of the 'consensus model' in terms of strategy rather than with respect to economic analysis. For these authors, the endogenous or exogenous nature of money supply derives from the choice of the control variable for monetary policy.[16] Assuming that the central bank behaves in a monopolistic manner with regard to the money market, they consider that the short-term interest rate has replaced the quantity of money as the relevant variable in this respect. This implies acknowledging the endogenous nature of money supply, albeit within a context of neoclassical inspiration. This theoretical result, however, has not led to a different interpretation of the role played by the central bank (see King, 2001, p. 120).

Now, the implications stemming from accepting the views of Keynes (and Schumpeter) would be completely different. The action of the central bank must be reconsidered in light of the fact that the quantity of money, as shown by the theory of the monetary circuit and the monetary theory of production, has 'a strictly endogenous nature' (Graziani, 1994, p. 31). The central bank is not free to modify the quantity of money in circulation or the interest rate, in view of attaining pre-established objectives. These limitations must be counterbalanced by the specification and redefinition of the tasks that monetary authorities are expected to fulfil. Some years ago, Fischer (1996, 1997) focused his attention on a double function of the central bank: combating inflation and ensuring financial stability. It is the latter issue that has become urgent at the time of writing.

The increasing fragility and interdependence of national financial systems call for an intervention that must become more careful and far-seeing, in view of which the central bank's role may prove decisive. There is no doubt that in this perspective the functions of supervision of the system of commercial banks and other financial intermediaries must be intensified; moreover, interventions of a preventive nature are indispensable (see Goodhart, 1989).

The term 'Minsky moment' could be used to characterize the 2007 crisis that hit bank loans in the United States. Whalen (2007, p. 14) points out an analogy between this situation and others considered by Minsky in his analysis of financial fragility. It was a 'Minsky-type' intervention of central banks (issuing liquidity in their quality of lenders of last resort) that prevented the situation from deteriorating further. If this can lead us to hope for a flexible monetary policy in such circumstances, it is impossible not to observe that further money emissions by the central bank (as shown by both monetary circuit theory and the monetary theory of production) can only result in costs to be paid by society as a whole.

## Acknowledgements

The author is grateful to Giuseppe Fontana, Guglielmo Forges Davanzati, Marco Passarella, and Sergio Rossi for their comments on a previous version of this chapter. Clearly the author alone is responsible for any errors this chapter contains.

## Notes

1. See notably Minsky (1957), Davidson (1965, 1972), and Kaldor (1970). These 'first-generation' post-Keynesian authors have been followed by others who have recently developed the profile of endogeneity of money supply as an antithesis to the dominant neoclassical vision (see Lavoie, 1992).
2. The LM curve of the first neoclassical synthesis is replaced by a function of MP (monetary policy). The model IS–LM–AS is substituted by the model IS–MP–IA, with the IA (inflation adjustment) schedule parallel to the axis of the ordinates (see Romer, 2000).
3. The position of Weber (2006), president of the Deutsche Bundesbank, is significant in this regard.
4. Keynes (1914, p. 622) had caustic comments for those who considered gold reserves as a sign of respectability of the central bank.
5. On the criteria for determining the interest rate in Keynesian analysis, see Robinson (1951, pp. 102–3). See also Shackle (1961, p. 234).
6. In this chapter we do not enter the debate between the 'horizontalist' approach (whose principal supporters are Moore, Rousseas, and Lavoie) and the 'structuralist' approach (adopted by Arestis, Dow, Howells, Palley, among others) to money supply. Let us note however that Fontana's (2004) contribution is interesting and useful to settle this controversy.

7. In this view, the distinction between endogenous and exogenous money proposed by Desai (1987) appears impossible to share.
8. Figuera (2001) discusses a number of elements for a comparison of Graziani's theory with that of the Dijon School.
9. On this subject matter, Realfonzo (2006) recalls the existence of an 'Italian circuitist approach'.
10. According to this approach (Graziani, 1994, p. 153), there are two possible causes for crisis: failure to open and failure to close the monetary circuit.
11. 'The implicit conclusion [...] is that there is no conceivable case in which banks can act as intermediaries between savers and investors. Banks do control the supply of money but they have no direct control over the supply of saving. The commonplace according to which banks, by selling deposits, would be collecting savings and by granting loans would be financing investment is but a myth' (Graziani, 1996a, p. 151).
12. Marx (1885, p. 225) pointed out how an account, in terms of work, paid by the worker to the capitalist was mistakenly seen as an account in terms of money paid by the capitalist to the worker.
13. 'In the monetary theory of production, the root of the interest lies not in saving or abstinence, but in the fact that, in a monetary economy, access to credit and money is a key factor: the producers of money and credit, that is the banking sector, therefore enjoy a privileged position which permits them to take for themselves a quota of the total product' (Graziani, 1994, pp. 150–1).
14. For Hayek (1976, p. 107), consistently with what he stated on the theme of money emission, the 'disappearance of what is called "interest policy" is wholly desirable'.
15. Forges Davanzati and Realfonzo (Chapter 7, this volume) consider that banks, like the central bank, may in fact carry out redistribution functions.
16. We cannot omit to mention Poole (1970) in this respect. On this point see also Blinder (1997a, p. 7).

## References


Arestis, P. and Sawyer, M. (2003), 'Reinventing fiscal policy', *Journal of Post Keynesian Economics*, 26 (1), 3–25.

Arestis, P. and Sawyer, M. (2004), 'On the effectiveness of monetary policy and of fiscal policy', *Review of Social Economy*, 62 (4), 441–63.

Berti, L. (1987), 'Alle origini della teoria monetaria contemporanea. Il contributo di Gunnar Myrdal', in G. Myrdal (1939), *Monetary Equilibrium* (London: Hodge), translated into Italian as *L'equilibrio monetario* (Rome: Istituto dell'Enciclopedia Italiana).

Bibow, J. (2002), 'Keynes on central banking and the structure of monetary policy', *History of Political Economy*, 34 (4), 749–87.

Blinder, A. (1997a), 'Distinguished lecture on economics in government: what central bankers could learn from academics – and vice versa', *Journal of Economic Perspectives*, 11 (2), 3–19.

Blinder, A. (1997b), 'Is there a core of practical macroeconomics that we should all believe?', *American Economic Review*, 87 (2), 240–3.

Chiodi, G. (1983), *La teoria monetaria di Wicksell* (Rome: La Nuova Italia Scientifica).

Davidson, P. (1965), 'Keynes' finance motive', *Oxford Economic Papers*, 17 (1), 47–65.

Davidson, P. (1972), *Money and the Real World* (London: Macmillan).

De Cecco, M. (1986), 'Innovazione finanziaria e teoria monetaria', *Note Economiche*, 3–4, 167–77.

Desai, M. (1982), 'The task of monetary theory: the Hayek–Sraffa debate in a modern perspective', in *Macroeconomics and Monetary Theory: the Selected Essays of Meghnad Desai* (Aldershot: Edward Elgar), vol. I.

Desai, M. (1987), 'Endogenous and exogenous money', in J. Eatwell, M. Milgate and P. Newman (eds), *The New Palgrave: a Dictionary of Economics* (London: Macmillan), vol. II.

Figuera, S. (2001), *Théorie monétaire dans l'économie capitaliste* (Paris: L'Harmattan).

Fischer, S. (1996), 'Central banking: the challenges ahead – maintaining price stability', *Finance and Development*, 33 (4), 34–7.

Fischer, S. (1997), 'Central banking: the challenges ahead – financial system soundness', *Finance and Development*, 34 (1), 14–16.

Fontana, G. (2004), 'Rethinking endogenous money: a constructive interpretation between horizontalists and structuralists', *Metroeconomica*, 55 (4), 367–85.

Fontana, G. (2006), 'The "new consensus" view of monetary policy: a new Wicksellian connection?', Jerome Levy Economics Institute of Bard College Working Paper no. 476.

Fontana, G. (2007), 'Why money matters: Wicksell, Keynes, and the new consensus view on monetary policy', *Journal of Post Keynesian Economics*, 30 (1), 43–60.

Friedman, M. (1968), 'The role of monetary policy', *American Economic Review*, 58 (1), 1–17.

Goodfriend, M. (2004), 'Monetary policy in the new neoclassical synthesis: a primer', *Federal Reserve Bank of Richmond Economic Quarterly*, 90 (3), 21–45.

Goodfriend, M. and King, R. (1997), 'The new neoclassical synthesis and the role of monetary policy', *National Bureau of Economic Research Macroeconomics Annual*, 12, 231–83.

Goodhart, C.A.E. (1989), 'The conduct of monetary policy', *Economic Journal*, 99 (396), 293–346.

Goodhart, C.A.E. (1994), 'What should central banks do? What should be their macroeconomic objectives and operations?', *Economic Journal*, 104 (435), 1424–36.

Goodhart, C.A.E. (2004), 'Review of Woodford's *Interest and Prices*', *Journal of Economics*, 82 (2), 195–200.

Graziani, A. (1977), 'Recensione a mo' di premessa', in R. Convenevole, *Processo inflazionistico e redistribuzione del reddito* (Turin: Einaudi).

Graziani, A. (1980), 'Malthus e la teoria della domanda effettiva', foreword to L. Costabile, *Malthus* (Turin: Einaudi).

Graziani, A. (1981), *Teoria economica: macroeconomia* (Naples: Edizioni Scientifiche Italiane).

Graziani, A. (1983), 'Aspetti della dottrina monetaria di Keynes', *Piemonte vivo*, special issue, 49–66.

Graziani, A. (1984), 'Moneta senza crisi', *Studi Economici*, 39 (24), 3–37.

Graziani, A. (1985), 'Le débat sur le "motif de financement" de J.M. Keynes', *Économie Appliquée*, 38 (1), 159–75.
Graziani, A. (1989), 'The theory of the monetary circuit', *Thames Papers in Political Economy*, Spring.
Graziani, A. (1994), *La teoria monetaria della produzione* (Arezzo: Banca Popolare dell'Etruria e del Lazio).
Graziani, A. (1996a), 'Money as purchasing power and money as a stock of wealth in Keynesian economic thought', in G. Deleplace and E.J. Nell (eds), *Money in Motion: the Post Keynesian and Circulation Approaches* (London: Macmillan).
Graziani, A. (1996b), *La teoria del circuito monetario* (Milan: Jaca Book).
Hayek, F.A. (1976), *Denationalisation of Money: the Argument Refined* (London: Institute of Economic Affairs).
Hicks, J.R. (1937), 'Mr. Keynes and the "Classics": a suggested interpretation', *Econometrica*, 5 (2), 147–59.
Kaldor, N. (1970), 'The new monetarism', *Lloyds Bank Review*, 97, 1–18.
Keynes, J.M. (1913), *Indian Currency and Finance* (London: Macmillan).
Keynes, J.M. (1914), 'The prospects of money', *Economic Journal*, 24 (96), 610–34.
Keynes, J.M. (1928), 'The amalgamation of the British note issues', *Economic Journal*, 38 (150), 321–8.
Keynes, J.M. (1930), *A Treatise on Money* (London: Macmillan).
Keynes, J.M. (1931), *Essays in Persuasion* (London: Macmillan).
Keynes, J.M. (1932), 'The monetary policy of the Labour Party', *The New Statesman and Nation*, reprinted in *The Collected Writings of John Maynard Keynes* (London: Macmillan, 1982), vol. XXI.
Keynes, J.M. (1933), 'The monetary theory of production', in *The Collected Writings of John Maynard Keynes* (London: Macmillan, 1973), vol. XIII.
Keynes, J.M. (1936), *The General Theory of Employment, Interest and Money* (London: Macmillan).
Keynes, J.M. (1937a), 'Alternative theories of the rate of interest', *Economic Journal*, 47 (186), 241–52. Reprinted in *The Collected Writings of John Maynard Keynes* (vol. XIV *The General Theory and After: Part II, Defence and Development*) (London: Macmillan, 1973).
Keynes, J.M. (1937b), 'The "ex ante" theory of the rate of interest', *Economic Journal*, 47 (188), 663–9. Reprinted in *The Collected Writings of John Maynard Keynes* (vol. XIV *The General Theory and After: Part II, Defence and Development*) (London: Macmillan, 1973).
Keynes, J.M. (1937c), 'To G. Myrdal', reprinted in *The Collected Writings of John Maynard Keynes* (London: Macmillan, 1979), vol. XXIX.
King, M. (2001), 'No money, no inflation: the role of money in the economy', *Économie Internationale*, 88 (4), 111–32.
Laidler, D. (2004), 'Woodford and Wicksell on interest and prices: the place of the pure credit economy in the theory of monetary policy', University of Western Ontario EPRI Working Paper no. 5.
Lavoie, M. (1992), *Foundations of Post-Keynesian Economic Analysis* (Aldershot: Edward Elgar).
Leijonhufvud, A. (1981), 'The Wicksell connection: variations on a theme', in *Information and Coordination: Essays in Macroeconomic Theory* (New York: Oxford University Press).

McCallum, B.T. (1995), 'Two fallacies concerning central bank independence', *American Economic Review*, 85 (2), 207–11.
McCallum, B.T. (2001), 'Monetary policy analysis in models without money', *Federal Reserve Bank of St. Louis Review*, 83 (4), 145–60.
McCallum, B.T. (2005), 'Michael Woodford's *Interest and Prices*: a review article', paper presented at the Monetary Economics Conference, 10–13 March, London, Ontario.
Marx, K. (1885), *Das Kapital: Kritik der politischen Ökonomie* (Hamburg: Verlag von Otto Meissner), vol. II.
Meyer, L.H. (2001), 'Does money matter?', *Federal Reserve Bank of St. Louis Review*, 83 (5), 1–15.
Minsky, H.P. (1957), 'Central banking and money market changes', *Quarterly Journal of Economics*, 71 (2), 171–87.
Modigliani, F. (1944), 'Liquidity preference and the theory of interest and money', *Econometrica*, 12 (1), 45–88.
Ohlin, B. (1936), 'Introduction' to the English translation of Wicksell (1898) *Geldzins und Güterpreise* (Jena: Verlag von Gustav Fischer).
Pasinetti, L.L. (1997), 'Macroeconomia dopo Keynes (e i vincoli dei parametri di Maastricht)', *Rendiconti Classe Scienze Morali dell'Accademia Nazionale dei Lincei*, 9 (8), 763–807.
Patinkin, D. (1948), 'Price flexibility and full employment', *American Economic Review*, 38 (4), 543–64.
Patinkin, D. (1952), 'Wicksell's "cumulative process"', *Economic Journal*, 62 (248), 835–47.
Patinkin, D. (1965), *Money, Interest and Prices*, 2nd edn (New York: Harper).
Poole, W. (1970), 'Optimal choice of monetary policy instruments in a simple stochastic macro model', *Quarterly Journal of Economics*, 84 (2), 197–216.
Realfonzo, R. (1998), *Money and Banking, Theory and Debate (1900–1940)* (Cheltenham: Edward Elgar).
Realfonzo, R. (2006), 'Italian circuitist approach', in P. Arestis and M. Sawyer (eds), *A Handbook of Alternative Monetary Economics* (Cheltenham: Edward Elgar).
Robinson, J. (1951), 'The rate of interest', *Econometrica*, 19 (2), 92–111.
Romer, D. (2000), 'Keynesian macroeconomics without the LM curve', *Journal of Economic Perspectives*, 14 (2), 149–69.
Sawyer, M. (2006), 'Inflation targeting and central bank independence: we are all Keynesians now! or are we?', *Journal of Post Keynesian Economics*, 28 (4), 639–52.
Schmitt, B. (1960), *La formation du pouvoir d'achat* (Paris: Sirey).
Schmitt, B. (1966a), 'La monnaie au centre de la répartition', *Revue d'économie politique*, 76 (1), 92–114.
Schmitt, B. (1966b), *Monnaie, salaires et profits* (Paris: Presses Universitaires de France).
Schmitt, B. (1975), *Théorie unitaire de la monnaie, nationale et internationale* (Albeuve: Castella).
Schumpeter, J.A. (1912), *Theorie der wirtschaftlichen Entwicklung* (Munich and Leipzig: Duncker and Humblot).
Schumpeter, J.A. (1954), *History of Economic Analysis* (New York: Oxford University Press).
Shackle, G.L.S. (1961), 'Recent theories concerning the nature and role of interest', *Economic Journal*, 71 (282), 209–54.

Tamborini, R. (2006), 'Back to Wicksell? In search of the foundations of practical monetary policy', Università degli Studi di Trento, Dipartimento di Economia, Discussion Paper no. 2.

Taylor, J.B. (1993), 'Discretion versus policy rules in practice', *Carnegie–Rochester Conference Series on Public Policy*, 39, 195–214.

Taylor, J.B. (1998), 'An historical analysis of monetary policy rules', National Bureau of Economic Research Working Paper no. 6768.

Weber, A. (2006), 'The role of interest rates in theory and practice: how useful is the concept of the natural real rate of interest for monetary policy?', G.L.S. Shackle Memorial Lecture, Deutsche Bundesbank, Frankfurt am Main, 9 March.

Whalen, C. (2007), 'The U.S. credit crunch of 2007: a Minsky moment', *Jerome Levy Economics Institute of Bard College Public Policy Brief*, no. 92.

Wicksell, K. (1897), 'Der Bankzins als Regulator der Warenpreise', *Jahrbücher für Nationalökonomie und Statistik*, 68, 228–43.

Wicksell, K. (1898), *Geldzins und Güterpreise* (Jena: Verlag von Gustav Fischer).

Wicksell, K. (1907), 'The influence of the rate of interest on prices', *Economic Journal*, 17 (66), 213–20.

Woodford, M. (2003), *Interest and Prices: Foundations of a Theory of Monetary Policy* (Princeton: Princeton University Press).

Woodford, M. (2006), 'Comments on the symposium on interest and prices', *Journal of the History of Economic Thought*, 28 (2), 187–98.

# 9

# The Dynamics of the Monetary Circuit

*Steve Keen*

## Introduction

As is well known, Keynes (1936) asserted that a monetary economy differs fundamentally from a barter economy. However, he provided no a priori foundation for his analysis that clearly ruled out a barter framework, which left the way open for Hicks's Walrasian interpretation of *The General Theory*, and the ultimate decline of Keynesian economics.

It is an undoubted strength of the monetary circuit approach to have improved upon Keynes's analysis in this regard, by giving a definitive basis on which a monetary economy cannot be analysed from a barter perspective. This is that, in a truly monetary economy, a token – and not a commodity – is accepted as the final means of payment. From this it also follows that banks are an essential component of a monetary economy (they cannot be simply subsumed within the firm sector); and that transactions are not bilateral – that is, an exchange of two commodities between two agents at a price that is fundamentally relative – but tripartite, with a buyer A purchasing a commodity from a seller B by directing the bank C to transfer money 'tokens' from the buyer's account to the seller's. This is an exchange of one commodity between two agents, mediated by a third, at a price that is fundamentally monetary. All payments are, in essence, transfers between bank accounts.

Unfortunately, this substantial conceptual advance appeared to lead to an impasse. Attempts by many (though not all) authors to put Graziani's (1989) insights into a mathematical model reached the conclusion that net profit was zero in a monetary production economy.

Rochon's (2005) thoughtful survey of this literature put the dilemma nicely:

> The existence of monetary profits at the macroeconomic (aggregate) level has always been a conundrum for theoreticians of the monetary circuit. [...] Indeed, not only are firms unable to create profits, they also cannot raise sufficient funds to cover the payment of interest. In other words, how can $M$ become $M'$? (Rochon, 2005, p. 125)

This is a paradoxical result, since, as Rochon (2005) makes evident, Marx also looms large in the monetary circuit tradition. In Marx's schema, net profits are positive and represent the surplus from production. How could it be that the attempt to give Marx's analysis an explicitly monetary flavour could end up destroying one of Marx's key insights, that profit emanates from the surplus generated in production?[1]

In this chapter, we show that this paradox is in fact an illusion, which results mainly from the use of inappropriate modelling techniques – and also, we argue, from a misspecification of the nature of debt. With an appropriate dynamic framework, and an appropriate understanding of debt, it is easily shown that positive profits are compatible with the monetary circuit in a pure credit economy – so long as that economy generates a physical surplus in Marx's sense. Many other currently accepted circuitist impressions about the monetary circuit – such as the need for continuous injections of money to sustain constant economic activity, and the destruction of money by the repayment of debt – are also shown to be erroneous. The correction of these errors substantially strengthens monetary circuit analysis, even though it requires the abandonment of several established circuitist conventions.

## The framework

The appropriate modelling framework is deceptively simple, and a natural extension of the insight that, in a monetary economy, payments for goods and services are made via transfers between bank accounts. The monetary circuit can be modelled by considering why the firm sector takes out loans – to finance production in the expectation of making a profit – and then detailing the money flows between bank accounts that loans give rise to, from the point of view of the banking sector, in a double-entry bookkeeping system. Each column in the accounting table records the flows that determine the value of an account at any point in time, and each row represents a particular type of transaction between accounts.

This technique bears a familiar resemblance to the social accounting matrix (SAM) or stock–flow consistent (SFC) approach championed by Godley and Lavoie (2007), in that, as with the SFC approach, the intention is to accurately account for all relations in the system. But there are substantive differences:

1. Time is modelled continuously rather than discretely.
2. The model-system states are bank transaction accounts (with assets and liabilities accounted for separately).
3. Wage, profit, and rentier incomes are not aggregated.
4. The system does not have the restrictions that are applied to the SFC approach, though we apply a principle analogous to the SFC approach, which considers that '[e]ach row and column of the flow matrix sums to zero on the principle that every flow comes from somewhere and goes somewhere' (Godley, 1999, p. 394; see also Godley and Lavoie, 2007, p. 9):
   (a) The columns of the table do not sum to zero, but instead return the equations of the model.
   (b) Entries in the rows of the table do not necessarily sum to zero.
   (c) There is no '*n*th equation rule', as in the SFC framework.

## Continuous time

A continuous time formulation is inherently superior to the discrete time approach commonly used in economics, on at least four grounds:

1. While every individual economic transaction, like every birth, is a discrete event, these transactions – also like births – are dispersed through time. Aggregate economic processes are thus better captured by continuous-time equations – as indeed is population growth in biology, radioactive decay in physics, and so on.
2. Time dependencies in discrete-time models often force unrealistic compromises on the modeller – as Godley (1999, p. 409) noted when he pointed out that '[he has] introduced lags [...] whenever simultaneous interdependence threatened to generate meaningless oscillations'. No such problem exists in a continuous-time model – in part because of the third, and major, advantage of this approach over discrete-time modelling.
3. In a continuous-time model, all entries in the equations are flows. In a discrete-time formulation, while most entries are flows, some

are stocks (for example, Table 1 in Godley (1999) lists 11 flow variables and 6 stocks), and stocks have to be explicitly linked with flows via equations of the form: $Stock_{t+1} = Stock_t + Flow_t$. Stocks in a continuous-time model are the value of its system states, which are given by the integral of the flows, and the basic equation is $d/dt\ Stock = \Sigma Flows$. There is thus no danger of misspecifying a stock as a flow – a perennial problem in economic modelling.[2] Nor is there a danger of not properly linking a flow to a stock variable: once a flow is introduced into the model, it is automatically linked to the appropriate stock via its differential equation.

4. Finally, time dependencies are much more easily handled in continuous-time form. For example, consumption is subject to a much shorter time delay than investment. However, accounting for this in a discrete-time framework means having difference equations of the form $C_{t+1} = F(Y_t)$ for consumption and $I_{t+52} = F(\Pi_t)$ for investment (indicating a week's lag for consumption and a year's lag for investment). In practice, to make their models tractable, researchers frequently use the same time delays (typically a year) for variables that beat to a very different drum, leading to serious distortions of the underlying dynamics. No such problem exists with continuous-time modelling, where very different time lags can easily be mixed – and they can even be variable, as shown below.

### Transaction accounts rather than economic entities

The transactions approach is a natural expression of the monetary circuit view. A crucial advantage of having bank accounts as the fundamental system states – rather than aggregate economic agents like 'households' – is that the actual financial transactions of the system are explicitly shown, and separated from physical transfers. This includes the endogenous creation of money: in a credit-money system, money is created in bank accounts, and the transactions paradigm allows this to be modelled directly. In contrast, even in Godley's sophisticated SFC framework, the modelling of endogenous money creation is implicit rather than explicit.

The transactions paradigm is also the basis of the next three points of difference between our work and Godley's.

### No household sector

In most SAM-based work, profits from firms, net interest income from financial transactions, and wages are aggregated into the income of a household sector (see again Table 1 in Godley, 1999). We accept Graziani's (1989) stricture that the behaviour of different entities and social classes is different, and this is lost by aggregating all classes into the amorphous unit 'households'. The transactions-accounts basis of the model facilitates this disaggregated approach.

### Absence of column–row restrictions

Since the columns sum the flows into and out of any given transaction account (and the dynamics of the record of debt), the model's differential equations are derived simply by adding up the columns: the columns therefore do not sum to zero. The major departure from the SFC approach, however, is that while rows normally do sum to zero, this is no longer compulsory. Though transactions between deposit accounts necessarily sum to zero, not all entries in bank accounts are in fact transactions (while others affect transfers between bank assets and bank liabilities, which must be separated for analytic reasons). In particular, when Moore's (1988) 'line of credit' concept of endogenous money growth is introduced, an entry occurs in the credit account of firms for which there is a matching entry in firms' record of debt, but no matching transaction transfer from any other account. This is the source of endogenous money growth, which is explicitly modelled in this framework.

### No *n*th equation rule

As Godley and Lavoie (2007) remark, the fact that the *n*th equation is determined by the other $n-1$ equations in their models is related to the same rule that applies in Walrasian economics, where the *n*th market's equilibrium is automatic if the other $n-1$ markets are in equilibrium. This feature arises from the mixed stock–flow nature of the SAM framework. No such closure rule is required in differential-equation models, where the model is fully specified by its flows and a set of initial conditions – of which there is one per system state (or stock).

### Debt as a data record versus 'negative money'

One crucial way in which our analysis differs from the norm for researchers in the endogenous-money tradition is that we treat debt, not as a bank account as such, nor as 'negative money', but as a data record of the legal obligations of a borrower to a bank. The argument that repaying debt destroys money – and therefore that debt is, in effect, 'negative money' – is commonplace in the endogenous-money literature, with writers routinely surmising that money is destroyed when debt is repaid:

> As soon as firms repay their debt to the banks, the money initially created is destroyed. (Graziani, 1989, p. 5)

> If debts are to banks, then the payments which fulfill commitments on debts destroy 'money'. In a normally functioning capitalist economy, in which money is mainly debts to banks, money is constantly being created and destroyed. (Minsky, 1980, p. 506)

This implies that money used to repay a debt goes into a debt account, and negates the equivalent sum of debt. While this is intuitively appealing, we believe that it is a fundamental misspecification of the nature of debt.

First, one of the essential differences between commodities and money is that the former are destroyed – or at least depreciated – in use, whereas money does not depreciate by use. To treat money as effectively indestructible when used in transactions, and yet destroyed when used to repay debt, is incongruous.

Secondly, though the apt framework for considering the models below is a purely electronic payments system, consider, as a thought experiment, a pure credit banking system using an entirely paper money, and issuing its own notes as money.[3] If a debt to a bank were repaid, would it make sense for the bank to duly destroy the returned notes? Of course not: the bank would instead record that the outstanding debt has been reduced, and store the returned notes in its vault, ready for relending. The one stricture, to avoid the problem of seigniorage identified by Graziani (1989), is that the notes that repay debt must be treated differently from those that represent the bank's income from the spread between its loan and deposit rates of interest. The latter can be used by the bank to finance the purchase of goods (whether as intermediate inputs or consumption expenditure by bankers); the former cannot.

This same stricture applies to electronically generated and stored money today. Repayments must be treated differently from interest payments: the latter can be used to finance bank expenditure, the former cannot.

Finally, if debt were truly an account holding 'negative money', then the only way it could be reduced would be by paying 'positive money' into it – in other words, by repaying the debt. Debt, however, can also be reduced by bankruptcy, when a lender is forced to write off a debt that the borrower is unable to repay. Equally, as illustrated later in this chapter, debt can grow via compound interest if the borrower (or, more correctly, the borrowing sector) does not meet all of its debt-servicing obligations – and this growth of debt is not matched by any corresponding growth in money. These manifest realities of debt emphasize that the debt account is not a repository for money – negative or otherwise – as are other accounts in the system, but a data record of the amount owed.

## The model

In all the models presented in this chapter, we consider the Wicksellian ideal of a pure credit economy, with no government sector – and therefore no fiat money and no money multiplier. There are three classes of agents, namely, capitalists (that is, the firm sector), bankers (that is, the banking sector), and workers. In the initial models, production is not explicitly modelled (a simple labour-only production model is introduced later), but is assumed to take place in the background to the financial flows.

At its very simplest, a loan necessitates the paying of interest on outstanding debt and deposit balances, enables the firm to hire workers to produce commodities for sale, gives the workers wages with which to purchase commodities, and gives the bank income for the purchase of intermediate goods and consumption expenditure (from the spread between loan and deposit interest charges on outstanding balances). Three deposit accounts are needed – one for each of the three classes of capitalists, workers, and bankers – while one record of debt is also required, to record lending from bankers to capitalists.

The balanced flows that are needed to capture this financial activity are proportional to the outstanding balances in the accounts at any given time. Using $F_L$, $F_D$, $B_D$, and $W_D$ as symbols for the firm loan, firm deposit, bank deposit, and worker deposit accounts respectively, $r_L$ for the rate of interest on loans, and $r_D$ for the rate of interest on deposits, $w$ as the parameter for the flow of wages payments from firms to workers, $\beta$ as the parameter for banks' purchases from firms, and $\omega$ as the parameter for workers' purchases, we derive Table 9.1 (we assume that the interest

*Table 9.1* Basic model without money growth

| | *Assets* | | *Liabilities* | | | |
|---|---|---|---|---|---|---|
| | *Loans* ($F_L$) | *Sum* ($\Sigma$) | *Deposits* ($F_D$) | ($B_D$) | ($W_D$) | *Sum* ($\Sigma$) |
| Interest | $r_L \cdot F_L - r_L \cdot F_L$ | 0 | $r_D \cdot F_D - r_L \cdot F_L$ | $r_L \cdot F_L - r_D \cdot F_D - r_D \cdot W_D$ | $r_D \cdot W_D$ | 0 |
| Wages | | | $-w \cdot F_D$ | | $w \cdot F_D$ | 0 |
| Consumption | | | $\beta \cdot B_D + \omega \cdot W_D$ | $-\beta \cdot B_D$ | $-\omega \cdot W_D$ | 0 |

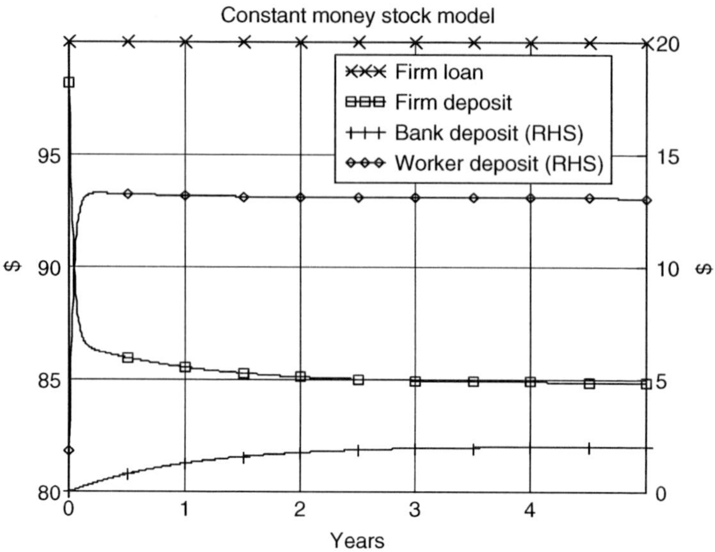


*Figure 9.1* Account dynamics with no debt repayment

the firm sector pays on its debt to the bank is such that the level of debt does not change).

This model is constructed by adding up the entries in each column and expressing them as the differential equation of each account:

$$\frac{d}{dt}F_L = 0$$

$$\frac{d}{dt}F_D = r_D \cdot F_D - r_L \cdot F_L - w \cdot F_D + \beta \cdot B_D + \omega \cdot W_D$$

$$\frac{d}{dt}B_D = r_L \cdot F_L - r_D \cdot F_D - r_D \cdot W_D - \beta \cdot B_D$$

$$\frac{d}{dt}W_D = r_D \cdot W_D + w \cdot F_D - \omega \cdot W_D$$

Given the initial condition of an initial loan of $L$ dollars, and values for the parameters, this model can be simulated as shown in Figure 9.1.[4]

A symbolic solution can also be found for account balances, and two of the three income flows in the model: wages, which equal $w \cdot F_D$, and gross interest payments of $r_L \cdot F_L$. However, to solve for the third income class – firms' profits – we need to unpack what the symbol $w$ stands for in the model considered.

Here we construct an explicit link between Graziani, Marx, and Sraffa – and an implicit link with production – by recognizing that the wage represents the workers' share in the surplus generated in production (in Sraffa's sense that wages and profits are shares in the surplus of output over inputs in a productive economy). This surplus is the product of two factors: (i) the relative shares of workers and capitalists in the surplus, and (ii) the turnover period between the financing of production and the sale of output. Using $s$ (where $0 < s < 1$) to represent the capitalists' share of the net surplus, and $S$ to represent how often production turns over in a year, we can note that $w = (1 - s) \cdot S$, and derive a symbolic solution for the equilibrium level of each account. Using an example value of $s = 1/3$, so that $S = 6$,[5] we get

$$\begin{bmatrix} F_{L_{Eq}} \\ F_{D_{Eq}} \\ B_{D_{Eq}} \\ W_{D_{Eq}} \end{bmatrix} = L \cdot \begin{bmatrix} 1 \\ \dfrac{(\beta - r_L) \cdot (\omega - r_D)}{(\beta - r_D) \cdot ((1-s) \cdot S + \omega - r_D)} \\ \dfrac{(r_L - r_D)}{(\beta - r_D)} \\ \dfrac{(\beta - r_L) \cdot (1-s) \cdot S}{(\beta - r_D) \cdot ((1-s) \cdot S + \omega - r_D)} \end{bmatrix} = \begin{bmatrix} 100 \\ 84.867 \\ 2.062 \\ 13.071 \end{bmatrix}$$

All classes of economic agents earn positive incomes, both from class incomes, and in terms of total income receipts including earnings from interest. The equilibrium yearly class earnings are

$$\begin{bmatrix} Wage_{Eq} \\ Profit_{Eq} \\ Interest_{Eq} \end{bmatrix} = \begin{bmatrix} (1-s) \cdot S \cdot F_{D_{Eq}} \\ s \cdot S \cdot F_{D_{Eq}} \\ r_L \cdot F_{L_{Ee}} \end{bmatrix} = \begin{bmatrix} 339.467 \\ 169.733 \\ 5 \end{bmatrix}$$

while the equilibrium yearly incomes are

$$\begin{bmatrix} Workers_{Eq} \\ Capitalists_{Eq} \\ Bankers_{Eq} \end{bmatrix} = \begin{bmatrix} (1-s) \cdot S \cdot F_{D_E} + r_D \cdot W_{DE} \\ s \cdot S \cdot F_{D_E} + r_D \cdot F_{DE} - r_L \cdot F_{LE} \\ r_L \cdot F_{LE} - r_D \cdot (W_{DE} + F_{DE}) \end{bmatrix} = \begin{bmatrix} 339.859 \\ 167.279 \\ 2.602 \end{bmatrix}$$

The results of this model contradict many circuitist papers on a range of issues. As can be seen from the matrix above, all classes of economic agents earn positive incomes, and these incomes substantially exceed the initial size of the loan. A constant level of economic activity is sustained with a constant level of money – there is no need for continuing injections of money to sustain economic activity. And clearly, firms' profits substantially exceed the interest bill on the outstanding debt: it is quite possible for firms to borrow money and make profits in the aggregate.

Our contrary results indicate the validity of Kalecki's wry engineer-based observation on economics when he first became acquainted with it, as recounted by Godley and Lavoie (2007, p. 1), that economics 'is the science of confusing stocks with flows'. The stock of debt at any point in time generates a stock of active money deposits that enables a flow of incomes. The sum of these flows over a year can easily exceed the outstanding stock of money at any point in time – and the ratio between the sum of income flows over a year and the money stock tells us the velocity of circulation of money.[6] The previous circuitist conclusions all arose from either mistaking a stock for a flow, or from the erroneous belief that the maximum value of a flow over time (income) was set by the size of the initial stock (money).

This is, however, prior to considering the repayment of debt. Here the flow table format makes it easy to consider the issue of how debt should be treated: as 'negative money' – the standard circuitist perspective (and indeed that of Minsky) – or as a data record, with the repaid money necessarily residing in another asset account.

## Repayment of debt: 'negative money' or a bank asset?

Table 9.2 models the conventional treatment of debt as 'negative money', and of the repayment of debt as necessarily destroying money. A flow of $l_R \cdot F_L$ is repaid,[7] which results in a deduction from the firms' deposit account and an identical deduction from the firms' loan account. Both bank liabilities (the sum of deposit accounts, including the bank's own deposits) and bank assets fall.

As Figure 9.2 shows, all accounts gradually taper to zero over time, and hence economic activity ceases – whereas if firms do not repay their debt, economic activity can continue indefinitely. This makes the repayment of debt rather foolish from everyone's point of view: if debt really is negative money, then it is in everyone's interest (bankers, capitalists, and workers alike) that it never be repaid.

However, if debt is in fact a record of a legal obligation, and money is not destroyed when debt is repaid, but instead stored as an asset of the bank – in the bank vault ($B_V$), so to speak – then a very different picture emerges. The repayment of debt keeps bank assets constant, but alters their form from active loans to passive reserves. Once the bank has reserves, they can be relent at the rate $m_R \cdot B_V$, enabling a constant level of economic activity to be maintained, as in the original model

*Table 9.2* Model with debt as negative money

| | *Assets* | | *Liabilities* | | | |
|---|---|---|---|---|---|---|
| | *Loans* $(F_L)$ | *Sum* $(\Sigma)$ | *Deposits* $(F_D)$ | $(B_D)$ | $(W_D)$ | *Sum* $(\Sigma)$ |
| Interest | $r_L \cdot F_L - r_L \cdot F_L$ | 0 | $r_D \cdot F_D - r_L \cdot F_L$ | $r_L \cdot F_L - r_D \cdot F_D - r_D \cdot W_D$ | $r_D \cdot W_D$ | 0 |
| Wages | | | $-(1-s) \cdot S \cdot F_D$ | | $(1-s) \cdot S \cdot F_D$ | 0 |
| Consumption | | | $\beta \cdot B_D + \omega \cdot W_D$ | $-\beta \cdot B_D$ | $-\omega \cdot W_D$ | 0 |
| Repayment | $-l_R \cdot F_L$ | $-l_R \cdot F_L$ | $-l_R \cdot F_L$ | | | $-l_R \cdot F_L$ |

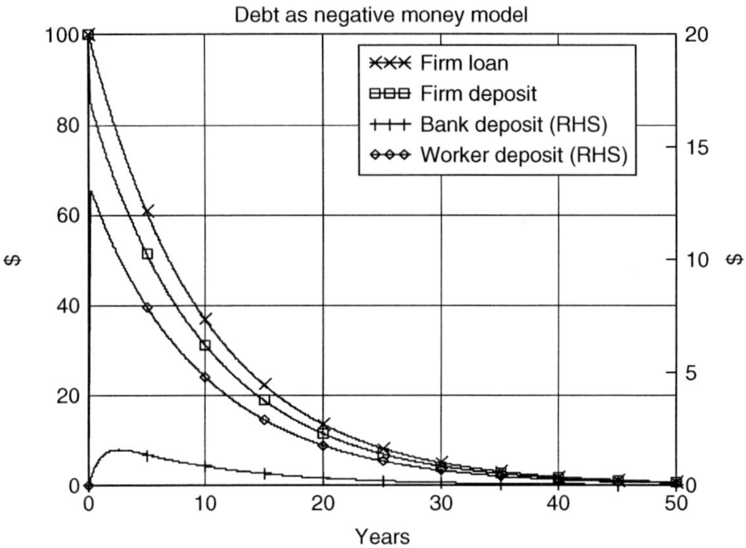


*Figure 9.2* Debt as negative money

without debt repayment (though at a lower level of activity, since the level of active deposits falls).[8] This preferred perspective is shown in Table 9.3.

In contrast to the 'debt as negative money' model, the model shown in Table 9.3 behaves similarly to the previous model without debt repayment, in that a constant level of economic activity is sustained

*Table 9.3* Model with debt as ledger entry

| | *Assets* | | | *Liabilities* | | | |
|---|---|---|---|---|---|---|---|
| | *Loans* $(F_L)$ | *Vault* $(B_V)$ | *Sum* $(\Sigma)$ | *Deposits* $(F_D)$ | $(B_D)$ | $(W_D)$ | *Sum* $(\Sigma)$ |
| Interest | $r_L \cdot F_L - r_L \cdot F_L$ | | 0 | $r_D \cdot F_D - r_L \cdot F_L$ | $r_L \cdot F_L - r_D \cdot F_D - r_D \cdot W_D$ | $r_D \cdot W_D$ | 0 |
| Wages | | | | $-(1-s) \cdot S \cdot F_D$ | | $(1-s) \cdot S \cdot F_D$ | 0 |
| Consumption | | | | $\beta \cdot B_D + \omega \cdot W_D$ | $-\beta \cdot B_D$ | $-\omega \cdot W_D$ | 0 |
| Repayment | $-l_R \cdot F_L$ | $l_R \cdot F_L$ | 0 | $-l_R \cdot F_L$ | | | $-l_R \cdot F_L$ |
| Relending | $m_R \cdot B_V$ | $-m_R \cdot B_V$ | 0 | $m_R \cdot B_V$ | | | $m_R \cdot B_V$ |

from a single injection of money. The new account equilibria are as follows:

$$\begin{bmatrix} F_{L_{Eq}} \\ B_{V_{Eq}} \\ F_{D_{Eq}} \\ B_{D_{Eq}} \\ W_{D_{Eq}} \end{bmatrix} = \frac{L \cdot m_R}{l_R + m_R} \cdot \begin{bmatrix} 1 \\ l_R/m_R \\ \dfrac{(\beta - r_L) \cdot (\omega - r_D)}{(\beta - r_D) \cdot ((1-s) \cdot S + \omega - r_D)} \\ \dfrac{(r_L - r_D)}{(\beta - r_D)} \\ \dfrac{(\beta - r_L) \cdot (1-s) \cdot S}{(\beta - r_D) \cdot ((1-s) \cdot S + \omega - r_D)} \end{bmatrix} = \begin{bmatrix} 97.561 \\ 2.439 \\ 82.797 \\ 2.012 \\ 12.753 \end{bmatrix}$$

As before, these equilibria are consistent with positive (if lower) incomes for all classes of economic agents:

$$\begin{bmatrix} Wage_{Eq} \\ Profit_{Eq} \\ Interest_{Eq} \end{bmatrix} = \begin{bmatrix} (1-s) \cdot S \cdot F_{D_{Eq}} \\ s \cdot S \cdot F_{D_{Eq}} \\ r_L \cdot F_{L_{Ee}} \end{bmatrix} = \begin{bmatrix} 331.187 \\ 165.593 \\ 4.878 \end{bmatrix}$$

Let us now expand the model by relaxing one assumption above – that all debt-servicing commitments are met – and by modelling the creation of money. For the sake of clarity, let us also treat each stage in the money-circulation process separately, introduce a graphical formalism for representing the monetary circuit,[9] and – as a prelude to modelling a credit crunch – use time lags in place of the parameters $\beta$, $\omega$, $l_R$, and $m_R$.[10]

## The creation of money

The key step in the creation of money is deceptively simple: credit money is created when the banking sector grants the firm sector new purchasing power, in return for the firm sector accepting that its indebtedness to the banking sector has increased by the same amount. This is introduced by adding to the model a new parameter, $n_M$,[11] to represent the annual rate of creation of money. As before, the system is developed in a double-entry bookkeeping table, but this time each row represents a distinct stage in the monetary-circulation process. We also carefully note the nature of each stage, which enables four distinct types of monetary transactions to be identified:

1. Interest on the firm sector's outstanding debt $F_L$ accrues at the rate $r_L$. This is not a flow, but a ledger entry of compound interest: the right to add to the debt that is granted by the debt contract.
2. Interest is paid by the banking sector at the rate $r_D$ on the firm sector's outstanding deposit account balance $F_D$. This is a contractual flow: no purchase or goods exchange is affected by it, but it is necessitated by the banking sector's obligations to its depositors.
3. The firm sector's payments of interest at the rate of $r_L$ on its outstanding debt $F_L$ is another contractual flow. The term $(1 - \delta_d)$ allows for the possibility that the firm sector's payments are insufficient to pay the full interest due (which reflects the failure of some firms to repay their debts, and can be a precursor to bankruptcy), and therefore the remainder of the debt-servicing obligation that is not met $(\delta_d \cdot r_L \cdot F_L)$ is capitalized in a ledger entry, and added to the outstanding debt.
4. The firm uses a proportion of its account balance $F_D$ to hire workers, this proportion reflecting (i) the workers' share of the net surplus in production $(1 - s)$ (where $0 < s < 1$), and (ii) the time lag between laying out the money to finance production and receiving payment for commodities sold (shown here as $\tau_S$, where this represents the fraction of a year the process takes). This is a commodity/service purchase flow: money flows one way (firm to worker) in return for labour flowing the other way in the factory sector, to produce commodities for sale by the firm sector.
5. Once workers have positive bank balances $W_D$, the bank sector is obligated to pay interest to them at the rate $r_D$.
6. Bankers and workers then spend a proportion of their bank balances buying commodities from the firm sector at the rates $\tau_B$ and $\tau_W$ respectively; these, like (4), are commodity/service purchase flows,

*Table 9.4* Full model with money creation

| | *Assets* | | | *Liabilities* | | | |
|---|---|---|---|---|---|---|---|
| | *Loans* ($F_L$) | *Vault* ($B_V$) | *Sum* ($\Sigma$) | *Deposits* ($F_D$) | ($B_D$) | ($W_D$) | *Sum* ($\Sigma$) |
| Accumulation | $r_L \cdot F_L$ | | $r_L \cdot F_L$ | | | | |
| Interest $F_D$ | | | | $r_D \cdot F_D$ | $-r_D \cdot F_D$ | | 0 |
| Interest payment | $-(1-\delta_d)\cdot r_L \cdot F_L$ | | $-(1-\delta_d)\cdot r_L \cdot F_L$ | $-(1-\delta_d)\cdot r_L \cdot F_L$ | $(1-\delta_d)\cdot r_L \cdot F_L$ | | 0 |
| Wages | | | | $-(1-s)\cdot F_D/\tau_S$ | | $(1-s)\cdot F_D/\tau_S$ | 0 |
| Interest $W_D$ | | | | | $-r_D \cdot W_D$ | $r_D \cdot W_D$ | 0 |
| Consumption | | | | $B_D/\tau_\beta + W_D/\tau_\omega$ | $-B_D/\tau_\beta$ | $-W_D/\tau_\omega$ | 0 |
| Loan repayment | $-F_L/\tau_L$ | $F_L/\tau_L$ | 0 | $-F_L/\tau_L$ | | | $-F_L/\tau_L$ |
| Money relending | $B_V/\tau_M$ | $-B_V/\tau_M$ | 0 | $B_V/\tau_M$ | | | $B_V/\tau_M$ |
| Money | $n_M \cdot F_D$ | | $n_M \cdot F_D$ | $n_M \cdot F_D$ | | | $n_M \cdot F_D$ |

with money flowing from workers and bankers to firms in return for commodities flowing in the other direction.

7. The firm sector can repay a proportion of its debt $F_L$ at the rate $\tau_L$.
8. The bank sector relends at the rate $\tau_M$ from its vault; this loan is a transfer of money from $B_V$ to $F_D$, which the bank then records on its debt ledger $F_L$ as a corresponding increase in the firm sector's indebtedness.
9. Lastly, the bank sector can grant new credit to the firm sector at the rate $n_M \cdot F_D$.[12] The additional debt is shown by an equivalent entry in the debt ledger, so that both bank assets and bank liabilities grow by the same amount.

The relevant book entries are shown in Table 9.4.

These nine stages can be represented by four distinct types of transfers:

1. Ledger entries, which are not actual flows of money but are obligated by the contractual relations in the monetary system. Thus compound interest on a loan is not a flow, but a legally enforced right that the loan contract gives to the bank to compound the level of debt at the agreed rate of interest. For this class of relationship we use the symbol - - -▸.
2. Flows of money that are driven, not by the amount of money in either the source or recipient account, but by the amount outstanding on the debt ledger. Here we use the symbol ■—▹.

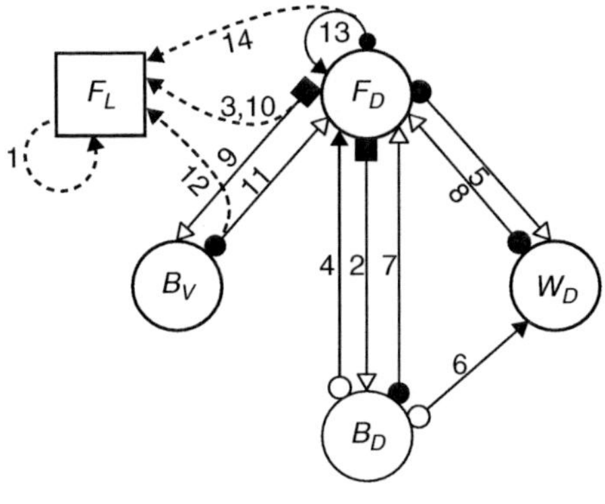


*Figure 9.3* The four types of flow dynamics: - - -▸: ledger entry induced by source variable; ■—▹: cash flow induced by destination variable; ○—▸: cash flow induced by source variable; ●—▹: cash flow induced by ledger entry

3. Flows where the rate of flow is a function of the amount of money in the recipient account, indicated by ○—▸ in Figure 9.3. These again are not flows as economists have conventionally thought about them – that is, as money flowing in one direction in return for goods flowing in the other direction – but instead are a function of the legal relationships in finance, where in return for depositing funds at a bank, the bank is obliged to pay interest on the amount of the deposit.
4. Flows where the rate of flow is a function of the amount of money in the source account are indicated by ●—▹. These alone are flows as economists conventionally think of them: money flows from one account to another in return for work (payment of wages), goods (consumption by workers and bankers), or in return for accepting the legal responsibility of new debt.

Table 9.5 shows the 14 relationships in the monetary circuit using this graphical system. These 14 related flows are represented graphically in Figure 9.3.

As before, the equations of motion of this system can be constructed by simply adding up the columns of Table 9.4:

$$\frac{d}{dt}F_L = r_L \cdot F_L - (1-\delta_d) \cdot r_L \cdot F_L - \frac{F_L}{\tau_L} + \frac{B_V}{\tau_M} + n_M \cdot F_D$$

$$\frac{d}{dt}B_V = \frac{F_L}{\tau_L} - \frac{B_V}{\tau_M}$$

*Table 9.5* Links and types of links in full model

| *Number* | *Source* | *Link* | *Type* | *Destination* | *Formula* | *Description* |
|---|---|---|---|---|---|---|
| 1 | $F_L$ | - - -▸ | 1 | $F_L$ | $r_L \cdot F_L$ | Ledger recording of compound interest |
| 2 | $F_D$ | ■—▷ | 2 | $B_D$ | $(1-\delta_d) \cdot r_L \cdot F_L$ | Payment of interest on outstanding debt |
| 3 | $F_D$ | - - -▸ | 1 | $F_L$ | $(1-\delta_d) \cdot r_L \cdot F_L$ | Ledger recording of interest payment |
| 4 | $B_D$ | ○—▸ | 3 | $F_D$ | $r_D \cdot F_D$ | Interest on firm sector's deposit account |
| 5 | $F_D$ | ●—▷ | 4 | $W_D$ | $\frac{1-s}{\tau_S} \cdot F_D$ | Wages paid to workers |
| 6 | $B_D$ | ○—▸ | 3 | $W_D$ | $r_D \cdot W_D$ | Interest on workers' deposit accounts |
| 7 | $B_D$ | ●—▷ | 4 | $F_D$ | $\frac{B_D}{\tau_\beta}$ | Consumption by bankers |
| 8 | $W_D$ | ●—▷ | 4 | $F_D$ | $\frac{W_D}{\tau_\omega}$ | Consumption by workers |
| 9 | $F_D$ | ■—▷ | 2 | $B_V$ | $\frac{F_L}{\tau_L}$ | Repayment of debt |
| 10 | $F_D$ | - - -▸ | 1 | $F_L$ | $-\frac{F_L}{\tau_L}$ | Ledger recording of repayment of debt |
| 11 | $B_V$ | ●—▷ | 4 | $F_D$ | $\frac{B_V}{\tau_M}$ | Relending from bank vault |
| 12 | $B_V$ | - - -▸ | 1 | $F_L$ | $\frac{B_V}{\tau_M}$ | Ledger recording of bank relending |
| 13 | $F_D$ | ●—▷ | 4 | $F_D$ | $n_M \cdot F_D$ | Creation of money |
| 14 | $F_L$ | - - -▸ | 1 | $F_L$ | $n_M \cdot F_D$ | Creation of new debt |

$$\frac{d}{dt}F_D = r_D \cdot F_D - (1-\delta_d) \cdot r_L \cdot F_L - \frac{1-s}{\tau_S} \cdot F_D + \frac{B_D}{\tau_\beta} + \frac{W_D}{\tau_\omega} - \frac{F_L}{\tau_L} + \frac{B_V}{\tau_M} + n_M \cdot F_D$$

$$\frac{d}{dt}B_D = -r_D \cdot F_D + (1-\delta_d) \cdot r_L \cdot F_L - r_D \cdot W_D - \frac{B_D}{\tau_\beta}$$

$$\frac{d}{dt}W_D = \frac{1-s}{\tau_S} \cdot F_D + r_D \cdot W_D - \frac{W_D}{\tau_\omega}$$

The transaction-account dynamics of this model are shown in Figure 9.4, and the income dynamics in Figure 9.5.

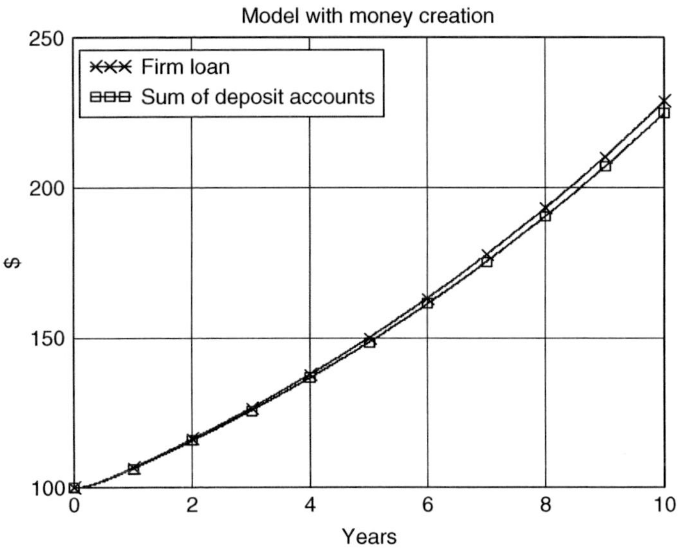


*Figure 9.4* Loan and deposit dynamics with money creation

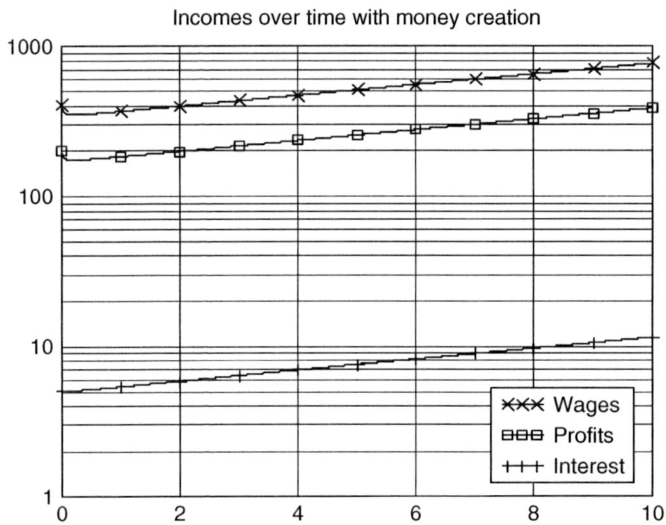


*Figure 9.5* Income dynamics with money creation

As is obvious, both transaction-account balances and incomes grow over time, so that a growing stock of money finances a growing level of real economic activity – which, in this model, is treated as implicit (the increasing stock of money is enabling an increasing level of employment and flow of goods). One realistic difference between this and the previous no-growth model is the divergence between loans and deposits. Loans equalled deposits in the previous model because of the unrealistic assumption that the firm sector precisely met its debt-repayment obligations. Relaxing this assumption, by allowing that a proportion $\delta_d$ of repayments are not made, gives a result which accords with actual economic data, namely, that loans exceed deposits.[13]

As it stands, this model shows that the circuitist vision fills its objectives of showing the essentially monetary nature of capitalism, and explaining how the surplus generated in production is monetized by the process of monetary circulation. It is, however, a skeletal model, in that the behavioural parameters in the model – the values of $\tau_B$, $\tau_W$, $\tau_L$, and so on – are constant. Flesh can be added to the skeleton by making these values functions of time, and of other system states. The full development of this model is a work in progress, but its potential can be demonstrated here by using it to model a credit crunch.

## A 'credit crunch'

There is no doubt that the US economy began to experience a 'credit crunch' in late 2007 – a process marked by a sudden switch from the willing provision of new debt to an unwillingness by lenders to lend, and a sudden switch from risk-seeking to risk-averse behaviour by borrowers.

These basic phenomena can be modelled in this framework by changing several of the model's key parameters:

1. Reducing the value of the money-creation parameter $n_M$, to signify a reduced willingness by lenders to lend.
2. Increasing the time lag for the relending of repaid debt $\tau_M$, to signify the same reluctance.
3. Reducing the time lag for debt repayment $\tau_L$, to signify a desire by borrowers to reduce their debt exposure.
4. Increasing the value of $\delta_d$, to signify an increase in the proportion of firms that fail to meet their interest-payment commitments.

In the following simulations, all key parameters were altered by a multiplier of 3: thus at the time of the credit crunch, the rate of money

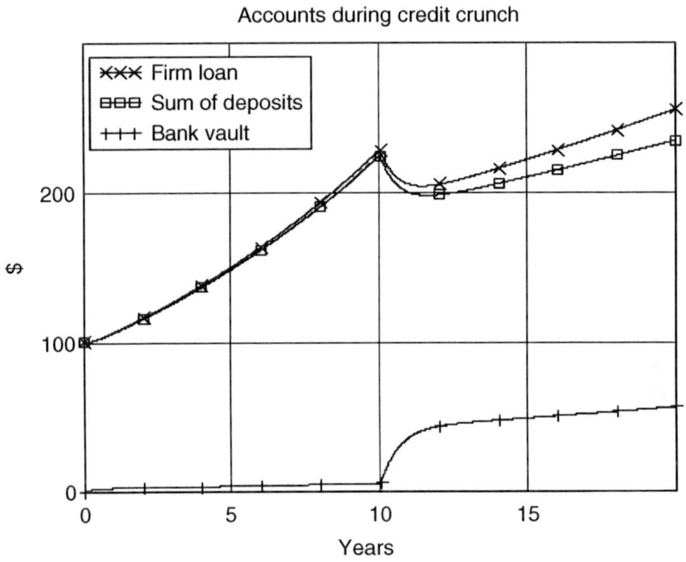


*Figure 9.6* Loan and deposit dynamics during a credit crunch

creation and the rate of recycling were reduced by two-thirds, while the rate of repayment of outstanding debt and the level of non-payment of interest tripled.

As Figures 9.6 and 9.7 indicate, the changes to these parameters do indeed simulate a 'credit crunch', with a sudden and sharp drop in both the amount of money in circulation and loans, and a sudden rise in the level of inactive funds in the bank vault. As accounts drop, so do incomes; ultimately, both accounts and incomes return to pre-crunch levels, but after a substantial time lag and with a slower rate of growth (given the lower monetary-parameter values).

It is also possible to show, with a rudimentary production system, that this monetary phenomenon has real effects.

## The monetary to real transmission mechanism

Linking this model of monetary dynamics to a model of real output necessarily raises the vexed issue of a price mechanism. As is well known, there is a sharp divide between neoclassical economists, who posit a supply and demand mechanism for price determination, and post-Keynesian economists who, in line with Kalecki, posit a

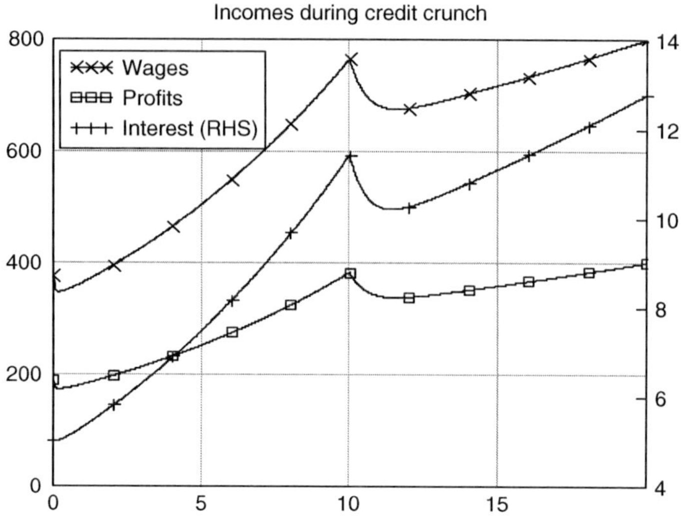


*Figure 9.7* Income dynamics during a credit crunch

cost-plus analysis,[14] – with empirical research strongly supporting the latter perspective (see Lee, 1998). For the sake of simplicity, the model presented below uses a 'neoclassical' mechanism, but with a surprisingly non-neoclassical outcome.

The key links between the monetary sector and the real sector in this model are as follows:

1. The flow of wages sustains a stock $L$ of workers hired for a wage $W$ who produce output $Q$ in factories, so that $Q = a \cdot L$, where $a$ represents labour productivity.[15]
2. The output is then sold to capitalists, workers, and bankers with a price level $P$ that responds with a lag $\tau_P$ to the gap between the monetary value of output $(P \cdot Q)$ and demand, where this is the sum of the commodity-expenditure flows from the three classes of agents in the model.[16]

The equations needed to include these links are three algebraic relations for output, labour, and demand,[17] and one additional differential equation for prices:

$$Q = a \cdot L$$

$$L = \frac{s}{\tau_S} \cdot \frac{F_D}{W}$$

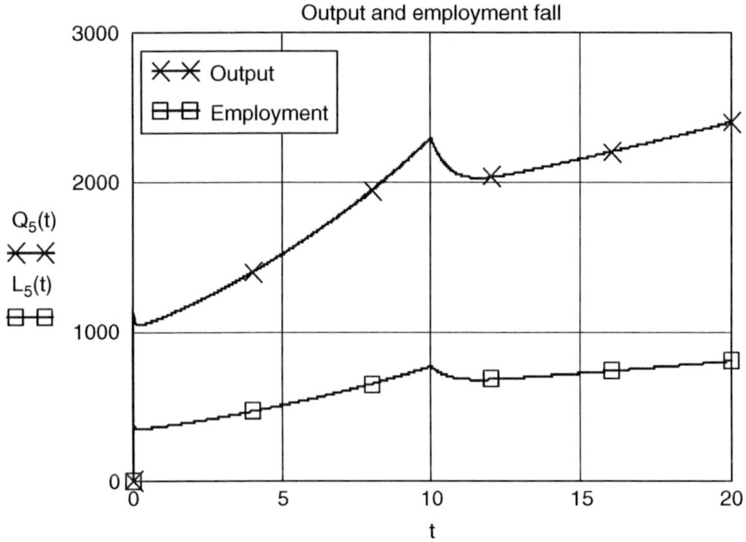


*Figure 9.8* Output and employment with a credit crunch

$$\frac{d}{dt}P = -\frac{1}{\tau_P} \cdot P \cdot \left(\frac{Q - D/P}{Q}\right)$$

$$D = \frac{s}{\tau_S} \cdot F_D + \frac{B_D}{\tau_\beta} + \frac{W_D}{\tau_\omega}$$

Output and employment behave as one would expect in a credit crunch, falling abruptly (Figure 9.8). Against expectations, the price index rises rather than falls because of the credit crunch (Figure 9.9). A neoclassical pricing mechanism thus has a distinctly non-neoclassical outcome in this dynamic setting. Neoclassical economists might surmise that this is an artefact of the wage rate $W$ being a constant in this model, and that were the wage flexible downwards, the credit crunch would indeed be absorbed by a price adjustment with little or no effect on output and employment. A more general model would be needed to theoretically evaluate this likely rebuttal, but a very strong empirical case can be made that falling wages would only exacerbate the impact of a credit crunch.

## The real-world credit crunch

As Keynes (1936, pp. 268–9) argued:

> [t]he method of increasing the quantity of money in terms of wage-units by decreasing the wage-unit increases proportionately the

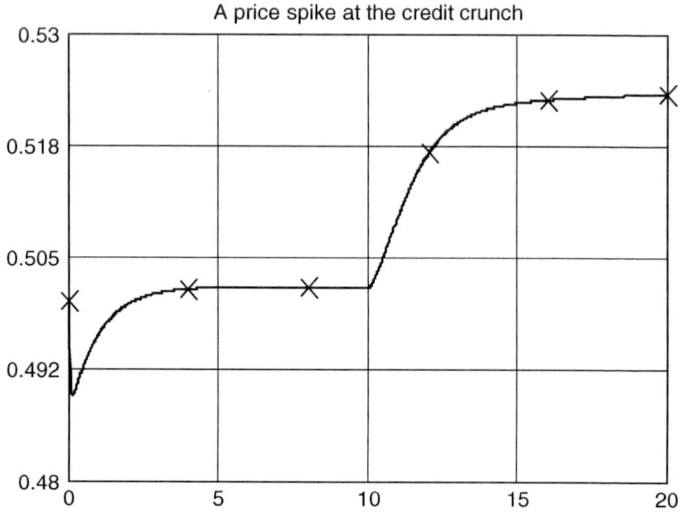


*Figure 9.9* Price dynamics with a credit crunch

> burden of debt; whereas the method of producing the same result by increasing the quantity of money whilst leaving the wage-unit unchanged has the opposite effect. Having regard to the excessive burden of many types of debt, it can only be an inexperienced person who would prefer the former.

Keynes's stricture against reducing money wages during a debt-induced downturn is all the more valid today. Not only would a reduction in money wages reduce the price level – and thus increase the debt-repayment burden – but also today, workers are debtors to an unprecedented degree.

The United States is tottering under the weight of the greatest debt burden in its financial history (and several OECD countries are in a similar or worse state). As Figure 9.10 indicates, the US current debt levels (relative to GDP) exceed even that reached during the Great Depression, when plunging real output and deflation running at over 10 per cent per year increased the private-debt-to-GDP ratio from 175 per cent in late 1929 to 215 per cent by 1932.

That burden is disproportionately borne by households, and workers, when compared to any previous speculative bubble. At the time of writing the ratio of household debt to GDP is almost twice the peak it reached during the Great Depression, and courtesy of the 'subprime

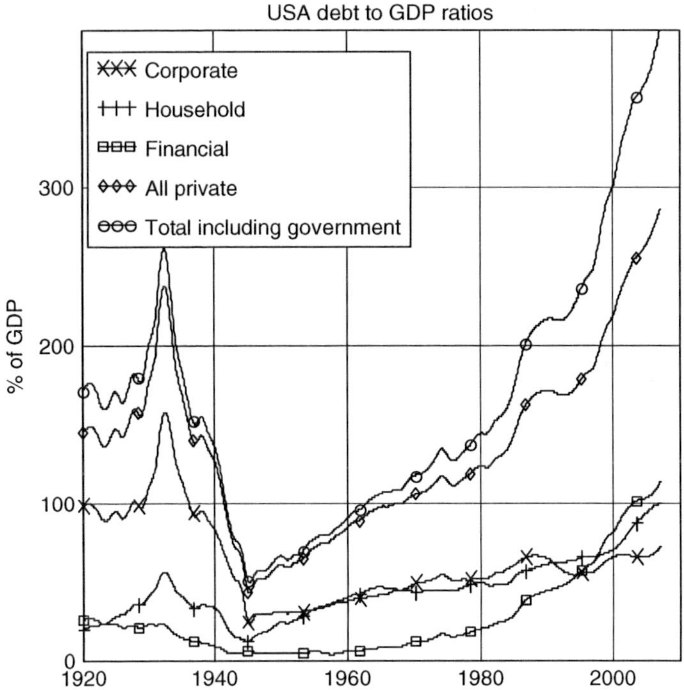


*Figure 9.10* Long-term US debt-to-GDP ratios

loans' phenomenon, a large proportion of that debt is owed by middle-to-low-income earners. A reduction in money wages would further reduce their capacity to service their debts, which would only add to the deflationary impact of the US excessive debt.

## Concluding remarks

This chapter has shown how the monetary circuit framework can explain what Graziani (1989) set out to explain: the process by which the surplus generated in production is monetized. This, however, is merely the first step in explaining the dynamics of a monetary production economy. The basic skeleton of a pure credit economy given here can be enriched further by disaggregating the banking sector – and therefore introducing another set of triangular relations between banks and a central bank that fulfils the role of a settlement institution between banks – and by disaggregating production to capture intersectoral financial dynamics.

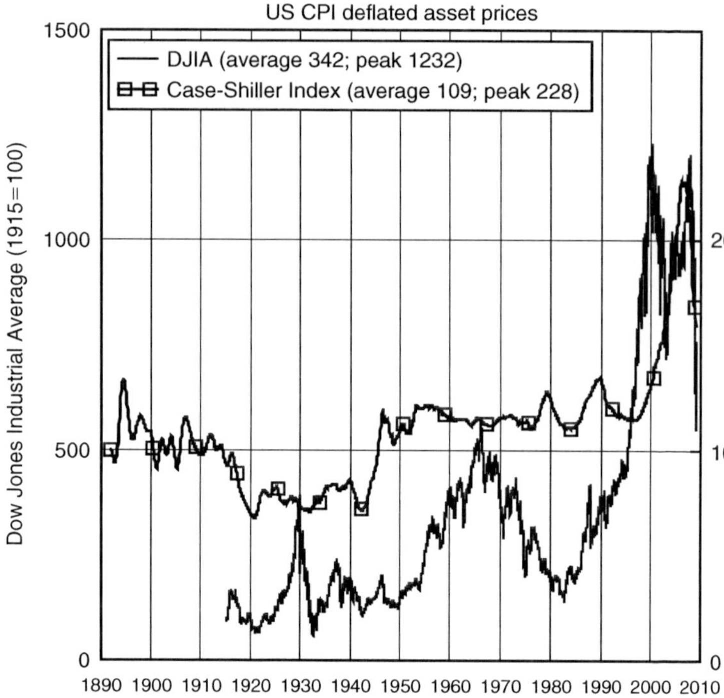


*Figure 9.11* US asset prices deflated by CPI

The creation of fiat money has to be added to model the actual mixed credit–fiat economy in which we live.

Most important, from the point of view of explaining the modern phenomenon of what is surely the greatest speculative bubble of all time, borrowing purely for the sake of speculation has to be added to the production-oriented borrowing that is the focus of this model. Ponzi-financing, which plays such a key role in Minsky's 'financial instability hypothesis', has been the driving force behind the unprecedented accumulation of debt (relative to income) that is the hallmark of our times.

This borrowing is driven by expectations of asset-price appreciation, and the bubble itself drives that price appreciation. The scale of the debt is obvious from Figure 9.10; the scale of the asset-price-appreciation bubble can best be seen by applying one key aspect of Minsky's hypothesis, namely, that there are two price levels in capitalism – one for commodities, the other for capital assets – and deflating asset prices by the consumer price index (Figure 9.11). The results are truly dramatic. In stark contrast to Greenspan's well-known remark that an asset bubble cannot be identified until after it has burst, the bubbles in both the share and housing markets were obvious by mid-1994 and 1996 respectively. By mid-1995 and 2000, they had reached levels that had never previously been experienced. By the time they burst, they were 3.7 and 2.1 times their long-term averages. What is opaque from a neoclassical/Austrian perspective is obvious from a Minskian standpoint.

The endogenous creation of credit money – fuelled by appreciating asset prices that are themselves a product of the expansion of credit money – is an essential aspect of this process. For that reason alone, our model of capitalism must be a monetary one. Keynes made the case, Minsky explained the dynamics, and Graziani gave us the *ab initio* principles on which a monetary analysis of capitalism must be based. The current, almost surely secular crisis adds urgency to the task of developing a true understanding of the monetary dynamics of capitalism.

## Notes

1. We are not endorsing a labour theory of value here, which in fact we explicitly reject (see Keen, 1993). However, Marx's insight that surplus is the source of profit transcends the veracity of the labour theory of value.
2. The volume written by Godley and Lavoie (2007, p. 1) opens with the wonderful remark by Kalecki that economics 'is the science of confusing stocks with flows'.
3. As Yakovenko (2007, p. 5) notes, '[t]he physical medium of money is not essential here', and a more natural analogy for the pure credit system outlined here is a completely electronic banking system. The physical analogy, however, better makes the mental point that the destruction of money when a debt is repaid does not make sense. Such systems existed in nineteenth-century America (Chown, 1944, pp. 181–90) – though many such banks clearly behaved in ways that amounted to seigniorage.
4. The fact that some parameter values exceed 1 is explained later.
5. This means that the time lag between producing output and earning revenue from selling it is equal to two months.
6. With the parameter values used in this simulation, the velocity of money commences at 6.05 and converges to 5.142 – so annual incomes are equivalent to 5.142 times the stock of deposits.
7. In this simulation $l_R$ equals 10 per cent.
8. These are not reserves in the modern institutional sense – as they cannot be lent out – but the reservoir of funds that would accumulate as loans were repaid in a pure credit system, which could then be lent out again. In the following simulation, we set $m_R$ equal to 4, which means that the stock of inactive money turns over four times per year.
9. This method was developed for another paper in conjunction with Dr Jeffrey Dambacher of Australia's CSIRO (Commonwealth Scientific and Industrial

Research Organization), and is based on the qualitative dynamic modelling approach developed in mathematical biology.

10. The term $\omega$ represented how many times workers' expenditure turned over in the time frame of the model. Thus $\omega = 26$ meant that workers spent their wages 26 times per year. In a time lag formulation, this is restated as '$\tau_W = 1/26$', so that the turnover period for workers' expenditure is 1/26th of a year – or equivalently that workers spend their wages every two weeks.
11. We assume that $n_M = 0.1$, so that the rate of creation of money is 10 per cent per year.
12. This could equally be shown as being proportional to debt ($n_M \cdot F_L$).
13. In a more complete model, this would in part be attenuated by incorporating bankruptcy (which reduces debt without reducing money), and amplified by capital raisings by the banking sector – which increases bank reserves by transferring funds from deposits (thus reducing them) without reducing the level of loans.
14. Kalecki's position is much richer than just this of course, with an allowance for at least two price mechanisms, and variable mark-ups (Kalecki, 1942, pp. 126–7). See Kriesler (1987) for a thorough exposition and Keen (1998) for a proof that contra Kalecki's price dynamics are compatible with input–output dynamics.
15. Capital is taken for granted in this simple model. Of course, in a more realistic and necessarily multi-sectoral model, production would depend as well on a stock of machinery and a flow of commodity inputs.
16. In this simple model, capitalists are assumed to spend their share of the monetized value of the surplus $s/\tau_S \cdot F_D$ on commodities.
17. A more complete model would make these differential equations with their own time lags.

## References

Chown, J.F. (1944), *A History of Money* (London: Routledge).

Godley, W. (1999), 'Money and credit in a Keynesian model of income determination', *Cambridge Journal of Economics*, 23 (4), 393–411.

Godley, W. and Lavoie, M. (2007), *Monetary Economics: an Integrated Approach to Credit, Money, Income, Production and Wealth* (Basingstoke: Palgrave Macmillan).

Graziani, A. (1989), 'The theory of the monetary circuit', *Thames Papers in Political Economy*, Spring. Reprinted in M. Musella and C. Panico (eds) (1995), *The Money Supply in the Economic Process* (Aldershot: Edward Elgar).

Kalecki, M. (1942), 'Mr Whitman on the concept of "degree of monopoly": a comment', *Economic Journal*, 52 (205), 121–7.

Keen, S. (1993), 'Use-value, exchange-value, and the demise of Marx's labor theory of value', *Journal of the History of Economic Thought*, 15 (1), 107–21.

Keen, S. (1998), 'Answers (and questions) for Sraffians (and Kaleckians)', *Review of Political Economy*, 10 (1), 73–87.

Keynes, J.M. (1936), *The General Theory of Employment, Interest and Money* (London: Macmillan).

Kriesler, P. (1987), *Kalecki's Microanalysis: the Development of Kalecki's Analysis of Pricing and Distribution* (Cambridge: Cambridge University Press).

Lee, F. (1998), *Post Keynesian Price Theory* (Cambridge: Cambridge University Press).

Minsky, H. (1980), 'Capitalist financial processes and the instability of capitalism', *Journal of Economic Issues*, 14 (2), 505–23.

Moore, B.J. (1988), *Horizontalists and Verticalists: the Macroeconomics of Credit Money* (Cambridge: Cambridge University Press).

Rochon, L.-P. (2005), 'The existence of monetary profits within the monetary circuit', in G. Fontana and R. Realfonzo (eds), *The Monetary Theory of Production: Tradition and Perspectives* (Basingstoke: Palgrave Macmillan).

Yakovenko, V.M. (2007), 'Econophysics, statistical mechanics approach to' (arXiv:0709.3662; 23 September 2007).

# 10
# The Financialization of Modern Economies in Monetary Circuit Theory

*Marc Pilkington*

## Introduction

It is an accepted fact at the time of writing that financial phenomena have the ability to wreak havoc on the economy. As Fahrer (2007, p. 21) notes:

> the financial economy is growing to a level where it is starting to influence more profoundly the fundamentals of the real economy [...]. Regulators are focusing much more on asset bubble risks or a potential hedge fund crisis with risks crystallising in the financial economy because of the wash-over effects on the real economy.

Interestingly, the International Monetary Fund (2006) also shares the fears of systemic risk entailed by the rapid growth of those complex financial institutions using increasingly sophisticated instruments.

In this chapter, we aim at conceptualizing an additional macroeconomic sector, defined as a broad accounting category in the stock–flow consistent framework developed by Lavoie (2004), and by Lavoie and Godley (2001–2, 2007). Starting from the methodological observation that many financial services supplied by banks today do not fit into the categories of monetary intermediation or financial intermediation as defined by the theory of money emissions (TME hereafter), we argue that the theoretical distinction between banks and non-bank financial institutions (NBFIs hereafter) – such as hedge funds,[1] insurance companies, venture capital firms, private equity firms, pension and mutual funds, and so on – is blurred in both post-Keynesian and monetary circuit literature.

Following the fundamental insights of the TME (Schmitt, 1984, 1996; Rossi, 1998, 2006; Gnos, 2003, 2005) on monetary and financial intermediation, we consider the current process of financialization in the world economy. Further, we draw on Karl Polanyi's groundbreaking work in the twentieth century on *haute finance*. Although we abstract from the geopolitical, institutional, and historical setting of his time, we nevertheless retain some of the features of Polanyi's concept of *haute finance* that pertain to the current world economic system. We finally attempt to redefine *haute finance* as a new macroeconomic sector in the Lavoie–Godley [LG from now on] model in order to single out the far-reaching macroeconomic consequences of the financialization of modern economies.

## Money and financial intermediation in monetary circuit theory

### The function of banks

*The function of banks in Keynesian literature*

Major Keynesian economists (Tobin and Golub, 1998) have often modelled banks as mere financial intermediaries. Likewise, a common statement in post-Keynesian monetary analysis is that 'banks, after all, are essentially in the business of selling credit' (Moore, 1988b, p. 46). To be precise, commercial banks participate in the process of financial intermediation, by means of which deficit-spending units borrow from saving units the resources they need to finance their net flow of expenditures (Ball, 1964, p. 168). Even though banks are seen by post-Keynesians as the main actors in the process of financial intermediation, the latter authors overlook a fundamental feature of banks in a monetary economy of production, namely, monetary intermediation. Arguably, both mainstream and post-Keynesian economists also fail to emphasize the central role played by double-entry bookkeeping in governing banking activity.

*The function of banks in monetary circuit literature*

The TME is a fundamental component of monetary circuit theory. In this framework, banks are interposed between households and firms. The fusion of real and monetary emissions (both viewed as instantaneous events) enables the monetization of production.[2] Banks actually emit a number of money units for the remuneration of current workers, whose product is the very 'content' of the newly formed deposits (Schmitt, 1984, pp. 484–92). In this respect, banks are no longer primarily characterized by their function of financial intermediary, which they now share in practice with NBFIs. In contrast with the latter, banks are the only institutions endowed with the right to accept money deposits (withdrawable on demand) from the general public and to issue legally acceptable payments within the economic system. This function of monetary intermediation distinguishes banks from other financial institutions in monetary circuit literature. As Rossi (1998, p. 38) points out, 'the distinguishing feature of modern banking – in contrast to non-bank financial intermediation – is to issue payments within the economy'. Payments are indeed made possible because money is a mere numerical form issued by banks that perform a monetary intermediation, thereby enabling the measurement of economic output: 'without it, physical output would simply be a heap of heterogeneous objects' (Cencini, 2003b, p. 314).

A powerful way to apprehend banking activity is through a fundamental accounting principle known as double-entry bookkeeping. It is indeed a historical characteristic of banks, which has greatly facilitated the circulation of money debts within the economic system. As Innes (1913, pp. 402–3) already noted a century ago:

> debts and credits are perpetually trying to get in touch with one another, and it is the business of the banker to bring them together [...]. There is thus a constant circulation of debts and credits through the medium of the banker who brings them together and clears them as the debts fall due. This is the whole business of banking as it was three thousand years before Christ, and as it is today.

## Double-entry bookkeeping and the creation of purchasing power

### *Do banks create credit* ex nihilo *and do they create purchasing power on their own?*

In a description of the money-creation process, post-Keynesians often explain that money is a mere liability (that is to say, bank deposits) that commercial banks issue on themselves. The latter are then supposed to lend these deposits, legally accepted[3] as money, to firms and households. Can we thus infer that banks create purchasing power *ex nihilo* on their own? The answer is clearly negative if we adopt the perspective of monetary circuit theory. According to the TME, banks do not create credit *ex nihilo* as the credit granted by banks to firms to finance production has its ultimate origin in the credit granted by workers to banks, at the very moment current wages are paid (Schmitt, 1984). In this theory, the factors of production own a positive purchasing power over current output in the form of a bank deposit following the payment of wages (ibid.). This description of the way factors of production acquire a positive purchasing power over economic output holds true even when firms try to circumvent bank intermediation by financing production out of their own cash flows (Gnos, 2003) or on capital markets.

Schmitt (1984, 1996) has thoroughly analysed the way bank money intervenes in the monetary circuit by observing that, strictly speaking, banks do not start to issue the deposits that they subsequently lend to firms. On the contrary, as the old saying goes, 'loans make deposits' (Withers, 1909). In fact, when they create money, banks debit and credit accounts with purely numerical units (Cencini, 1997, pp. 273–4). The distinction between *ex nihilo* money creation and double-entry bookkeeping indeed has some far-reaching implications. Being composed of purely numerical units, bank money can never be the actual object (or 'content') of workers' income. In the TME, wage earners are fundamentally paid in real goods and services. Of course, this is necessarily the case in the reflux stage of the circuit of wages, as firms have to sell goods to households in order to repay bank loans. Nonetheless, it is also true in the initial stage of the monetary circuit. In the real world, workers do not obtain goods physically when they are paid in wage units.[4] However, at the moment wages are paid, wage earners immediately save their income in the form of bank deposits defined as a stock of income corresponding to a drawing right over a fraction of output (Schmitt, 1984, pp. 484–92), until they finally spend it on buying goods and services in the product market. Therefore, the very 'content' of workers' income is made of the goods and services that firms and workers have produced together in the production process (ibid.).

### *Banks and firms participate together in the same macroeconomic reality*

As Lavoie (1984, p. 774) puts it, '[a]ny production in a modern or in an "entrepreneur" economy is of a *monetary nature*'. When banks grant new loans that take the form of flows of credit, '[t]he additional debts of banks are issued and used to accept and pay for additional offer contracts of producers and workers' (Davidson, 1988, p. 164). More than 20 years ago, Lavoie (1984, p. 774) clearly understood the double-sided nature of income formation and the role of double-entry bookkeeping in this macroeconomic process, when he wrote that '[t]hese flows of credit then reappear as deposits on the liability side of the balance sheet of banks when firms use these loans to remunerate their factors of production'. In the so-called Dijon School, led by Schmitt, the emphasis on double-entry bookkeeping in the process of money creation has successfully enabled the conceptual integration of money and output, which demonstrates the fact that banks and firms indeed participate in the same macroeconomic reality:

> bank deposits are [. . .] the organic *result* (that is, a stock magnitude) of two intimately related *actions* (or flows): (1) creation, on the monetary side, of the numerical form of payments (money proper) by the banking system, and (2) production, on the real side, of physical output (money's worth) by the non-bank public, that is, firms and workers taken together. (Rossi, 2001, p. 7)

The emphasis is on the macroeconomic structure of the economic system, wherein 'the monetary sector and the real sector operate concomitantly to determine the macroeconomic magnitude par excellence: money-income' (Cencini, 1997, pp. 273–4). The role of banks, firms, and wage earners is therefore examined in light of a holistic macroeconomic structure (Cencini, 1997, p. 276) logically independent of microeconomic theory (Cencini, 2003a).

*Is an unidentifiable leakage from banks to NBFIs possible?*

Although bank loans make deposits (Withers, 1909), Cencini (1997, p. 275) notes that:

> [t]he reality of our modern monetary systems is based on the simultaneous application of the two principles, 'loans make deposits' and 'deposits make loans', where the first refers to the fact that deposits are created through the loans granted by banks to firms, while the second states that the deposits earned by workers are immediately lent to firms to cover financially their costs of production.

Further, as Chick (1986, pp. 13–14, emphasis added) recognizes, '[t]hese newly created deposits must be held *somewhere in the economy*, willingly or unwillingly, and the increased holdings count as saving, voluntary or involuntary'.

What is more, the distinction between financial circulation and industrial circulation in the *Treatise on Money* (Keynes, 1930, p. 243) casts light on the 2007–9 turmoil in international financial markets. Keynes had foreseen that the monetary flows between the two sectors might result in a 'speculative boom' wherein the financial sector could end up 'stealing resources from the industrial sector' (p. 254). The autonomous circulation of financial-business deposits within the financial sphere might indeed divert income from the industrial sphere. However, we argue here for purely logical and accounting reasons that the fear of an unidentifiable leakage from banks towards NBFIs, in the process of financial disintermediation, is a contradiction in terms even when financialization is brought into the picture as we will see in the next section.

## The analysis of financialization in modern economies

### The characterization of financialization in modern economies

*The meaning of financialization*

The term 'financialization' is used to describe a multifaceted reality that reflects complex phenomena (Epstein, 2005, p. 3) such as the shift towards the maximization of 'shareholder value' in corporate-governance mechanisms, the growing dominance of capital and financial markets over the traditional banking sector, the increasing political and economic power of the owners of financial assets (sometimes called the 'rentier class'), the spectacular growth of trading and innovation on financial markets, and, finally, a general pattern of accumulation in which profit-making occurs increasingly through financial channels (Krippner, 2004, p. 14).

We endorse here the broad definition used by Epstein (2005, p. 3), encompassing all the previously mentioned aspects: 'financialization means the increasing role of financial motives, financial markets, financial actors and financial institutions in the operation of the domestic and international economies'. According to many economists, the process of financialization – understood in a broad sense – is deeply rooted in the international political economy of our time, since it has considerably reshaped the balance of power between public monetary institutions (such as central banks) and the most influential private operators taking the form of global-spanning financial conglomerates and acting as powerful individual investors on financial markets (Dombrowski, 1998, p. 1).

*The increasing weight of household debt*

Figure 10.1 shows the exponential rise of household debt over the period 1950–2007 in the United States. In fact, this crucial macroeconomic variable started skyrocketing at the end of the 1990s. Fuelled by low interest rates decided by the US Federal Reserve as a result of the major shocks

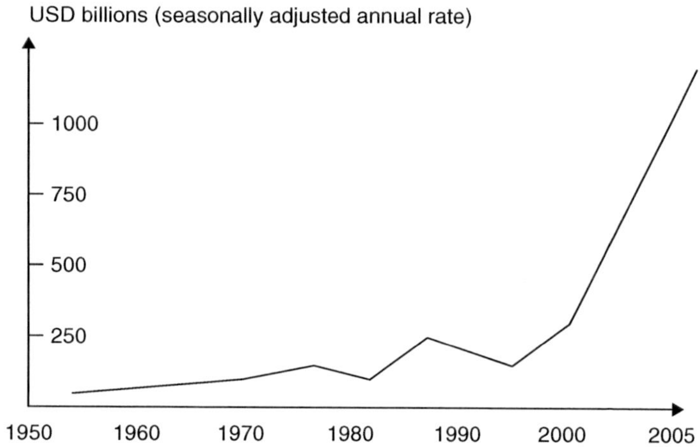


*Figure 10.1* Evolution of household liabilities in the US credit market (billion US dollars, seasonally adjusted annual rate)
*Source:* Federal Reserve Board/Haver Analytics

caused by the explosion of the Internet bubble and the terrorists attacks of 11 September 2001,

> the US consumer rushed into a frenzy of purchases of consumer goods. Encouraged by banks and the whole US financial system, he exceeded his own financing capacities and plunged since 2004 into generalized debt and into a situation not seen in the United States since the dip of the Great Depression post 1929, namely a negative saving rate. (*Global European Anticipation Bulletin*, 2006, Internet)

Under the impulse of financialization, households modified their attitude towards debt: 'now people often pay their mortgage off quickly and use it as a revolving line of credit to invest into other assets. That would have been unheard of a decade ago when the idea was to pay off the mortgage to become debt-free' (Fahrer, 2007, p. 21). The massive securitization of household debt has enabled the autonomous circulation of enormous amounts of liquidities within the financial sphere reminiscent of the financial-business deposits once singled out by Keynes (1930, p. 243). Following this explosion of household debt (Palley, 2007, p. 3), the bulk of the resulting liquidities were channelled to the housing industry and led to a sharp increase in house prices (and arguably to the subprime crisis), which calls for a renewed reflection on endogenous finance (Palley, 1996).

### *The shifting function of portfolio managers and the decreasing share of bank credit*

The exponential rise of financial and capital markets worldwide[5] is characterized by massive deregulation trends, sophisticated financial innovations, financial disintermediation, and the resulting decreasing share of bank credit in the financing of firms. Fama (1980, p. 44) once emphasized the function of banks as portfolio managers:

> the concern with banks in macroeconomics centers on their role as portfolio managers, whereby they purchase securities from individuals and firms (and a loan is, after all, just a purchase of securities), which they then offer as portfolio holdings (deposits) to other individuals and firms.

This central function has been thoroughly described in mainstream and post-Keynesian literature with the recent revival of Keynes's liquidity preference applied to banks (Le Heron, 2002). We argue, however, that it is no longer possible to define banks exclusively with regard to this sole function of portfolio manager. As a matter of fact, this role, once confined to commercial banks, has been partly transferred, in the process of financialization, to other NBFIs operating on international capital markets. In the economic system taken as a whole, the transfer of this function accounts for substantial monetary flows that need to be captured within a stock–flow consistent framework.

## The changing nature of finance in the context of bank disintermediation

### *Securitization and financial engineering*

Under the broad discipline of financial engineering, securitization is the process of creating a new financial instrument by combining other financial assets and then marketing them to investors:

> banks used to make loans to borrowers whose credit-worthiness they had carefully evaluated and then keep the loans on their books until they were paid off. Today, big banks are almost credit intermediaries. They make loans, bundle them together, and sell securities that are claims not on individual loans but on the bundle of loans. (Leijonhufvud, 2007, p. 2)

The principal and interest of the newly created securities are derived from the cash flows generated by a pool of assets acting as collaterals.

According to the Securities Industry and Financial Markets Association (2008, p. 1), an estimated 4.01 trillion US dollars of securitized assets were issued in 2007 in the United States. Further, securitization in modern finance often goes hand in hand with the fact that

> credit intermediation has been vastly facilitated by the proliferation of complex risk transfer instruments [...]. One consequence is that a growing number of banks have been shifting to 'originate and distribute' business models, transferring risks to other investors. (Knight, 2007, Internet)

Financial engineering can thus be seen as a set of practices aimed both at sophisticated portfolio management and effective credit-risk transfer. For instance, the recent and controversial subprime mortgage-backed securities consisted in the securitization of mortgage loans collected in tailor-made portfolios and placed in *ad hoc* independent legal bodies called structured investment vehicles or special purpose entities.

*Financial disintermediation*

Today, productive activities are often financed with the help of new financial instruments without drawing on credit lines and using traditional bank loans. Financial disintermediation refers (1) to consumers (firms and households) investing directly in securities rather than leaving their money in the form of bank deposits withdrawable on demand, then (2) to borrowers obtaining financial resources in capital markets rather than through banks. Can we claim that the financial function of banks is transferred to capital markets in this new scheme? In fact, our answer is slightly subtler. Instead of altering the inner logic of monetary circuit theory, we argue that the structure of modern finance has merely been extended and complexified with the addition of numerous financial institutions bearing credit risk in lieu of commercial banks, and acting as sophisticated and sometimes unidentifiable middlemen in the realm of the opaque world of capital markets. A fundamental shift is the increasing role of financial markets in the process of financial intermediation. Banks have largely ceased to fund the loans[6] that they traditionally granted to their customers (in accordance *ex post facto* with their reserve and/or capital requirements). Instead, they simply originate the loans and quickly shift them off their balance sheet (through the instantaneous process of double-entry bookkeeping) by packaging them into sophisticated high-yield securities and distributing them to investors such as hedge funds (Markman, 2007). Paradoxically, these massive securitization operations have not undermined the extent of securities investments by banks that continue to be involved in risky asset-management activities (Knight, 2007). There is thus a conceptual necessity to deal with an increasingly blurred distinction between banks and NBFIs: 'there has been an important trend for dissolution of functional boundaries, particularly between banking and securities activities. This has led to the creation of increasingly complex institutions, which integrate both types of activities' (Griffith-Jones, 1998, p. 23).

After this brief analysis of some of the defining characteristics of financialization, let us consider in the next section the integration of this global evolution in a macroeconomic stock–flow framework.

## An attempt to integrate financial globalization in a macroeconomic stock–flow framework: towards a redefinition of Karl Polanyi's *haute finance*

### Polanyi's original concept of *haute finance*: a historical perspective

*Haute finance* in Polanyi's (2001 [1944]) theoretical framework was a *sui generis* institution of the end of the nineteenth and the beginning of the twentieth century. Independent of single governments, regardless of their geopolitical influence, the *haute finance* sector was nevertheless interacting with all; *haute finance* was arguably the most complex institution in the history of mankind (Polanyi, 2001 [1944], p. 11). The functional motive of *haute finance* was gain:

> nineteenth-century civilization [...] chose to base itself on a motive only rarely acknowledged as valid in the history of human societies, and certainly never before raised to the level of justification of action and behaviour in everyday life, namely, gain. (Polanyi, 2001 [1944], p. 31)

Further, the very existence of *haute finance* entailed a subtle dialectic with governments, whose end was political power and conquest. The global spread of markets was associated with 'a phenomenon unheard of in the annals of Western civilization, namely, a hundred years' peace – 1815–1914' (Polanyi, 2001 [1944], pp. 9–11). The first half of this period rested primarily on political mechanisms. In its second half,[7] however, the peace came to rely increasingly on a 'mysterious institution [...]

[that] functioned as the main link between the political and economic organization of the world' (p. 10).

> Although its leading members had made their fortunes in the financing of wars [...] and had no objection to any number of minor, short, or localized wars [...] their business would be impaired if a general war between the Great Powers should interfere with the monetary foundations of the system. (Polanyi, 2001 [1944], p. 11)

Hence, from a historical and geopolitical perspective, despite its *raison d'être* based on profit accumulation, the institutionalization of self-interest and the political legitimation of financial gain by the rentier class, *haute finance* nevertheless rested on a curious paradox: its continuous existence was ensured by the safeguarding of world peace.

## The modern definition of *haute finance*

### Haute finance *as a functional economic principle that pertains to modern economies*

The term 'rentier' is sometimes used in reference to economic agents who derive all their income from the ownership of financial assets. Keynes (1936, Ch. 24) once defined the famous 'rentier class' as a class of functionless investors. Although this popular definition clearly conveys the idea of a purely passive role played by these economic agents (the rentier class), we nonetheless agree with Epstein and Jayadev (2005, p. 48), who argue that the process of financialization in modern economies is indeed very active. Therefore, the corresponding institutional sector needs to be defined positively with regard to an unambiguous function. Hence, we opt here for a clear-cut methodological choice consisting in the introduction of a new macroeconomic sector as well as a broad accounting category under the *haute finance* label in a revisited LG stock–flow framework. This is a major step towards the elaboration of a coherent theory of the monetary circuit that captures the way 'an industrial capitalist economy works as an *organic whole*' (Lavoie and Godley, 2007, p. 3). This methodological choice, albeit very ambitious, will indeed play a key theoretical role in the enhancement of our understanding of the global evolution commonly referred to as 'the financialization of modern economies'.

For Polanyi, industrial capitalism was a unique mode of economic organization in human history in elevating gain to a fundamental principle. We argue that this feature of industrial capitalism (the central role of gain as a functional and institutionalized economic principle) now applies to a fuller extent to financial capitalism.[8] Therefore, we argue that there is a need to define *haute finance* anew as an independent conceptual entity, and therefore as a new macroeconomic sector *per se* in the LG framework.

Dumenil and Lévy (2005, p. 17) argue that, in modern economies, 'the term "finance" itself refers to a framework of institutions interlocked in a complex network'. It is sometimes claimed that this term can hardly be used as a 'scientific concept despite the obvious conceptual convergences found in the literature' (p. 21). As a matter of fact, a very high level of complexity characterizes modern finance.[9] However, monetary macroeconomists are not always at ease with the existence of such a complex and ill-defined entity when it comes to the conceptual integration of its macroeconomic consequences: '[t]here is to date no consensus on the appropriate definition of financialization, never mind agreement as to the logic or laws of motion – or even the existence – of a new system of rentier or finance capitalism' (Crotty, 2005, p. 85).

Owing to the lack of a single and consensual definition of *haute finance*, the corresponding macroeconomic sector that we wish to define should be the result of a methodological choice deeply rooted in the theory of the monetary circuit that is outside mainstream theory.[10]

In line with the institutionalized economic principle governing the very existence of *haute finance* identified in the twentieth century by Polanyi, we put forward a general (and hopefully consensual) definition of the macroeconomic function performed by the *haute finance* sector, which is simply to generate profits derived from financial market activity. This definition nevertheless requires further clarification with regard to the underlying meaning of financial profits. Schmitt (1984, p. 288) has argued that, from a macroeconomic perspective, the profits of non-financial corporations (NFCs hereafter) are self-contained in wages in the national income. This proposition stems from the statement by Keynes (1936, pp. 213–14), according to whom labour is the sole factor of production. In his interpretation of Keynes's monetary theory, Schmitt (1984) defines profits as income having been 'captured' in the production process (and not additional incomes merely added to wages). Profits come into existence when output is sold at a price that exceeds factor cost, that is to say, wages. However, in our analysis, it must be pointed out that the financial profits (or gains) generated by *haute finance* are purely microeconomic, and must therefore be distinguished from the profits of productive firms. Whether or not *haute finance* is in a position to divert resources from other macroeconomic sectors is a crucial question albeit almost premature at this stage.[11] However, one might wonder how the theoretical existence of a new macroeconomic sector can be derived from the observation of a wide range of purely microeconomic profit-seekers operating on international financial markets and characterized by increasingly sophisticated individualistic optimizing behaviour? We argue that the answer to this puzzling question can only be the outcome of the critical assessment of the methodology adopted by mainstream economics.

Haute finance: *a concept in sharp contrast with mainstream theory*

In mainstream economics,

> models abstract heavily from reality. [...] The existence of equilibrium in turn requires the prior assumption that all agents within the model display the character traits of a 'representative individual' who is concerned only about deriving personal maximum gain. This is standard characterization of agential behavior within the economic worldview but it contains precious few insights into concrete economic practices. (Watson, 2007, p. 65)

We abide by the widely held view that the personal gain motive, sometimes equated to psychological egoism (Slote, 1964), is a defining characteristic of financial capitalism. However, we propound an alternative to the mainstream view with its 'representative individual agent', and decide instead to define gain as an abstract and functional motive of the *haute finance* sector rather than a sacralized individual characteristic that governs the optimizing behaviour under constraints of economic agents under all circumstances. In fact, how does one reconcile the existence of gain as a defining characteristic of financial capitalism with the methodological rejection of strict neoclassical individualistic optimizing behaviour? We suggest borrowing a historical example by referring to the famous alleged words '*Enrichissez-vous*' by Guizot, Louis Philippe's prime minister, aimed at the French bourgeoisie class in 1848 (Rosanvallon, 1985). The holistic meaning of gain is understood insofar as it is viewed as the functional characteristic of a social group. Its subsequent conceptualization will be achieved by drawing a parallel between the French bourgeoisie in the nineteenth century and *haute finance* in the twenty-first century.

> Further, we need to acknowledge the limitations of the ability of so-called rational economic agents to predict future asset prices on

> financial markets. In spite of the impressive mathematical arsenal at the disposal of mainstream economists (Keynes, 1936, p. 297), the truth is that 'it has become increasingly difficult to know who the ultimate holders of risk are and how the prices of specific asset classes will evolve going forward'. (Knight, 2007, Internet)

> [Keynes] once recognized that allowances must be made for the interactions among the independent variables of his analysis. Changes in one variable can lead to changes in other variables, and the full effects of any initial change depend on these interactions. The complexity of these interrelations means that the analysis of changes over time cannot be adequately handled by mathematical equations. (Asimakopulos, 1991, pp. 136–7)

A fundamental error in economic theory is to derive all economic analysis from purely individualistic behaviour – through the aggregation of some postulated and sophisticated utility functions – therefore confining its validity to mere microeconomic theory (Graziani, 2003, p. 18). However, the ontological nature of macroeconomics requires a distinctive mindset in order to cast light on the holistic dimension of the economic system and explain its functional interdependencies (Arestis, 1996, p. 116): '[t]he starting point for a construction of a macroeconomic model can only be the identification of the social groups present in the community, followed by the definition of the conditions necessary for their reproduction and perpetuation over time' (Graziani, 2003, p. 19).

Despite the limitations of mathematical modelling, we nonetheless aim to build solid macroeconomic foundations for an explanatory framework resting on purely logical principles:

> we must exploit logic so far as we possibly can. Every purchase implies a sale: every money flow comes from somewhere and goes somewhere [...]. The aim here is to show how logic can help to organize information in a way that enables us to learn as much from it as possible. That is what we mean by macroeconomic theory. (Godley and Cripps, 1983, p. 44)

### *The case for a supranational* haute finance *sector*

The financial and technological innovations of the past decades have globalized and shrunk the financial system. The supranational nature of *haute finance* in our argumentation derives from the increasingly complex restructuration of global financial portfolios worldwide (Knight, 2007). Ramonet (1997, Internet) argues that '[f]inancial globalization is a law unto itself and it has established a separate supranational state with its own administrative apparatus, its own spheres of influence, its own means of action'.

We disagree with this assertion, which has currently no political and legal basis in the world. Although we posit the supranational nature of our newly defined institutional sector, we argue that *haute finance* remains a highly unstable and fragmented system. Moreover, the aforementioned supranational dimension and the blurring of the distinction between banks and NBFIs (sometimes purposely circumvented for regulatory motives) can be viewed as overlapping phenomena: 'banks have created separate entities known as conduits or "special investments vehicles" (SIVs), usually located offshore in Cayman islands or some such place where regulators are not much in evidence' (Leijonhufvud, 2007, p. 7). Paradoxically, when national regulators aim to safeguard the legal distinction between banks and NBFIs, the supranational dimension of *haute finance* is reinforced: 'in those countries where barriers remain [between banks and NBFIs], banks are however free to combine banking and securities abroad, and are increasingly finding ways around the law in their home market' (Griffith-Jones, 1998, p. 23).

Therefore *haute finance* is characterized by considerable regulatory difficulties when conducted on a mere domestic scale. This is illustrated by the following description of the global interconnectedness of banks' liabilities[12] in light of the complex mechanisms that triggered the 2007–8 subprime crisis:

> a German bank in Leipzig, for example, holds an (indirect) claim on some poor fellow in California – half a world away – who had borrowed up to the hilt at a very low 'starter rate' and who could not possibly meet his mortgage payments when the rate was raised to market level, but lived on the vain hope that the value of the house would continue to appreciate indefinitely. (Leijonhufvud, 2007, p. 3)

With a multitude of financial actors dispersed in numerous countries and interlinked through innovative, complex, and often opaque credit-risk transfer mechanisms, we argue that no single government (or central bank) was able to exercise sufficient power to impact effectively on the course of actions that led to this global crisis.

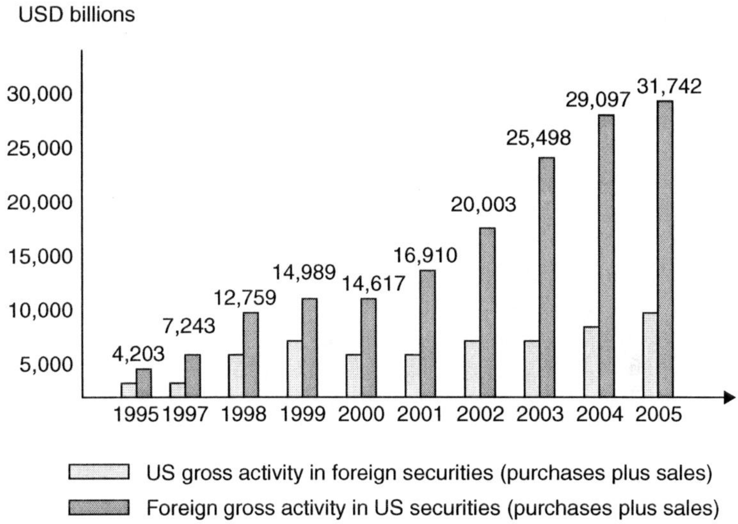


*Figure 10.2* The globalization trends in investment activities: the example of US securities
*Source:* US Treasury

Hereafter, we illustrate our case for a supranational[13] *haute finance* sector with the description of the globalization trends in the US securities market (Figure 10.2). The investment activity in foreign securities by residents in the United States[14] has increased at an incredibly fast pace over the last three decades. From 1980 onwards, US gross activity (purchases and sales) in foreign securities grew dramatically (140-fold) from 53 billion US dollars to almost 7.4 trillion US dollars in 2004. Foreign gross activity in US securities has also grown exponentially (166-fold) from 198 billion US dollars in 1980 to 32.95 trillion US dollars in 2004.

## The components of *haute finance*

We consider *haute finance* as a conceptual entity defined as a supranational institutional sector[15] constantly interacting with the traditional domestic sectors of the economy.

First, the *haute finance* sector is made of all NBFIs (regardless of their nationality) operating on international financial markets such as insurance and finance companies, investment banks, securitization firms, mutual funds, private pension funds, and public sovereign funds.[16] These NBFIs are not always distinguished from traditional banks in the literature, since financial innovation is constantly blurring the distinction between them. NBFIs[17] carry out financing activities but their resources (that is, their liabilities) are never directly obtained from savers in the form of perfectly liquid debt (that is to say, deposits withdrawable on demand). Instead, these institutions mobilize the public savings (by issuing tradable securities) for rendering other financial services including investment. All such institutions become financial intermediaries when they engage in lending activities.

Secondly, we need to include in *haute finance* the asset-management activities carried out by traditional banks that correspond neither to monetary intermediation in the TME (Rossi, 1998) nor to financial intermediation in the sense of the transfer of perfectly liquid resources (that is, resources withdrawable on demand) obtained directly from savers and supplied to deficit-spending units.[18] As we previously saw, there exists a fundamental distinction between monetary and financial intermediation, the former being performed when banks issue payments in the economy, and the latter when they bridge the gap between deficit-spending units and saving units. Banks often act as financial intermediaries, of course, but they also supply additional financial services (such as asset management), which can alternatively be provided by NBFIs. As a consequence, international[19] banking activities that pertain neither to monetary intermediation (when banks issue legally acceptable payments drawn on deposit accounts) nor to pure financial intermediation can legitimately be included in the *haute finance* sector.

Thirdly, certain activities of NFCs paradoxically need to be integrated in the *haute finance* sector. In fact, under the impulse of the new shareholder-value-maximization philosophy triggered by the 1980s takeover movement and the subsequent 'portfolio view of the firm' (Crotty, 2005, p. 90), NFCs have been actively involved in financial portfolio investment[20] independently of their real activities such as domestic productive investments and outward FDI (p. 105). Along with traditional banks, NFCs now engage in securitization and asset-management activities (both internally and externally). These activities should be included in *haute finance* regardless of the legal identity of the entity managing the financial assets in its own books. The challenge lies in the statistical integration of this component of *haute finance*, which will be of utmost importance in our endeavour to extend the LG framework, if we are to obtain one day a set of meaningful and computable data in macroeconometric terms.

## The inclusion of *haute finance* in a stock–flow consistent framework

How can we integrate financialization in a stock–flow consistent framework? Our perspective in this chapter is the modern theory of the monetary circuit. Therefore, we focus on the implications of financialization on the very structure of the macroeconomic stock–flow consistent framework put forward by LG that offers a coherent circuitist vision of endogenous money and sets proper accounting foundations for monetary macroeconomics that does not leave financial phenomena in the dark (Denizet, 1969), and ensures that there is no black hole (Godley, 1996, p. 7) in the economic system. Credit flows and money stocks are reconciled in a coherent framework enabling macroeconomists to work on comprehensive accounts, thereby providing an exhaustive description of the economic process.

As a full-fledged economic sector, *haute finance* can be integrated in the balance sheet and the transaction-flow matrices of the LG model. The additional transaction flows are simply the monetary *quid pro quo* of the securities and the financial services exchanged between the existing institutional sectors and the newly defined *haute finance* sector. These financial services generate both gains and losses, which are the aggregate of (1) the interests, dividends, and other contractual payments received by all agents of the different macroeconomic sectors; (2) the gains/losses resulting from the evolution of financial markets; (3) minus the devalorization of economic agents' financial portfolio resulting from inflation; (4) minus the management and administrative costs incurred by these financial services.

We only provide hereafter the premises of an extended LG framework including *haute finance*, but this model is not yet fully operational. The next step will be to turn this theoretical skeleton into a dynamic system of equations calibrated to real-world data with a set of relevant exogenous variables in order to account for complex macroeconomic phenomena such as the changes in the reserve ratio and the capital requirements of lending institutions, the variations in firms' inventories and stocks of capital goods, households' target of wealth relative to income, the reactions to fiscal shocks and interest-rate policy decisions, firms' expectations of sales, and households' expectations of inflation (Godley, 2004). Regardless of the quality of the subsequent modelling techniques employed, the thorough quantification of the monetary flows originating from *haute finance* will necessarily involve a clear understanding of the numerous factors regulating modern financial markets,

*Table 10.1* Aggregate balance sheet of the institutional sectors

| | *Households* | *Firms* | *Banks* | *Government* | Haute finance | *Total* |
|---|---|---|---|---|---|---|
| 1. Bank deposits | $+D$ | | $-D$ | | | 0 |
| 2. Bank loans | $-Lh_b$ | $-Lf_b$ | $+L_b$ | | | 0 |
| 3. *Haute finance* loans | $-Lh_{hf}$ | $-Lf_{hf}$ | $-Lb_{hf}$ | $-Lg_{hf}$ | $+L_{hf}$ | 0 |
| 4. *Haute finance* securities | $+Sh_{hf}$ | $+Sf_{hf}$ | $+Sb_{hf}$ | $+Sg_{hf}$ | $-S_{hf}$ | 0 |
| 5. Government bills | $+G_h$ | $+G_f$ | $+G_b$ | $-G$ | $+G_{hf}$ | 0 |
| 6. Capital goods | $-Pk$ | $+Pk$ | | | | 0 |
| 7. Equities | $+peE_h$ | $-peE$ | $+peE_b$ | $+peE_g$ | $+peE_{hf}$ | 0 |

*Notes:*
1. *pe* stands for the unit price of equity.
2. Positive figures denote assets, while negative figures denote liabilities.
3. *Pk* stands for capital goods generated by the reinvestment of net profits equivalent to a transfer of money income from households to firms, which is nothing more than 'the conversion of wage goods into new capital goods within firms' (Schmitt, 1984, p. 166). In a more orderly system of payments, 'the part of profits invested in the production of fixed capital goods should no longer be available on the financial market' (Baranzini and Cencini, in Rossi, 2001, p. xvi).
4. We amalgamate the Treasury with the central bank for present purposes.
5. All sectors buy equities, government bills, and *haute finance* securities (we abstract from firms' commercial bills).
6. Banks grant loans to firms to finance production (that is, money is endogenous) and also to households, but we assume that only the latter agents save a significant share of their income in the form of bank deposits.

that is to say, 'little more than their own pricing dynamics' (Watson, 2007, p. 97). Even with the assumption of a non-ergodic world (Davidson, 1994), the analysis of these increasingly complex pricing dynamics remains beyond the scope of the present chapter.

A good example of transaction flows arising out of the traditional banking sector and entering the *haute finance* sector is given by credit-risk transfer enabling banks to shift credit risk (assessed in monetary terms) off their balance sheets into the hands of investors. In the process of financial circulation, the resulting fungible securities will very likely be traded and reshaped into increasingly sophisticated instruments within *haute finance*, where they will continue to circulate.

*Haute finance* institutions issue securities and grant loans. The resulting assets and liabilities reappear in the balance sheets of the other institutional sectors (Table 10.1). In fact, the existence of *haute finance* is assumed to be neutral at first, since it does not change the totals of

*Table 10.2* A simplified current transactions matrix

| | *Households (current account)* | *Firms (capital account)* | *Firms* | *Banks* | *Government* | Haute finance | *Total* |
|---|---|---|---|---|---|---|---|
| Consumption | $-C$ | $+C$ | | | | | 0 |
| Government expenditure | | $+G$ | | | $-G$ | | 0 |
| Investment in fixed capital | | $+p\Delta K$ | $-p\Delta K$ | | | | 0 |
| Wages | $+W$ | $-W$ | | | | | 0 |
| Taxes | $-Tw$ | $-Tf$ | | $-Tb$ | $+T$ | $-Thf$ | 0 |
| Interest on bank loans | $-iLh_{(t-1)}$ | $-iLf_{(t-1)}$ | | $+iL_{t-1}$ | | | 0 |
| Interest on *haute finance* securities | $+iSh_{(t-1)}$ | $+iSf_{(t-1)}$ | | $+iSb_{(t-1)}$ | $+iSg_{(t-1)}$ | $-iS_{(t-1)}$ | 0 |
| Interest on *haute finance* loans | $-iSh_{(t-1)}$ | $-iSf_{(t-1)}$ | | $-iSb_{(t-1)}$ | $-iSg_{(t-1)}$ | $+iS_{(t-1)}$ | 0 |
| Interest on government bills | $+iGh_{(t-1)}$ | $+iGf_{(t-1)}$ | | $+iGb_{(t-1)}$ | $-iG_{(t-1)}$ | $+iGhf_{(t-1)}$ | 0 |
| Interest on bank deposits | $+iB_{(t-1)}$ | | | $-iB_{(t-1)}$ | | | |
| Dividends | $+Fd+Fb+Fhf$ | $-Fd$ | | $-Fb$ | | $-Fhf$ | 0 |
| Total | 0 | 0 | 0 | 0 | 0 | 0 | 0 |

*Note:* Positive figures denote sources of funds, while negative figures denote uses of funds.

the different lines and columns of the table (total interest on securities equals total interest on loans). Of course, as soon as we enter dynamic analysis, this assumption will be relaxed. The 'current flows' are shown in Table 10.2.

All sectors receive interest on *haute finance* securities and government bills, and they pay interest on their lagged stock of *haute finance* loans. All sectors pay taxes to the government. Only households receive interest on bank deposits, income in form of wages, distributed profits of banks, firms and *haute finance* institutions, and use it to purchase goods and services, pay taxes and interest on their loans, and buy securities. The government, in turn, receives money from taxes and uses it to buy goods from firms and pay interest on its lagged stock of debt, while firms use sales receipts to pay wages, taxes, interest on their lagged stock of loans, and dividends, retaining the rest to finance investment. Finally, banks receive interest on loans granted to firms and households that they use to pay interest on households' deposits, taxes, and dividends. As in previous

*Table 10.3* Flows of funds

| | *Households* | *Firms* | *Banks* | *Government* | Haute Finance | *Total* |
|---|---|---|---|---|---|---|
| Δ bank deposits | $-\Delta D$ | | $+\Delta D$ | | | 0 |
| Δ bank loans | $+\Delta Lh_b$ | $+\Delta Lf_b$ | $-\Delta L_b$ | | | 0 |
| Δ *haute finance* loans | $+\Delta Lh_{HF}$ | $+\Delta Lf_{HF}$ | $+\Delta Lb_{HF}$ | $+\Delta Lg_{HF}$ | $-\Delta L_{HF}$ | 0 |
| Δ *haute finance* securities | $-\Delta Sh_{HF}$ | $-\Delta Sf_{HF}$ | $-\Delta Sb_{HF}$ | $-\Delta Sg_{HF}$ | $+\Delta S_{HF}$ | 0 |
| Δ government bills | $-\Delta G_h$ | $-\Delta G_f$ | $-\Delta G_b$ | $+\Delta G$ | $-\Delta G_{hf}$ | 0 |
| Δ equities | $-pe\Delta E_h$ | $+pe\Delta E$ | $-pe\Delta E_b$ | $-pe\Delta E_g$ | $-pe\Delta E_{hf}$ | 0 |

*Table 10.4* Simplified balance sheet of households

| *Households* | |
|---|---|
| *Assets* | *Liabilities* |
| Securities owned by households purchased from firms (equities, corporate bonds, and so on) | Outstanding debt (bank loans and *haute finance* loans) |
| Securities owned by households purchased from banks (deposit certificates) | |
| Securities owned by households purchased from *haute finance* (for instance, share in mutual funds) | |
| Funds lent by *haute finance* (for example, loans granted by NBFIs) | |
| Securities owned by households purchased from the government (Treasury bonds) | |
| Bank deposits owned by households (if positive) | |
| Real assets owned by households | |

LG models, every monetary flow has to 'come from somewhere and go somewhere' (Godley, 1999, p. 394), and this is why all row and column totals are zero.

Table 10.3 emphasizes the dynamic nature of the model with the flows of funds for each institutional sector.

## The simplified balance sheet of households, firms, and banks

According to Dos Santos (2007, p. 5), 'the size and the desired composition of the balance sheets of the various institutional sectors [...]

*Table 10.5* Simplified balance sheet of firms

| *Firms* | |
|---|---|
| *Assets* | *Liabilities* |
| Securities owned by firms purchased from other firms (equities, corporate bonds, and so on) | Own equity funds and capital reserves |
| Securities owned by firms purchased from *haute finance* (for instance, share in mutual funds) | Outstanding debt (bank loans, *haute finance* loans, inter-firm liability, and tax liability) |
| Cash reserves supplied by *haute finance* (contractual payments made by NBFIs) | |
| Funds lent by *haute finance* (for instance, venture capital funds) | |
| Securities owned by firms purchased from banks (for instance, certificates of deposit) | |
| Securities owned by firms purchased from the government (Treasury bonds) | |
| Bank deposits owned by firms (if positive) | |
| Cash reserves as a result of internal liquidity management and retained profits | |
| Real assets owned by firms | |

determine (short period) equilibrium asset prices which, in turn, crucially affect real [macroeconomic] variables'. Drawing on this idea, we consider the structure of the balance sheet of households (Table 10.4), firms (Table 10.5), and banks (Table 10.6), including assets and liabilities originating from *haute finance*. We omit the balance sheet of the government and *haute finance* for present purposes.

The composition of the simplified balance sheets shown in Tables 10.4, 10.5, and 10.6 should be investigated in further research work, in order to analyse the macroeconomic consequences of their structural evolution as a result of the constant interactions between all the main institutional sectors of the economy.

## Conclusion

We have aimed in this chapter to cast light on the current process of financialization in the framework of monetary circuit theory. In the light

*Table 10.6* Simplified balance sheet of banks

| *Banks* | |
|---|---|
| *Assets* | *Liabilities* |
| Securities owned by banks purchased from other banks (for instance, certificates of deposit) | Own equity funds and capital reserves |
| Securities owned by banks purchased from firms (equities, corporate bonds, and so on) | Outstanding debt (deposits, *haute finance* loans, interbank liability, and tax liability) |
| Securities owned by banks purchased from *haute finance* (for example, share in mutual funds) | |
| Financial services purchased from *haute finance* (for instance, credit-risk transfer instruments) | |
| Cash reserves supplied by *haute finance* (for example, contractual payments made by NBFIs) | |
| Funds lent by *haute finance* (special loans granted by NBFIs) | |
| Securities owned by banks purchased from the government (Treasury bonds) | |
| Loans granted to firms, households, and other banks | |
| Cash reserves as a result of internal liquidity management and retained profits | |
| Real assets owned by banks | |

of Karl Polanyi's groundbreaking work in the twentieth century on *haute finance*, this renewed endeavour has led us to define a new institutional sector that was integrated into the premises of the Lavoie–Godley model. Further elaboration on the *haute finance* sector will certainly give rise to major modelling and statistical difficulties that stem from its postulated supranational nature. In an open-economy framework, this methodological assumption will require some complex accounting procedures. For instance, the existence of this new macro-accounting entity implies that the financial services supplied by commercial banks that do not fit into the categories of monetary and financial intermediation (as defined in the TME) be included in *haute finance* and withdrawn from the traditional domestic banking sector in national statistics. Moreover, the creation of a supranational *haute finance* sector entails the aggregation of national statistics on NBFIs (and on other selected international banking activities) that will be excluded from our revisited definition of the domestic banking sector. Finally, data inadequacies might impede our conceptual attempt to include in *haute finance* all the financial activities of multinational NFCs (Crotty, 2005, p. 106). Despite all these reservations, we are convinced that the recognition of *haute finance* as a full-fledged macroeconomic sector is now a conceptual necessity. Let us hope that the joint efforts of researchers in the future will contribute to its successful integration into a fully operational model that will improve our understanding of the workings of modern economies.

## Notes

1. In 2006, hedge funds accounted for half the trading on the New York and London stock exchanges (Anderson, 2006).
2. This macroeconomic operation concomitantly involves banks, households, and firms (Gnos and Rasera, 1985).
3. The origin of the acceptability of bank deposits as money by economic agents (their 'moneyness') is a source of contention between post-Keynesians and circuitists. While the former have adopted, along with leading monetary practitioners (Goodhart, 1989 [1975], p. 111; Aglietta and Orléan, 2002) the convention-based analysis derived from the view that modern banking systems function on the bedrock of confidence, the latter try to explain the objective purchasing power of money (Schmitt, 1988, p. 89) through the conceptual integration of money and output.
4. The payment of wages is seen as an instantaneous and circular flow of money that gives rise to the formation of a stock of money income (Schmitt, 1984; Gnos, 1998, 2005; Rossi, 1998, 2006).
5. Approximately 3.2 trillion US dollars are exchanged *each day* on the foreign exchange market (Bank for International Settlements, 2007, p. 1). In comparison, *annual* world merchandise exports in 2006 were 11.76 trillion US dollars (World Trade Organization, 2007, p. 6). Another example of the exponential rise of financial markets is given by the growth of the credit derivatives markets. From almost nothing in the mid-1990s, the notional amount outstanding of credit derivatives as of mid-year 2007 was estimated to be 45.46 trillion US dollars (International Swaps and Derivatives Association, 2007, Internet).
6. Following Le Bourva (1962), we dismiss the idea that money creation is dependent on a pre-existing monetary base. Instead, we endorse the theory of the credit divider, which puts the emphasis on the endogenous nature of bank money characterized by the leading role of the demand for bank credit by firms (in order to finance production) and the subsequent refinancing of commercial banks by the central bank whose behaviour is mainly accommodating and defensive (Moore, 1988a).
7. According to Arestis and Basu (2003, p. 183), this period (that is, the second half of Polanyi's 100-year peace) was in fact '[t]he first age of unregulated

financial globalization that spans over the period from the 1870s to 1913 when London arguably acted as the center of financial activity'.

8. Not all financial services serve the direct and primary purpose of gain. Other important functions exist (hedging, insurance, risk-sharing, capital raising and funding of real-world projects, credit rating, debt restructuring, and so on). However, from a holistic perspective, the essence of this wide variety of financial services can only be understood in light of a broader financial-profit motive. The necessity to conceptualize financial phenomena in monetary circuit theory justifies the introduction in the LG framework of *haute finance* defined as a full-fledged macroeconomic sector and a broad accounting category with regard to its postulated functional *raison d'être*: gain (that is to say, the realization of profits on financial markets).
9. This is a fascinating discussion that lies beyond the scope of this chapter, but the level of complexity of the present world financial system is probably much higher than Polanyi's *haute finance*. With regard to the existing balance of power in the international political economy, we argue that the conceptualization of a modern *haute finance* sector is indeed of utmost importance today.
10. Mainstream theory is often characterized by its repetitive and questionable emphasis on the maximization of utility functions by a representative individual agent.
11. One should not extrapolate at the exploratory stage; if the capture by *haute finance* of incomes from other sectors is to be scientifically singled out one day by macroeconomists, it will only be the outcome of a rigorous modelling process within a stock–flow consistent framework.
12. The reason why the subprime crisis (that originated on a specific segment in the United States) propagated so quickly to the rest of the world is due to those interconnected *haute finance* liabilities in the balance sheet of banks worldwide.
13. We have in mind the following meaning for the term 'supranational': 'extending beyond or transcending established borders or spheres of influence held by separate nations' (*American Heritage Dictionary*, 2007, Internet).
14. National statistics in other countries would also show massive cross-border flows in financial markets and therefore call for the recognition of *haute finance* as a *supranational* sector (see the previous note for a definition of the term 'supranational').
15. The definition is conceptual and holds regardless of the country of incorporation of NBFIs. From a legal point of view, these institutions may be incorporated in any country without affecting their postulated supranational nature from a methodological and macroeconomic point of view. Paradoxically, we include the purely financial activities of multinational NFCs in the *haute finance* sector.
16. One might be tempted to emphasize the geopolitical dimension of sovereign funds to justify their inclusion in the government sector. However, for obvious reasons, we decide to include sovereign funds in the *haute finance* sector in our revisited LG framework.
17. NBFIs act as suppliers of loans and credit facilities. However, they are not allowed to take bank deposits from the general public and have to find other means of funding their operations such as issuing debt instruments.

18. We use the expression 'to bridge the gap between deficit-spending units and saving units' to characterize financial intermediation. However, we have shown in our description of double-entry bookkeeping in monetary circuit theory that banks, in reality, do not create unilaterally the deposits that they lend to households or firms.
19. The integration of banks' cross-border activities into *haute finance* provides them with a supranational dimension by making them conceptually independent of any single government. This is not a denial of the national rootedness of banks from a statistical, legal, and regulatory perspective. To a very large extent, governments and banking supervision systems still continue to determine the activities of commercial banks and therefore justify their inclusion in national financial statistics. However, the postulated supranational nature of *haute finance* is a methodological choice that stems from the observation of the massive globalization trends in the financial sector over the last few decades. In fact, the current weight of *haute finance* questions the ability of any single government to exert a significant influence on its future evolution.
20. Multinational NFCs often open purely financial subsidiaries abroad (for example, car makers).

## References

Aglietta, M. and Orléan, A. (2002), *La monnaie, entre violence et confiance* (Paris: Odile Jacob).

*American Heritage Dictionary of the English Language, The* (2007), 4th edn, published by Houghton Mifflin Company, available at http://www.answers.com/topic/supranational?cat=biz-fin.

Anderson, J. (2006), 'As lenders, hedge funds draw insider scrutiny', *New York Times*, 16 October, available at http://www.nytimes.com/2006/10/16/business/16hedge.html?ref=business.

Arestis, P. (1996), 'Post-Keynesian economics: towards coherence', *Cambridge Journal of Economics*, 20 (1), 111–35.

Arestis, P. and Basu, S. (2003), 'Financial globalization: some conceptual problems', *Eastern Economic Journal*, 29 (2), 183–9.

Asimakopulos, A. (1991), *Keynes's General Theory and Accumulation* (New York: Cambridge University Press).

Ball, R.J. (1964), 'Money and assets', in *Inflation and the Theory of Money* (London: George Allen and Unwin).

Bank for International Settlements (2007), *Triennial Central Bank Survey of Foreign Exchange and Derivatives Market Activity in April 2007* (Basle: Bank for International Settlements).

Cencini, A. (1997), *Monetary Theory, National and International*, 2nd rev. edn (London: Routledge) (first published 1995).

Cencini, A. (2003a), 'Micro, macro et l'analyse du circuit', in P. Piégay and L.-P. Rochon (eds), *Théories monétaires post Keynésiennes* (Paris: Economica).

Cencini, A. (2003b), 'IS-LM: a final rejection', in L.-P. Rochon and S. Rossi (eds), *Modern Theories of Money: the Nature and Role of Money in Capitalist Economies* (Cheltenham: Edward Elgar).

Chick, V. (1986), 'The evolution of the banking system and the theory of saving, investment and interest', *Économies et Sociétés* (Série Monnaie et Production, 3), 20 (8–9), 111–26.

Crotty, J. (2005), 'The neoliberal paradox: the impact of destructive product market competition and "modern" financial markets on nonfinancial corporation performance in the neoliberal era', in G. Epstein (ed.), *Financialization and the World Economy* (Cheltenham: Edward Elgar).

Davidson, P. (1988), 'Endogenous money, the production process, and inflation analysis', *Économie Appliquée*, 41 (1), 151–69.

Davidson, P. (1994), *Post Keynesian Macroeconomic Theory: a Foundation for Successful Economic Policies for the Twenty-First Century* (Cheltenham: Edward Elgar).

Denizet, J. (1969), *Monnaie et financement: essai de théorie dans un cadre de comptabilité économique* (Paris: Dunod).

Dombrowski, P. (1998), 'Haute finance and high theory: recent scholarship on global financial relations', *Mershon International Studies Review*, 42 (1), 1–28.

Dos Santos, C.H. (2007), 'A simplified "benchmark" stock–flow consistent (SFC) post-Keynesian growth model', Jerome Levy Institute Working Paper no. 503.

Dumenil, G. and Lévy, D. (2005), 'Costs and benefits of neoliberalism', in G. Epstein (ed.), *Financialization and the World Economy* (Cheltenham: Edward Elgar).

Epstein, G. (2005), 'Introduction', in G. Epstein (ed.), *Financialization and the World Economy* (Cheltenham: Edward Elgar).

Epstein, G. and Jayadev, A. (2005), 'The rise of rentier incomes in OECD countries: financialization, central bank policy and labor solidarity', in G. Epstein (ed.), *Financialization and the World Economy* (Cheltenham: Edward Elgar).

Fahrer, M. (2007), 'Robert Elstone: exchange consolidation – balancing global markets and local regulation', *Melbourne Review*, 3 (1), 16–23.

Fama, E.F. (1980), 'Banking in the theory of finance', *Journal of Monetary Economics*, 6 (1), 39–57.

Global European Anticipation Bulletin (2006), 'Dollar/real estate/stock markets: US consumer's insolvency, a catalyst of the impact phase of the global systemic crisis', Public Announcement, no. 9, available at http:// www.leap2020.eu/December-2006-Dollar-Real-Estate-Stock-Markets-US-consumer-s-insolvency,-a-catalyst-of-the-impact-phase-of-the- global_a233.html.

Gnos, C. (1998), 'The Keynesian identity of income and output', in A. Jolink and P. Fontaine (eds), *Historical Perspectives on Macroeconomics: Sixty Years after the General Theory* (London: Routledge).

Gnos, C. (2003), 'Circuit theory as an explanation of the complex real world', in L.-P. Rochon and S. Rossi (eds), *Modern Theories of Money: the Nature and Role of Money in Capitalist Economies* (Cheltenham: Edward Elgar).

Gnos, C. (2005), 'French circuit theory', in P. Arestis and M. Sawyer (eds), *A Handbook of Alternative Monetary Economics* (Cheltenham: Edward Elgar).

Gnos, C. and Rasera, J.-B. (1985), 'Circuit et circulation: une fausse analogie', *Cahiers de la Revue d'Économie Politique*, special issue, 41–57.

Godley, W. (1996), 'Money, finance, and national income determination: an integrated approach', Jerome Levy Institute Working Paper no. 167.

Godley, W. (1999), 'Money and credit in a Keynesian model of income determination', *Cambridge Journal of Economics*, 23 (2), 393–411.

Godley, W. (2004), 'Towards a reconstruction of macroeconomics using a stock–flow consistent (SFC) model', Cambridge Endowment for Research in Finance Working Paper no. 16.

Godley, W. and Cripps, F. (1983), *Macroeconomics* (London: Fontana Books).

Goodhart, C.A.E. (1989), *Money, Information and Uncertainty*, 2nd rev. edn (London: Macmillan) (first published 1975).

Graziani, A. (2003), *The Monetary Theory of Production* (Cambridge: Cambridge University Press).

Griffith-Jones, S. (1998), *Global Capital Flows: Should They Be Regulated?* (New York: St. Martin's Press).

Innes, A.M. (1913), 'What is money', *Banking Law Journal*, May, 377–408.

International Swaps and Derivatives Association (2007), 'ISDA mid-year 2007 market survey: credit derivatives at $45.46 trillion', available at http://www.isda.org/press/press092607.html.

International Monetary Fund (2006), *The Global Financial Stability Report* (Washington, DC: International Monetary Fund).

Keynes, J.M. (1930), *A Treatise on Money* (vol. 1 *The Pure Theory of Money*) (London: Macmillan).

Keynes, J.M. (1936), *The General Theory of Employment, Interest and Money* (London: Macmillan).

Knight, M.D. (2007), 'Financial risks: a view from the BIS', Speech at the Central Bank of Argentina 2007 Money and Banking Conference, Buenos Aires, 4–5 June 2007, available at http://www.bis.org/speeches/sp070606a.htm.

Krippner, G. (2004), 'What is financialization?', Department of Sociology, University of California Los Angeles, mimeo.

Lavoie, M. (1984), 'The endogenous flow of credit and the post-Keynesian theory of money', *Journal of Economic Issues*, 18 (3), 771–97.

Lavoie, M. (2004), 'Circuit and coherent stock–flow accounting', in R. Arena and N. Salvadori (eds), *Money, Credit, and the Role of the State* (Aldershot: Ashgate).

Lavoie, M. and Godley, W. (2001–2), 'Kaleckian models of growth in a coherent stock–flow monetary framework: a Kaldorian view', *Journal of Post Keynesian Economics*, 24 (2), 277–311.

Lavoie, M. and Godley, W. (2007), *Monetary Economics: an Integrated Approach to Credit, Money, Income, Production and Wealth* (Basingstoke: Palgrave Macmillan).

Le Bourva, J. (1962), 'Création de la monnaie et multiplicateur du crédit', *Revue Économique*, 13 (1), 29–56.

Le Heron, E. (2002), 'La préférence pour la liquidité des banques: une analyse post-keynésienne du comportement bancaire', *Cahiers lillois d'économie et de sociologie*, 38, 97–131.

Leijonhufvud, A. (2007), 'Monetary and financial stability', *Center for Economic Policy Research Policy Insight*, no. 14, available at http://www.cepr.org/pubs/PolicyInsights/PolicyInsight14.pdf.

Markman, J.D. (2007), 'The credit crisis could be just beginning', available at http://www.thestreet.com/newsanalysis/investing/10380613.html.

Moore, B. (1988a), 'The endogenous money supply', *Journal of Post Keynesian Economics*, 10 (3), 372–85.

Moore, B. (1988b), *Horizontalists and Verticalists: the Macroeconomics of Credit Money* (Cambridge: Cambridge University Press).

Palley, T. (1996), *Post Keynesian Economics: Debt, Distribution and the Macro Economy* (London: Macmillan).
Palley, T. (2007), 'Financialization: what it is and why it matters', Jerome Levy Economics Institute Working Paper no. 525.
Polanyi, K. (2001 [1944]), *The Great Transformation* (Boston: Beacon Press, 1944).
Ramonet, I. (1997), 'Disarming the markets', *Le Monde Diplomatique*, December, available at http://mondediplo.com/1997/12/leader.
Rosanvallon, P. (1985), *Le moment Guizot* (Paris: Gallimard).
Rossi, S. (1998), 'Endogenous money and banking activity: some notes on the workings of modern payment systems', *Studi Economici*, 53 (3), 23–56.
Rossi, S. (2001), 'The meaning of bank deposits', Research Laboratory of Monetary Economics Working Paper no. 6.
Rossi, S. (2006), 'The theory of money emissions', in P. Arestis and M. Sawyer (eds), *A Handbook of Alternative Monetary Economics* (Cheltenham: Edward Elgar).
Schmitt, B. (1984), *Inflation, chômage et malformations du capital: macroéconomie quantique* (Paris and Albeuve: Economica and Castella).
Schmitt, B. (1988), *L'Écu et les souverainetés nationales en Europe* (Paris: Dunod).
Schmitt, B. (1996), 'A new paradigm for the determination of money prices', in G. Deleplace and E.J. Nell (eds), *Money in Motion: the Post Keynesian and Circulation Approaches* (Basingstoke: Macmillan).
Securities Industry and Financial Markets Association (2008), 'US market outlook', available at http://www.sifma.org/research/pdf/usMktOutlook0108.pdf.
Slote, M.A. (1964), 'An empirical basis for psychological egoism', *Journal of Philosophy*, 61, 530–7.
Tobin, J. and Golub, S.S. (1998), *Money, Credit and Capital* (Irwin: McGraw-Hill).
Watson, M. (2007), *The Political Economy of International Capital Mobility* (Basingstoke: Palgrave Macmillan).
Withers, H. (1909), *The Meaning of Money* (London: Smith, Elder and Co.).
World Trade Organization (2007), *Annual Report* (Geneva: World Trade Organization).

# Name Index

# Subject Index